LOCAL GOVERNMENT IN LATIN AMERICA

LOCAL
GOVERNMENT
IN
LATIN AMERICA

R. ANDREW NICKSON

LYNNE
RIENNER
PUBLISHERS

BOULDER
LONDON

Published in the United States of America in 1995 by
Lynne Rienner Publishers, Inc.
1800 30th Street, Boulder, Colorado 80301

and in the United Kingdom by
Lynne Rienner Publishers, Inc.
3 Henrietta Street, Covent Garden, London WC2E 8LU

Library of Congress Cataloging-in-Publication Data
Nickson, R. Andrew.
 Local government in Latin America / by R. Andrew Nickson.
  p. cm.
 Includes bibliographical references and index.
 ISBN 1-55587-366-9
 1. Local government—Latin America. I. Title.
JS2061.2.N53 1995
352.08—dc20   94-43541
                                                    CIP

British Cataloguing in Publication Data
A Cataloguing in Publication record for this book
is available from the British Library.

Printed and bound in the United States of America

The paper used in this publication meets the requirements
of the American National Standard for Permanence of
Paper for Printed Library Materials Z39.48-1984.

5 4 3 2 1

To the forgotten revolutionaries of Latin America,
the unsung heroes of the municipalista *movement,*
who held high the banner of local government
contra viento y marea *at a time*
when it was neither fashionable nor advisable to do so—

Allen Brewer-Carias (Venezuela)
Diogo Lordello de Mello (Brazil)
Gustavo Martínez Cabañas (Mexico)
Manuel Montoya Ugarte (Peru)

and many others long forgotten in their own countries

CONTENTS

TABLES AND FIGURES

TABLES

FIGURES

Acknowledgments

I wish to thank the many colleagues in Latin America and elsewhere who have helped in the gathering of information for this book. Particular thanks go to Eduardo Azofeifa (IFAM, Costa Rica), Charles Boyce (consultant, International Development Programs, United States), Francois Bremaeker (IBAM, Brazil), Enrique Cabrera (CIDE, Mexico), Mayin Correa (ex-mayor of Panama City), Humberto Delgado (INIDEM, Bolivia), Charlotte Elton (CEASPA, Panama), Hilda Herzer and Pedro Pírez (CENTRO, Argentina), Ronald Jiménez (head of INFOM, Guatemala), Antonio Kawas and Patricia Falck de Nuñez (head and planning director, respectively, of BANMA, Honduras), Ulrich Kuenzel (GTZ, Ecuador), Liliana Miranda (IPADEL, Peru), Victor Orellana (head of ISAM, El Salvador), Samuel Ospina (head of ESAP, Colombia), Adolfo Pérez (CLAEH, Uruguay), Hector Pinilla (Panama), Roland Schwartz (head of the Ebert Foundation in Nicaragua), Franz Thedieck (PROADE, Bolivia), Celina Maria de Souza and Edmundo Werna (Brazil), Cristóbal Valdéz (head of Foro Urbano, Dominican Republic), and José Zarzosa (head of INDETEC, Mexico).

At the University of Birmingham, thanks go to Chris Davies and Nick Devas of the School of Public Policy, as well as to Nick Griffiths (Hispanic studies), Bob Gwynne (geography), and Iker de Luisa. I am particularly indebted to the encouragement and intellectual stimulation of Ken Davey and Richard Batley, both colleagues in the Development Administration Group. Their understanding of the financial and administrative systems of local government in Latin America, and the rest of the world, has been of invaluable help.

Finally, a special thanks to my wife, Louise Brown, who has been a constant source of support and encouragement throughout.

R. Andrew Nickson

Latin America

INTRODUCTION

The municipality is the formal institution of local government, the lowest tier of public administration within the nation-state. There are currently around 14,000 municipalities throughout Latin America. With the exception of parts of rural Bolivia and the rural areas of many Argentine provinces, a structure of local government covers the entire length and breadth of the region. It extends from the far north in the Municipality of Mexicali on the Mexican border with the United States to the far south in the Municipality of Navarino in the Chilean Antarctic, and from the Municipality of the Galapagos Islands off the west coast of Ecuador to the Municipality of João Pessoa on the northeastern tip of Brazil.

The economic and political significance of the municipal structure within Latin America is not inconsiderable. Local government typically accounts for between 5 and 15 percent of total public expenditure, and in most countries this share is growing. Municipalities have long provided a range of public services, albeit inadequately, to the rapidly growing urban population of the region. The share of the region's population living in urban settlements of more than 20,000 inhabitants is likely to rise from 72 percent in 1990 to 77 percent in 2000. Almost every municipality with a population of more than 20,000 already provides its citizens with some form of rudimentary solid waste management, city lighting, and road construction and maintenance, as well as cemeteries, public markets, slaughterhouses, and civil registration facilities. Furthermore, in some countries, municipalities have a long-standing tradition of providing basic public services such as water supply, sewerage, and urban transportation; whereas in others, recent decentralization programs have encouraged municipal involvement in primary health care and basic education for the first time. The breadth of service provision means that local government also makes a significant impact on economic activity and job creation in the local economy. It achieves this through its role as direct employer, as purchaser of local goods and services, and by the multiplier effect of municipal investment programs, which are still largely financed from central government transfers.

Today there is new interest in local government within Latin America. This follows several decades during which municipalities were stripped of their major functions by agencies of central government, stripped of their financial base by the removal of tax powers, and stripped of their political autonomy in many cases by the removal of the democratic election of local officeholders. During this period, decentralization was conceived of primarily in terms of administrative deconcentration to the regional level. Today it is primarily discussed in terms of devolution to local government.

Local government also has a growing political significance. The return to democracy during the 1980s exposed a gulf between the state and civil society that could no longer be attributed to military rule. This "dialogue of the deaf," as it became known, was the product of a centralist and exclusionary political culture that had endured for centuries. This led to a sudden concern for greater political accountability, which was viewed by political leaders primarily as a means to implant democratic norms of behavior and so to safeguard the democratization process. And local government, because of its closer proximity to civil society, was seen as a crucial mechanism for ensuring this greater political accountability. According to this view, municipalities had a strategic role to play in bridging the gap between the state and civil society, and in transforming hitherto marginalized groups into full-fledged citizens. Moves in this direction took place in many countries experiencing a transition to democracy, where an upsurge in community participation was increasingly channeled through local government. The extensive cooperation that subsequently developed between grassroots organizations and municipalities in the delivery of basic services in Latin America became impressive enough to attract considerable international interest. The most striking demonstration of this new political significance of local government is its own rapid democratization. From May 1994 municipal mayors were, for the first time in Latin American history, freely elected in every country except Cuba and Haiti. This was in marked contrast to the situation that had prevailed only twenty years earlier when most were appointed by central government.

Yet despite its growing economic and political significance, local government in Latin America remains a highly neglected area of study. The situation has changed little since 1954, when George Blanksten listed no English-language work on the subject in his *Bibliography on Latin American Politics and Government*. The standard textbooks in English on contemporary Latin American development still usually refer to local government only in passing. The extensive literature on the bureaucratic-authoritarian model of development that characterized much of Latin America during the 1970s virtually ignored the significance of local government in regime maintenance (Rehren:106). Similarly, the major studies of the transition in the region during the 1980s made no reference to the importance of enhanced local government powers in the process of democratization (Nickson:219). Countless books have been written on urban development in

Latin America, yet very few specifically on local government, apart from Mark Cannon's *Urban government for Valencia, Venezuela* (1973) and Arturo Valenzuela's *Political brokers in Chile: Local government in a centralized polity* (1977), both of which predate the current revival of local government. Many more studies of local government exist in the Spanish language, but most of these have tended toward a normative approach that focuses on administrative law. As such, they have been preoccupied with what "should" happen according to the prevailing legislation, and not with what actually transpires when these idealized municipal norms are applied in the context of turbulent political reality. In focusing attention on the reality rather than the rhetoric of the subject, this study has necessarily placed far less emphasis on the normative issues that have so enthralled municipal specialists within Latin America. Yet so strong is the legalistic tradition that pervades the world of local government in the region that reference will be made to municipal codes on many occasions.

This study attempts to fill the information gap on Latin American local government in the English-speaking world. But a disclaimer is in order. This is not a book about urban development, nor about decentralization, although both issues are addressed indirectly. Instead, its focus is on the operations of local government itself, a crucial ingredient that is all too often neglected in the wider discussion of decentralization and urban development in Latin America. In addressing the specific nature of "local" government, the study necessarily presents a partial view of the overall process of economic and social change at the local level. Other actors such as central government, state corporations, and private business impinge mightily on the municipal arena, in many cases swamping the powers of local government. However, the conventional view that local government in Latin America is simply the plaything of these more powerful actors is becoming less and less tenable.

Local government has remained invisible for far too long as a distinctive actor within the process of Latin American development. In seeking to redress this imbalance, this study presents a baseline survey of local government in the region, its history, its present structure, and its future prospects. By focusing on a partial view of the process of change at the local level, such a study necessarily runs the risk of not seeing the forest of national socioeconomic processes amongst the trees of municipal administration. However, this is an unavoidable price that must be paid in order to highlight the significant role local government seems destined to play in the future development of the region.

This book is divided into two parts. Part 1 provides a broad overview of local government in Latin America, emphasizing characteristics common to many countries. It examines the history of local government in the region, its legal status, its basic structure, the nature of local government service provision, local government finance, the electoral system, its internal organization, citizen participation in local government, and intermunicipal relations. Part 2 is divided into chapters that give detailed descriptions of local government in eighteen countries. These chapters have been written to a common format that addresses specifically each of the subject areas discussed in Part 1 in order to facilitate intercountry comparisons. Only two countries are omitted: Cuba because of the absence of pluralist democracy at the local level, and Haiti because of the distinctive political culture that sets it apart from the rest of the region. Appendixes provide two recent official pronouncements in favor of local government and a directory of major local government institutions and support bodies in Latin America. Finally, the bibliography is divided into general and country sections.

Effort has been made in the text to avoid the semantic arguments that bedevil the language of local government within Latin America. In order to minimize confusion to the non-Spanish speaker, English titles are preferred throughout. Hence, the elected executive head of the municipality, variously known in different countries as the *alcalde, intendente,* and *síndico,* is referred to throughout as the mayor. Similarly, the municipal legislature, variously known as the *consejo, concejo, junta,* and *corporación,* is referred to as the council, and its members as councillors.

PART 1

AN OVERVIEW OF LOCAL GOVERNMENT IN LATIN AMERICA

1

THE HISTORY
OF LOCAL GOVERNMENT

The history of local government in Latin America has been greatly romanticized by modern writers who have often attributed to it powers and features that it never possessed. Central to this process of mythologizing the past is the municipal administration during the colonial era, known as the *cabildo,* which was the forerunner of the local government councils of the postindependence period. The popularization of the alleged virtues of the cabildo has often been used as an instrument by those advocating decentralization. However, although widely portrayed as representing a "golden age" of local democracy, the reality of the cabildo was very different.

THE IBERIAN TRADITION

Spanish and Portuguese America inherited a strong tradition of urban government from the Iberian peninsula. The institution of the free city-state, implanted during the Roman occupation, had taken deep root, and during the twelfth, thirteenth, and fourteenth centuries, Iberian towns acquired considerable autonomy. Certain common principles guided their operation. These included equality before the law, administration of justice by resident judges elected by the people, popular participation in municipal affairs, and accountability of public administrators. The colonization of Spanish America took place before the centralizing forces had destroyed municipal autonomy in Spain. In a sense, the early municipal initiatives on American soil represented an attempt to recreate the very institutions that were increasingly under threat in Spain itself.

7

THE POSTCONQUEST PERIOD

The heyday of the cabildo was in the immediate aftermath of the conquest and before the Spanish Crown imposed the highly centralist system of imperial administration known as the Council of the Indies (Consejo de las Indias). During this brief period, which lasted little more than fifty years after the original conquest of 1492, the new colonial possessions were effectively ruled by self-governing groups of Spanish conquistadores, led by free-booting Spanish adventurers known as *adelantados*. Although the adelantados operated with a degree of royal blessing, they quickly sought to establish cabildos on conquered territory as an administrative device to ensure a degree of legal protection for activities not specifically authorized by the Crown. By 1600 some 250 cabildos had been created, although most were still little more than large villages. Although the first council members (*regidores*) were usually appointed by the adelantado, the cabildo had considerable autonomy and control over the newly acquired territory, and its members were often able to bypass the incipient colonial bureaucracy of the adelantados and royal governors.

The cabildo immediately became the main institution for defending and representing the interests of the conquistadores, and the means by which they could be rewarded financially for the risks undertaken during the conquest. Although the post of regidor carried no salary, it provided many opportunities for financial gain. The cabildo was responsible for distributing the land that the regidores, as settlers, craved. The regidores fixed the price of beef and other provisions that they, as ranchers, sold in the town. The regidores influenced the administration of indigenous labor, on which they, as landowners and mine-owners, depended. And as regidores they elected the very municipal magistrates before whom any lawsuits against them would first be heard (Parry:108).

The colonial system of local government was manufactured; it did not evolve naturally through a process of gradual urbanization. The new municipalities became miniature replicas of the Iberian city-states, consisting of an urban center (*cabecera*) and an extensive rural hinterland that invariably extended to the boundary with the adjoining municipality. This settlement pattern, and the territorial configuration of local government that derived from it, mirrored the colonial relationship between the Spanish invaders and the indigenous people. In marked contrast to the English settlement of North America, the Spanish colonists congregated in the new urban clusters, and the rural population remained almost exclusively indigenous, providing both labor and sustenance for the new urban settlements. In practice, the actions of the cabildo were confined to the urban area of the municipality, where the Spanish resided. As a result, the view was soon established that local government could legitimately abdicate any responsibility for service delivery in rural areas—a perception that would remain deeply ingrained well into the post-1945 period in many Latin American countries.

GRADUAL ROYAL CONTROL

It was not the policy of an absolute monarchy to nourish independent municipalities, and before long the Spanish Crown began to exert control over its newly acquired territorial possessions, initially through the appointment of royal governors. The 1521 defeat of the Comunero rebellion by Spanish towns against royal authority provided a catalyst, encouraging Charles V to clamp down on municipal autonomy on both sides of the Atlantic. Fearing the re-creation on American soil of the loose federation of towns known as the Santa Hermandad, communication between cabildos was banned altogether.

In 1480 the Crown had placed a royal official over each Spanish cabildo to enforce the authority of the monarchy at the local level. After 1521 this official, known as a *corregidor,* was introduced to the Americas as well. Henceforth, all legislation passed by the cabildo had to be ratified by the Crown. These new measures rapidly stripped the cabildo of most of its nominal powers and led to its decline throughout the rest of the colonial period. It became the lowest tier in an administrative hierarchy imposed on the colonies by the Hapsburg monarchs, Charles I and Philip II. The cabildo was beholden to the governor, the viceroy, and the captain-general, and the deadweight of this excessive political control was reinforced by the right of the royal governor or his nominee to attend and preside over its meetings.

Features of Local Administration

The essential features of local administration during the colonial era had a major influence upon the municipal governments established during the postindependence period. The Crown greatly limited the cabildo's powers of taxation. The cabildo could not tax directly, and property taxation did not exist. Hence its revenue derived from the rental or leasing of publicly owned land to cattle drovers and stall holders, as well as from fees and fines. Freedom of expenditure was equally restricted, and the cabildo's functions were reduced to the allocation of town lots, the issuance of building permits, the protection of the urban food supply, law and order, sanitation, street cleaning, supervision of markets, and the fixing of prices for basic commodities.

Administration and jurisprudence were closely interwoven at the local level, as elsewhere in the colonial system. The senior magistrate (*alcalde ordinario*) presided over the cabildo in addition to his judicial work, and this post gradually evolved into that of mayor. Other offices shared among the regidores were that of sheriff (*alguacil mayor*), standard bearer (*alférez*), public works commissioner (*obrero mayor*), and inspector of weights and measures (*fiel ejecutor*). Only the town clerk (*escribano de cabildo*) was not a member of the cabildo. The number of cabildo members was small. In the case of the largest ones, such as Mexico City and Lima, there were only twelve regidores, and numbers fell to as low as four in the smaller ones.

In the event of local emergencies, especially the need to organize defense against Indian attacks, or else for the celebration of royal occasions, the leading male citizens were invited to join the regidores in an open town meeting, known as the *cabildo abierto*. The democratic credentials of this institution have been greatly exaggerated by modern historians. Those who attended did so by invitation, not by right, and their opinions and suggestions were of an advisory nature and were not binding upon the cabildo.

The Colonial Inheritance

The cabildo failed to develop into a powerful expression of political opposition to royal autocracy. The authority of the watchful corregidor was rarely challenged, and there was little pressure from the regidores to expand the limited functions of the cabildo. This absence of political assertiveness, the legacy of which would have a profound effect upon the fortunes of local government during the postindependence period, derived from the essentially undemocratic composition of the cabildo. In particular, two interrelated features of the colonial system of local government—the sale of posts and its control by local elites—bequeathed a legacy of graft and corruption that has endured to the present day.

The Sale of Posts

In 1523 Charles V decreed a local electoral system for Spanish America that reflected the municipal tradition of medieval Spain. Under this arrangement, regidores would be elected annually from among local property owners (*vecinos*), and there was a prohibition on their immediate reelection. Alcaldes were to be elected by the regidores, with a prohibition on their reelection in the two years following the expiry of their term of office. But this "democratic" proposal was dropped in the face of the monarchy's pressing financial difficulties. Such was the political decline of the "free towns" of Castile that elected municipal posts in the Iberian peninsula were already being rapidly converted into proprietary ones. This process served to alleviate the pressing financial problems of local government. By removing accountability to an electorate, it also contributed to the political centralization pursued by the monarchy after the marriage of Isabella and Ferdinand. The practice was soon copied in Spanish America, where regidores were nominated by the governor, were chosen by outgoing regidores, or, increasingly, received their office directly from the king.

Under Philip II the efficiency of municipal institutions declined further, principally because official positions were sold as a means of increasing royal revenues. In response to the virtual bankruptcy of the monarchy, in 1557 the Castilian practice of auctioning lifetime offices to the highest bidder was extended to the Americas. Cabildo posts were the first to be affected by this measure, including that of regidor, which produced the phenomenon of the lifetime councillor (*regidor perpetuo*). In order to further increase its revenue, the Crown also increased the number of regidor posts. The auctioning of public office was soon extended to governors, to members of the regional law courts (known as *audiencias*), and eventually even to viceroys. The office of local magistrate, forerunner of the mayor, was the only office to remain elective. Although chosen by the regidores, but not from among them, the nominations for such posts were nevertheless subject to confirmation by the governor.

In 1606 the practice was broadened to enable officeholders to bequeath proprietary posts to their heirs upon payment of a special tax. As a result, by the early seventeenth century, most municipal offices had become both proprietary and hereditary:

> Municipal office thus became to all intents and purposes a piece of private property which passed freely by sale from one person to another, or between members of the same family, within the limitations stated. A vacancy might even be purchased for a minor, the post being held by the father or other suitable substitute until the coming-of-age (Haring:166).

The public auctioning and inheritance of the post of regidor raised much-needed finance for the Crown, but it had very negative consequences for the colonial administration. It strengthened the oligarchic nature of the cabildo, the membership of which became exclusively drawn from among the Creoles (American-born Spaniards) who stood to gain the most from control over the local administration. The sales enabled these local elite families to exert strong influence over judicial and political decisions. However, by increasing the pressure on incumbents to derive a profit from the initial investment made to secure the post, they also encouraged rampant corruption. The turnover in the bureaucracy was also reduced to a minimum because posts were sold on a lifetime basis. The absence of recruitment by merit led to gross mismanagement and effectively stifled the prospects of any significant social mobility through municipal officeholding.

Elite Control

Largely as a result of the sale and inheritance of posts, Spanish local administration in the Americas became synonymous with local elite interests. Although broad powers were legally concentrated in the hands of higher authorities such as the viceroys and captains-general, the actual force of law deriving from this arrangement was often limited. The inability to ensure close supervision because of communications difficulties meant that local Creole elites retained considerable de facto power over the isolated societies of the interior. Referring to the late Hapsburg period (1650–1700), one writer noted that this American participation in the colonial administration left a "historical deposit of compromise and consensus with elite interests which could not be effaced" (Lynch, 1992:81).

The problem was that the Creoles were not "modernizing elites." On the contrary, once posts could be inherited, the wealthiest Creoles were attracted to municipal office because of its associated prestige. As a consequence, the cabildo usually displayed a remarkable lack of social concern and a high degree of administrative incompetence. Paramount attention was granted to its ceremonial function, and the problem of growing urban squalor was largely ignored. Hence, despite the declining power of the cabildo in the seventeenth and eighteenth centuries, the position of regidor was still coveted because it enhanced social status.

Although the cabildo was starved of funds, its members were allowed to squander what little it had during fiestas and especially on royal birthday celebrations. These conspicuous displays underlined the social status of the regidores, and royal toleration of such financial irresponsibility was an important mechanism for ensuring cabildo loyalty to the Crown during the Hapsburg era (Pike, 1960b:411). Hence came the irony that, despite being the one institution of government in which Creoles were assured of influence, the cabildo became increasingly weaker as the colonial period progressed. By the mid-eighteenth century, its decline had assumed alarming proportions. Municipal finances were in disorder, corruption was universal, and the cabildo was unable to tackle the problems of urban growth.

THE PORTUGUESE SYSTEM

Portuguese colonialism produced a smaller and more regionally decentralized administrative system than in its Spanish counterpart in the Americas. The Brazilian *câmara,* like its Spanish equivalent, the cabildo, was also extremely elitist in composition. Its small number of councillors (*senadores*)—usually no more than four—were selected by a complex system of indirect election. Eligibility was restricted to property-owning males of high status and racial "purity," known as *homens bons,* who were not tainted by association with commerce or manual trades, nor by religious heterodoxy. As a result, the câmara initially represented the interests of local landed elites (sugar planters and cattle barons), although the growing influence of mercantile trade saw the gradual representation of traders on the coastal câmaras by the 1650s.

In pursuit of these elite interests, the câmara intervened more actively than the cabildo in areas of urban life, collecting taxes, leasing municipal property, controlling slaves, and policing the town. In so doing, it often clashed with royal prerogatives over matters of jurisdiction and taxation to a much greater degree than its counterpart in Spanish America. In particular, the câmaras spearheaded opposition to the royal ban on Indian slavery. The fact that the senadores were, however imperfectly, elected did prevent the câmaras from becoming the closed and self-perpetuating cliques that emerged from the sale and inheritance of the post of regidor in Spanish America (Burkholder and Johnson:83).

THE BOURBON REFORMS

The dismal situation of local administration in Spanish America changed radically as a result of the overhaul of imperial administration carried out under Charles III (1759–1788). The Bourbon Reforms, as they became known, introduced strong centralizing forces designed to control and modernize the colonial bureaucracy and to increase revenues at a time of a growing international threat to Spanish domination of the Americas. This new absolutism led to a rapid decline in the participation of Creoles in the higher echelons of the colonial administration. The audiencia system was abolished and replaced by intendancies (*intendencias*), headed exclusively by Spanish-born *peninsulares.*

Although often portrayed solely as a centralizing force, the period of the intendancies actually produced a new lease on life for the cabildo. Rather than removing the faculties of the cabildo, the intendants (*intendentes*) constantly pressured the cabildo to undertake its neglected responsibilities. In so doing, the intendants aroused the cabildo from its lethargy, and the Bourbon Reforms led to its political revitalization (Lynch, 1958:210, 211, 288). The sale of public offices was abolished, and commoners became eligible for office. The post of *síndico* (auditor) was created with the aim of defending municipal interests as well as protecting the citizens against abuses committed by the cabildo. In their zeal to root out disorder and improve efficiency, the intendants and their subordinates encouraged the cabildo to improve its financial administration and granted it greater powers of taxation. As a result, the amount of funds at its disposal increased sharply. In the

process, the final decades of the eighteenth century witnessed an apprecia-
ble improvement in basic urban services.

Although the relationship between cabildos and intendants was cooperative in the 1780s and 1790s, by the first decade of the nineteenth century
most cabildos were in dispute with their intendants. There are several reasons for this sudden change in attitude. First, by bringing an end to the old
patterns of financial irresponsibility, the reforms stripped cabildo members
of the opportunities for conspicuous display. Second, by providing a new
vista of economic opportunity through trade, the reforms and the influence
of the Enlightenment that they represented stimulated a new interest among
the cabildos for economic advancement and a measure of self-determina-
tion. Third, and perhaps most significant, the cabildos were fast becoming
the political conduit for the expression of Creole frustrations. Creoles
resented their exclusion from high office and the exclusive reliance on
Spanish-born administrators in the higher echelons of the colonial administration.

THE INDEPENDENCE MOVEMENT

The positive modern-day image of the cabildo derives from an overempha-
sis on its role during the final phase of its existence, when it briefly assumed
importance as a channel for the expression of growing local sentiment in
favor of independence from Spain. The cabildo had failed dismally as a
breeding ground for democratic values in American society during the colonial period. Yet despite its many failings, its significance lay in the fact that
it was the only colonial institution in which Creoles were well represented,
as well as the only one that retained a small measure of local autonomy.

Hence, when the Spanish monarchy collapsed in 1808 and the imperial
system teetered on the brink of disintegration, separatist sentiments were
first articulated through the cabildo. This was often due to pressure brought
to bear upon the cabildo by more radically minded members of the community (Haring:178). The near moribund institution quickly assumed a new
lease on life and soon became the midwife of the independence movement
itself. In 1810 cabildos elected revolutionary juntas in towns throughout the
subcontinent—Caracas (19 April), Buenos Aires (25 May), Bogotá (22
July), Santiago (18 September), and La Paz (16 November). Moreover, the
alleged democratic credentials of the cabildo were enhanced by the wider
representation of interests through the cabildo abierto, which was reintroduced to gather support for the independence movement. In contemporary
Latin America, the historical precedent of the cabildo abierto has been widely used by municipal authorities throughout the region in order to give legitimacy to a participatory and more directly accountable style of local democ-

racy, although its real significance has been greatly exaggerated in the process.

POSTINDEPENDENCE DECLINE

Spain's legacy to Latin America was a tradition of extreme centralization in governmental decisionmaking and an elitist social structure that impeded the implementation of central government policies. Local government was grossly neglected during the postindependence period as governments throughout the region strove to ensure national consolidation. There are hardly any studies of local government during this period (Hijano:84). Local government rapidly became subsumed under the powers of the newly emerging nation-states, whose leaders replicated the centralizing and elitist political tradition bequeathed to them by their colonial forebears. Local government was often suppressed altogether—for example, in Argentina (1820–1853), Bolivia (1843–1861), Chile (1830–1861), Mexico (1837–1857), and Paraguay (1824–1882).

The centralizing tendency was so strong that the capital cities of most Latin American countries were governed directly by the president of the republic, and two of them (Buenos Aires and Mexico City) still were in 1994. Meanwhile in Brazil, which had become a monarchy in its own right, the 1824 Constitution included provision for a municipal regime inspired to some extent by the Anglo-Saxon tradition of self-government. An 1834 amendment, however, placed municipalities under a suffocating centralization by provincial government, which was only gradually lessened by the 1891 and 1934 Constitutions.

Starting in the late nineteenth century, the completion of the process of national consolidation and the growing regional ascendancy of the United States led to the gradual receptivity of Latin America to Anglo-Saxon liberal philosophy. The classic early work on the U.S. political system, Alexis de Tocqueville's *Democracy in America,* first appeared in translation in Buenos Aires in 1864. Its fervent advocacy of decentralization and strong local government had a major impact on intellectual circles. This new influence was reflected in the promulgation in many countries of idealistic constitutions based on the North American model. Local government was granted formal autonomy and widespread powers that either were written directly into the constitution itself or were granted through separate municipal codes.

Despite this liberal ideal, with few exceptions, the enduring centralist tradition meant that local government lacked the financial resources to implement the wide range of functions to which it was formally committed. The constant abrogation of municipal elections by central government curtailed local government's political autonomy. At the same time, clientelism and the "spoils system" of recruitment greatly diminished its administrative capability. In the early decades of the twentieth century, a yawning gulf began to emerge between the rhetoric of local government autonomy and the reality of local government's gradual degeneration into an instrument for political control by central government. The cynical verbosity of speeches exalting the importance of the municipality (*municipalidad*) and its predecessor, the cabildo, in the democratic tradition of Latin America masked the dismal reality of incompetence, immorality, and impotence in municipal affairs.

DEMUNICIPALIZATION

From the 1930s onward, state-led strategies for import-substituting industrialization were introduced throughout most of Latin America. This produced a rapid urbanization process that soon revealed the gross deficiencies of the local government system. Municipalities were incapable of responding to the needs of migrants from rural areas who poured into the cities in search of new job opportunities. Virtually every government in the region reacted to this challenge not by strengthening municipal government, but by creating new central government bodies that stripped municipalities of their formal role as service providers at the local level (Harris:185).

This way of "resolving" the problem reflected the postwar ideological attraction of centralized planning as the most effective way to boost economic growth, an idea that dovetailed conveniently with the corporativist philosophy of the populist political regimes then in power. It also reflected the influence of the U.S. foreign aid program, USAID, whose technocratic managers invariably preferred to channel aid through these newly established agencies of central government, which could "get things done quickly" through bypassing the decrepit structures of local government. These agencies were viewed as incorporating the methods of technocratic rationality, ensuring a greater "functional" orientation to state action and greater cost-effectiveness through economies of scale. Their operations were also nationwide, allegedly providing a more uniform and standardized focus to state action.

As a result, in the 1950s and 1960s, a widespread process of "demunicipalization" took place throughout the subcontinent as responsibility for the delivery of such important services as urban water supply, transportation, public housing, primary health care, and education was transferred to central government. More generally, however, and contrary to the African and Asian experiences, at no point did this process of demunicipalization lead to abandonment of the formal structures of classical local government, even though the local institutions operated under heavy central pressure in the control of administration and resources (Mawhood:14).

Demunicipalization was nevertheless a selective process, and it had a differential impact on local government. The process of central government encroachment concentrated on those larger urban areas of strategic importance where new industries were located. Here the establishment of local branches of national utility companies did not allow for any significant representational role by municipal authorities. In this way, local political constraints to the decisionmaking process were effectively removed. But in large cities, local government was sometimes able to retain control over the provision of basic services by creating companies under municipal ownership. Many midsized towns also retained control over these services, although there was a marked tendency for the supply of water and electricity to be transferred to national agencies. The vast majority of smaller rural municipalities were hardly affected by this process and continued to be neglected by central government. They retained nominal responsibility for services that they were not able to provide and that central government was not interested in providing.

By the 1960s, both the left and the right of the political spectrum had tended to define democracy by reference to foreign rather than domestic considerations. For leftists, freedom from U.S. imperialism was paramount in the conceptualization of democracy, and for rightists freedom from Soviet communism assumed paramount importance. Despite their differences, however, both ends of the ideological spectrum deemphasized the importance of civil society, at the same time endorsing the importance of a highly centralized state in order to "defend" democracy. Furthermore, this approach stressed the positive contribution of the armed forces to the "defense of democracy" because of the identification of those forces with the independence movement and their subsequent self-assumed role as guardians of the national interest. During the 1970s a swathe of military regimes came to dominate the political system of Latin America, and by the end of the decade most countries in the region were ruled directly by the armed forces. In fact, the military soon came to personify the centralist tradition and proceeded, in the name of democracy, to deny the most basic democratic rights to citizens.

LOCAL GOVERNMENT IN CRISIS

By the 1970s, local government was in crisis in much of Latin America. The vast majority of municipalities had been reduced to historical relics—a nostalgic reminder of a bygone era that existed only in the imagination. Despite being referred to pompously as the bastion of Latin American democracy, and despite occupying a high-profile position in national constitutions, in reality the municipality had become obsolescent and fulfilled a purely ceremonial function. Following the centralist tradition, central government continued to exert control over municipalities, as expressed in the strict application of uniform laws and by the financial supervision over budgeting exercised by the auditor-general's office. Centralization produced a self-perpetuating cycle of municipal neglect. Central government did not grant local government a strong local revenue base or a significant share of national fiscal revenue. This shortage of finance meant that local government could not deliver a wide range of services and hence had little need—or financial ability—to recruit more technically qualified staff. In turn, central government then argued that it could not devolve service delivery responsibilities to local governments because they lacked the capacity to administer such services.

The extreme shortage of finance and lack of trained personnel combined to bring about a vicious circle of municipal decay that prevented local government from carrying out to a satisfactory degree even the limited range of activities (such as civil registration, beautification of the town, and solid waste management) to which it had been reduced. Growing financial dependency upon transfers from central government also encouraged the abdication by local government of its own responsibility for revenue generation, thereby encouraging further demunicipalization. It strengthened the culture of clientelism and political dependence on central government. The weak financial base also encouraged administrative instability, the symptoms of which were the lack of job stability and professionalism, the absence of a career and training structure, and the short terms of officeholders.

The popular image of local government became negative throughout the subcontinent. Citizens' experience of the nepotism, corruption, administrative inefficiency, lack of public accountability, and poor quality of service delivery led to the creation of a caricature of the municipal employee (*funcionario municipal*) that in several countries bordered on a term of personal abuse.

The prospects for reform appeared equally dismal. A major review of local government in the region in 1968 concluded that "the economic dependence of local government upon national governments appears to be an undeniable fact, which makes any tendency to increase the political and administrative autonomy of municipal governments seem utopian"; thus, in proposing possible solutions, "it is necessary to adopt a realistic position, viewing municipal government, not as an autonomous entity but rather as being autarchic, with decentralization taking place in the administrative instead of the political sense" (OAS:11, 21).

The reasons for this pessimistic assessment were not hard to find. One writer drew attention to the "pathological syndrome" of local government in

Latin America at the time (Lordello de Mello, 1983:188), which consisted of an interlocking and mutually reinforcing set of attributes that had produced a vicious circle of decline and decay. Foremost among these was the legacy of mistrust felt by the colonial authority toward its possessions. This legacy was so strong that it denied municipalities any significant role in the formulation and implementation of policies that had an impact on their area of jurisdiction. It also prevented municipalities from serving as effective mechanisms for transmitting local concerns to central government.

As late as 1983, a review of global trends in decentralization noted pessimistically that in Latin America, government structures generally remained highly centralized and that there appeared to be little prospect of any major change in the near future (Conyers:97). In the same year, one reviewer noted that the devolution of power from central to local government was not a major feature of contemporary administrative reforms in the region (Harris:194–195), and another described reforms within Latin American local government at the time as timid (Lordello de Mello, 1983:191).

At the very time that these assessments were being made, the disastrous consequences of neglecting local government during four decades of very rapid urbanization were fast becoming apparent in the burgeoning metropolises of Latin America. Urban planning by central government had turned out to be almost exclusively sectoral in nature, with little coordination among the unaccountable state agencies responsible for the delivery of different public services. The absence of comprehensive cross-sectoral urban planning was probably the single most important reason for the rapid decline in the quality of urban living; it had led to environmental pollution, traffic chaos, lack of green space, and a severe housing shortage. Only one institution—local government—was capable of providing urban planning that was both comprehensive and democratically accountable.

THE INVIGORATION OF LOCAL GOVERNMENT

By the beginning of the 1980s, the problems of local government in Latin America were well rehearsed. A wealth of national and regional studies carried out during the previous twenty years had dissected the sick corpus of the Latin American municipality and had graphically described its ailments. These studies were invariably accompanied by prescriptions for recovery. But few, if any, of these reforms had been implemented because of an absence of political will. During the 1980s, however, a remarkable improvement took place in the fortunes of local government, which influenced most countries in the region. Both external and internal factors played their part in this dramatic turnaround.

First, there was a growing worldwide movement toward decentralization, which was no longer seen simply as a means to improve service delivery. It was now regarded as a way of improving national planning, and especially the planning of rural development, by making policies more flexible, more relevant to local needs, and more effective in the coordination of the field activities of different government agencies. Decentralization was also seen as a way to attain basic needs objectives by improving popular participation in development. Here the writings of Jordi Borja on the French and Spanish experiences of decentralization were particularly influential (Borja:16–17). But more significant, after decades during which decentralization had received only rhetorical support in Latin America, two interrelated and mutually reinforcing factors were creating the political will to regenerate local government: a growing crisis of political legitimacy and the fiscal crisis of the state.

The Crisis of Political Legitimacy

The political argument in favor of local government is invariably stronger in countries that are emerging from autocracy. This was true in Latin America during the 1980s, as it would prove to be later in Eastern Europe. Until then, however, there had been a theoretical vacuum in the political culture of Latin America with regard to the significance of local democracy. This void was all the more surprising given that the technique of political consciousness raising, known as *concientización,* which gives great emphasis to decentralized and participatory forms of decisionmaking, originated within the region. This collective blind spot spanned the political spectrum. The political left, steeped in the Marxist orthodoxy of the command economy, lacked any tradition of decentralization. Likewise, populist parties such as the Mexican PRI and the Argentine Peronists neglected local government, and the political right remained wedded to the doctrine of national security, which served only to reinforce the prevailing centralist tradition.

As the 1970s wore on, it became apparent that the state faced a growing crisis of legitimacy, not only in countries under military rule, such as Brazil and Peru, but also in discredited democratic polities, such as Venezuela and Colombia. This realization encouraged intellectuals within the democratic opposition in many countries to initiate a thorough reevaluation of the traditional Latin American conceptualization of democracy, which had tended to be defined only by reference to international considerations—freedom from imperialism and from international communism. By placing a new emphasis on the domestic determinants of democracy, these intellectuals focused their attention increasingly on the influence that the centralist tradition continued to have in maintaining a chasm between the state and civil society.

A political strategy to decentralize the Latin American state was proposed as the most effective way to break this tradition. It was believed that diluting the power of the centralized state would also undermine the political, social, and economic bases on which autocratic rule had been built. Similarly, given that military rule had been facilitated by the weak structures of civil society, the construction of a strong and representative system of local government was viewed as crucial to sustaining democratic rule in the future.

The relationship between decentralization and participation in democracy was an important aspect of this new thinking. Strengthening local government was seen as the key to overcoming one of the central deficiencies of the Latin American state that derived from its centralism—its antiparticipatory nature. This incapacity for dialogue with civil society manifested itself through the limited scale and poor allocation of resources spent on social sectors. There was ample evidence that the exclusionary nature of Latin American political systems, by reducing citizen choice, had distorted expenditure priorities in a manner that had led to the inefficient and highly inequitable use of resources. Consequently, it was believed that genuine opportunities for participation in local decisionmaking processes would bring about a more "people-oriented" style of development. Hence, decentralization, by providing the necessary framework within which locally based citizen organizations could flourish, became an essential element in a participatory style of development that enhanced collective choice.

There was also a more explicitly political consideration that explained this new concern for the participatory rather than the purely representative aspects of democracy. It was widely feared that exclusive concentration on the formalities of representative democracy might make the system vulnerable to a resurgence of authoritarian rule if it did not bring about tangible improvements in living standards. To counter this threat, participation through local government was viewed as a means of political education and as the best way to deepen democratic culture in order to ensure the long-term viability of the transition process.

This revised conceptualization of the nature of Latin American democracy was particularly strong on the center-left of the political spectrum. Until the 1980s the "state can do it all" approach, encompassing central planning and the use of directives to lower tiers of government, had been the prevailing orthodoxy. Although this had been strongly influenced by the Soviet experience, it was in fact quite congruent with the centralist tradition within Latin America itself. But during the 1980s this approach was increasingly called into question as popular resistance to military rule expressed itself through community organizations. In those countries such as Brazil and Chile where municipalities became a "laboratory of resistance" to military rule, there was a new practical awareness of local government's potential contribution to the process of democratization. The collapse of the centralist model of Soviet communism in the late 1980s added fuel to the argument, compelling leftist parties to put forward local-level political programs, rather than just appealing for the conquest of power at a national level.

The Fiscal Crisis of the State

A surprising omission in studies of the Latin American debt crisis of the 1980s has been the impact that it had upon central-local financial relations, as well as the indirect contribution it made to the invigoration of local government in the region (Nickson:222). Starting with the Mexican default in August 1982, Latin American nations struggled to adjust to the lethal cocktail of a hike in real interest rates and a sharp deterioration in their terms of trade. Facing theoretical debt service ratios of over 100 percent, most countries in the region were forced to accept structural adjustment programs imposed by the International Monetary Fund (IMF) in order to obtain the agreement of creditor banks to debt rescheduling and refinancing packages.

This "fiscal crisis of the state," as it came to be known, had major consequences for service delivery at the local level. The central government bodies created during the demunicipalization period of the 1950s and 1960s had invariably operated on the basis of loans from foreign commercial banks that were on-lent through the financial intermediary of a parent ministry or a national development bank. These state corporations, which were notorious for defaulting on their repayment obligations, underwent a financial crisis during the 1980s as central banks refused to guarantee further foreign borrowing for fear of aggravating the debt burden.

Faced with a fiscal crisis and a continuing growth in demand for urban public services because of rapid migration from rural areas, governments were encouraged by the IMF to adopt a twin-track strategy. This involved the transfer of responsibility for service provision both horizontally to the private sector through privatization and vertically to local government through decentralization. The principal reason for the second prong of this strategy was the growing recognition by central governments of the enormous untapped fiscal potential of local government. Effective yields on most local taxes, especially property taxation, had fallen to derisory levels over the previous decades because of the failure of cadastral surveys to keep abreast with rapid urban growth, the failure to adjust tax rates in line with high rates of inflation, and widespread administrative inefficiency and corruption facilitated by the system of self-assessment for local taxation.

Although the overriding objective of this strategy was to correct a severe fiscal deficit, it was also argued that decentralization would raise the allocative and productive efficiency, the equity, and the effectiveness of service delivery as follows:

1. Allocative efficiency would be improved because resources could be allocated more efficiently by local government, which had a better understanding of local priorities than central government, and this would lead to a greater focus on human development expenditure that had a higher social priority ratio and was more labor-intensive in nature.
2. Productive efficiency could be improved through lower unit costs arising from the use of locally available resources in construction (e.g., user groups, rather than government contractors, could build water supply systems) and in maintenance (e.g., road maintenance could be carried out through intermunicipal pooling of equipment rather than by the ministry of public works).
3. Equity could be improved because local government had the detailed local knowledge to enable more effective targeting to identify, implement, and monitor programs designed to benefit the very poor. This was in contrast to the failure of traditional social programs administered by national agencies, the benefits of which did not accrue to those in greatest need.
4. Effectiveness would be improved because local government, through community organizations, was better able than central government to monitor the implementation and impact of public expenditure.

In addition to its contribution to the strengthening of local government "from above" through shifts in national fiscal policy, the debt crisis generated pressures "from below" that also contributed to its invigoration. The cutback in recurrent government expenditure brought about by IMF-imposed structural adjustment programs, especially the reductions in food and transport subsidies, had their greatest impact in the slums that ring the major cities of Latin America. The increasing level of absolute poverty this brought about was the main factor fueling the rapid growth in community organizations during the 1980s, which were heralded by sympathetic observers as the "new social movements." In particular, as the economic crisis deepened, self-help groups were formed to organize soup kitchens. As they grew in number, these community initiatives often coalesced into municipal-wide organizations that lobbied local government for financial and logistical support. A striking example was the Glass of Milk program initiated by community organizations in poor municipalities in Lima, Peru, which dramatically symbolized the relationship that was beginning to evolve between the local state and civil society in Latin America during the 1980s.

The Coalition for Change

By the mid-1980s, an uneasy domestic coalition had emerged in most Latin American countries in favor of decentralization. The main demands of these coalitions were greater political autonomy for local government, the devolution of responsibility for service delivery to the municipal level, and an associated strengthening of municipal finances. Three very different groups, with very different agendas, created this consensus because they all saw the decentralization process as a means to advance their aims. First, there were the neoliberals, who viewed decentralization as an essential part of a wider strategy for reducing the role of the public sector as a whole within the economy. Second, there were the radical reformers, who saw decentralization as a progressive measure designed to overcome the inegalitarian and undemocratic social structures inherited from the past. Third, there were the technocrats, who viewed decentralization primarily as a means to improve the overall efficiency of service delivery through better coordination at the local level.

The active encouragement of international development agencies was as important as the domestic coalitions for change. After two decades during which they had sought to bypass local government in their lending programs to Latin America, both the Inter-American Development Bank and the World Bank suddenly rediscovered the value of municipal endeavor. This volte-face was a reflection of their support for the harsh exigencies of IMF structural adjustment rather than an appreciation of the democratic virtues of decentralization. As such, these agencies lent support to the neoliberal elements within the domestic coalitions and emphasized the benefits of decentralization in terms of fiscal cleansing rather than citizen participation. According to this interpretation, local government was intended to play a purely instrumental role as a more efficient administrator of poverty alleviation programs. It would improve upon central government's performance by identifying target households, by coordinating centrally funded welfare programs, and by mobilizing community participation in social investment projects.

This support from international development agencies was demonstrated by shifts in their loan portfolios. In the early 1980s, the Inter-American Development Bank launched a new lending program for municipal development in Latin America. In order not to exacerbate the debt service problem of central government, municipalities became the final borrowers of these loans. They pledged their general revenues, or those generated by the project itself, as collateral for the credit, with the central government acting as financial intermediary only. By 1990 the bank was financing such projects in virtually every Latin American country. The World Bank also began to show a strong interest in municipal institution building during the 1980s (Guarda:118). It allocated significant funding for training in urban management and local government finance, through initiatives such as the Latin American Center for Training and Development of Local Government (CELCADEL), which was set up in Quito in 1983, and the global Urban Management Program established in the mid-1980s jointly with the United Nations Development Programme (UNDP) and the United Nations Centre for Human Settlements (HABITAT).

As the influence of this powerful domestic and international consensus in favor of decentralization was felt in the public policymaking process, a growing number of municipalities in the region increased the scale of their operations and changed the nature of their relationship with both central government and their own citizens. This process of municipal revitalization varied enormously from country to country. Costa Rica, the Dominican Republic, and Honduras proved the only exceptions. By the mid-1990s a clear regional trend that enhanced the role of local government in Latin American society had emerged.

2

THE LEGAL STATUS
OF LOCAL GOVERNMENT

A necessary starting point for comprehending contemporary local government in Latin America is to distinguish between the rhetoric and the reality of municipal autonomy in the region. The law pertaining to local government is embodied in national constitutions, as well as in separate municipal codes (see Table 2.1). Since 1984 new municipal codes have been

Table 2.1   National Legislation Concerning Local Government in Latin America

Country	Municipal Code
Argentina	Promulgated by each state government
Bolivia	Ley Orgánica de Municipalidades No. 696 (10 January 1985)
Brazil	Promulgated by each state government
Chile	Ley Orgánica Constitucional de Municipalidades No. 19130 (19 March 1992)
Colombia	Código de Régimen Municipal No. 1333 (25 April 1986)
Costa Rica	Código Municipal No. 4574 (30 April 1970)
Dominican Republic	Ley sobre Organización Municipal No. 3455 (21 December 1952)
Ecuador	Ley de Régimen Municipal No. 680 (31 January 1966)
El Salvador	Código Municipal No. 274 (31 January 1986)
Guatemala	Código Municipal No. 58 (12 October 1988)
Honduras	Ley de Municipalidades No. 13,490 (29 October 1990)
Mexico	Promulgated by each state government
Nicaragua	Ley de Municipios No. 40 (17 August 1988)
Panama	Ley sobre Régimen Municipal No. 106 (8 October 1973)
Paraguay	Ley Orgánica Municipal No. 1294 (9 December 1987)
Peru	Ley Orgánica de Municipalidades No. 23853 (28 May 1984)
Uruguay	Ley Orgánica Municipal No. 9515 (28 October 1935)
Venezuela	Ley Orgánica de Régimen Municipal No. 4,109 (15 June 1989)

promulgated in ten countries. The most striking examples were in Peru, where the 1984 municipal code replaced a body of municipal law that had been in force since 1892; in El Salvador, where the municipal code of 1986 replaced legislation that had been in existence since 1908; and in Colombia, where the 1986 municipal code replaced legislation from 1913. New municipal codes were also passed in Bolivia (1985), Paraguay (1987), Nicaragua (1988), Venezuela (1988), Guatemala (1988), Honduras (1990), and Chile (1992). In Mexico (1983), Guatemala (1986), and Paraguay (1992), major legislation reforming local government was introduced through articles in the respective national constitutions.

A cursory review of these laws conveys the false impression that in most countries local government is independent of central government. Wording to this effect, which defines the municipality as the primary and autonomous unit of government within the national political system, is now embedded in the constitution of virtually every country in the region. The opening articles of the recent constitutions of Colombia (1991) and Paraguay (1992) have even defined the nation itself as "decentralized." The 1987 amendment to the provincial constitution of Córdoba in Argentina granted municipalities with more than 10,000 inhabitants the right to draw up their own charters, and the new 1988 Brazilian constitution for the first time recognized municipalities as constitutional bodies.

Constitutions and associated municipal codes typically define local government autonomy in three major ways: politically, so that it is able to elect its own authorities; administratively, so that it may operate without interference in areas under its jurisdiction; and financially, so that it has the power to levy and collect its own sources of income. In addition, several constitutions state that municipal decisions can be challenged only through the courts.

This legal assertion of wide-ranging municipal autonomy, however, is largely a fiction. Latin American political culture remains highly centralized, and with the limited exception of Brazil, local government relations with central government are still characterized by subordination rather than equality. Laws approved by the national congress and decrees issued by the national executive invariably have an enormous bearing on municipal activities. The municipal codes approved by central government regulate the internal organization and functions of local government to a high degree. Municipalities have virtually no independent legislative function and can make regulations only within the framework of state and national laws.

Although the constitutional rhetoric of autonomy grants local government the power of general competence, in practice central government has significantly reduced this autonomy by abrogating functions that were formerly allocated to municipalities, as happened during the demunicipalization of the 1950s and 1960s. Municipal financial autonomy is severely constrained by a heavy dependence on transfers from central government, as well as by the need for local tax rates to be approved and accounts verified by central government audit bodies. Finally, the constitutional autonomy of local government is belied by the fact that in many countries municipal administrations (mayors and councils) may be suspended by a majority vote of the national congress for failure to discharge their duties.

So pervasive is this centralist tradition that it eclipses the formal distinction between local government's operation within either federal or unitary Latin American nations. The federal system of government established in four countries (Argentina, Brazil, Mexico, and Venezuela) did not derive from any commitment to decentralization, but rather from the urgent need to unite territory within which there was little semblance of national identity and within which regional (and even secessionist) tendencies were strong. Once national territorial integration had been ensured, both municipal autonomy and federalism were gradually suffocated. As a consequence, the federal norms imposed over the structure and functioning of local government soon differed little from those imposed by central government in the unitary nations of the region. Municipalities within federal nations have therefore tended to enjoy no greater degree of municipal autonomy than elsewhere in Latin America.

3

THE STRUCTURE
OF LOCAL GOVERNMENT

In 1994 there were 13,951 municipalities in Latin America, with an average population of 31,553 (see Table 3.1). The average population size of municipalities varied considerably among countries. National averages typically ranged between 20,000 and 55,000 (see Figure 3.1). The only exceptions were Uruguay, which had a much larger average size (168,421) because of the absence of any tier of government below that of the department, and Peru, which had a much smaller average size (12,736) because of its unique two-tier system of local government. These average municipal sizes are considerably higher than those found in the countries of southern Europe (France, 1,560; Spain, 4,700; Germany, 8,845) and North America (United States, 6,600; Canada, 5,594), but they are similar to those found in northern Europe (Netherlands, 17,860; Sweden, 30,249), Australia (19,114), and Japan (37,200) (Norton:40).

Such international comparisons are deceptive, however, because in every Latin American country except Costa Rica, these national averages mask enormous disparities in the population size of different municipalities. These differences are unusually pronounced by international standards. Population size ranges from the tiny Municipalities of Rosario Tasna in Bolivia (population 185) and Santiago Tepetlapa in the State of Oaxaca, Mexico (population 149) to the enormous Municipality of São Paolo in Brazil (population 9,627,000).

The conventional image of the typical Latin American municipality as a large city is false. Although a small minority are among the largest cities in the world, most are little more than large villages. The vast majority of municipalities in the region have fewer than 15,000 inhabitants, are

Table 3.1   Number and Average Size of Latin American Municipalities

Country	Number of Municipalities	Population in millions (mid-1994)	Average Population per Municipality
Argentina	1,100	33.9	30,818
Bolivia	296	8.2	27,703
Brazil	4,974	155.3	31,222
Chile	334	14.0	41,916
Colombia	1,034	35.6	34,429
Costa Rica	81	3.2	39,506
Dominican Republic	137	7.8	56,934
Ecuador	193	10.6	54,922
El Salvador	262	5.2	19,847
Guatemala	330	10.3	31,212
Honduras	291	5.3	18,213
Mexico	2,397	91.8	38,298
Nicaragua	143	4.3	30,070
Panama	67	2.5	37,313
Paraguay	213	4.8	22,535
Peru	1,798	22.9	12,736
Uruguay	19	3.2	168,421
Venezuela	282	21.3	75,532
All of Latin America	13,951	440.2	31,553

Source: Data from Chapters 10 through 27 in this book and Population Concern.

essentially rural in character, have low population densities, and are relatively poor by comparison with the national average income per head. At the other end of the scale, only around one hundred municipalities, less than 0.1 percent of the total, have more than 500,000 inhabitants. These are overwhelmingly urban in character, are densely populated, and have a relatively high income per head by comparison with the national average. Even in the small nations of Central America, only 1.5 percent of the 1,170 municipalities have more than 100,000 inhabitants; the vast majority (or 72 percent) have populations of 20,000 or fewer (Wheaton:15).

These disparities in municipal size have evolved largely because of the failure of municipal structures to respond to the changing pattern of human settlement in the region. Massive migration from rural areas, especially during the second half of the twentieth century, swelled the populations of historic urban centers, many of which had originally achieved their municipal status during the colonial period. At the same time, this migration contributed to the demographic stagnation, if not absolute decline, of the vast majority of small, rural municipalities. Yet nowhere in the region has the basic structure of local government been reformed to reflect these demographic changes. Municipal boundaries have not been reshaped to accommodate the rapidly changing pattern of human settlement. Nor have

Figure 3.1   Average Population Size of Latin American Municipalities

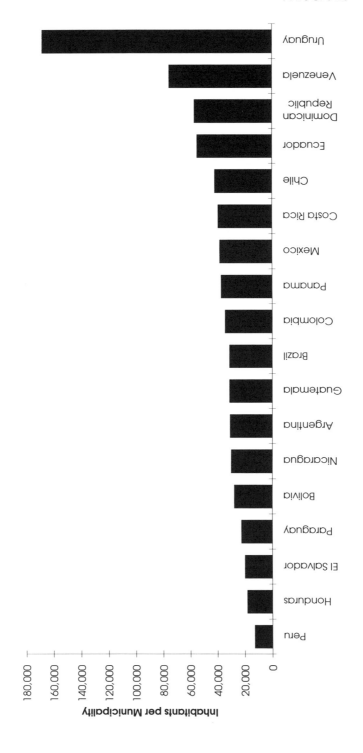

Source: Data from Table 3.1.

municipalities been divided into size categories according to their ability to provide different levels of service provision. Because any such moves would be interpreted as a flagrant violation of local government autonomy, municipal boundaries are effectively cast in stone, and all municipalities, large and small, are treated equally by the law in terms of the range of services for which they are responsible.

The unwillingness to contemplate the territorial restructuring of local government in the direction of amalgamation has undermined effective and efficient municipal service provision in both large and small municipalities. Latin America now contains some of the largest metropolitan areas in the world—in 1990 the region had eleven cities with more than three million inhabitants, as well as thirty-nine cities with more than one million inhabitants, of which no fewer than fourteen were in Brazil (Gilbert, 1994:34). Most of these large conurbations have long been designated as metropolitan areas, although none has a functioning metropolitan government (Edelman:9). This is often a result of the alleged threat amalgamation would pose to the autonomy of municipalities located within their boundaries. The absence of metropolitan government has led to lack of coordination, rivalry, and duplication in service provision between municipalities within large conurbations. This is especially noticeable with respect to solid waste disposal, transportation, and urban planning.

Meanwhile, small, low-density municipalities in rural areas lack the financial and human resources to operate a comprehensive range of services independently. Amalgamation makes available technically qualified municipal staff and enables the cost-effective provision of basic services such as road maintenance in rural areas through economies of scale. But this is almost always precluded by the refusal of municipalities to contemplate amalgamation on the grounds of municipal autonomy. Instead, central governments have often sought to address this problem indirectly by strengthening the intermediate or departmental tier of government and by granting it a measure of political autonomy through the direct election of governors and regional assemblies. Municipal subdivision has been a very common phenomenon in rural areas, a fact that largely explains the significant rise in the total number of municipalities during the twentieth century. The historic pattern of the Latin American municipality has been based on an urban center and surrounding rural territory. In areas of expanding colonization, new urban settlements emerged within the rural hinterland of existing municipalities. They usually lacked adequate political representation and were subordinated to political interests in the municipal headquarters. The prime motive for "breaking away" has invariably been to obtain better access to central government funding for basic rural services, especially feeder roads, primary schools, and electrification. Throughout the region this process of municipal fragmentation has unwittingly been encouraged by the growing use of transparent formulae for the allocation of central government financial transfers, which ensure a minimum amount for every municipality, irrespective of its size.

At a time when the number of municipalities in many parts of the world is being reduced in order to make service provision more cost-effective, the process of municipal fragmentation continues apace in Latin America, albeit at a slower rate since the 1980s. The political momentum of this process remains strong. It continues in flagrant violation of strict regulations in virtually all national municipal codes, which specify a minimum population size as a precondition for legal recognition of new municipalities. Its effect is to keep most Latin American municipalities well below the critical size needed in order to reap the economies of both scale and scope that would justify the trained personnel and capital investment necessary to provide adequate service provision to the citizens.

4

LOCAL GOVERNMENT SERVICES

An important consequence of the uniform treatment before the law that characterizes local government autonomy in Latin America is that all municipalities are granted the same legal mandate for service provision. Despite the enormous differences in population size, hardly anywhere are municipalities classified into size categories, with corresponding differential powers and responsibilities. This uniform mandate is determined by central government, sometimes in constitutional provisions, but more often in the form of municipal codes. This is the case in both unitary and federal nations, with the sole exception of Argentina, where the mandate for local government is established by provincial government. Yet the capacity of the vast majority of municipalities to carry out those functions mandated to them is severely constrained by a lack of financial and human resources. In contrast, a few larger municipalities have far greater access to revenue. This leads, in practice, to enormous differences between large and small municipalities in the range of services they actually provide.

DISCRETIONARY AND NONDISCRETIONARY FUNCTIONS

Municipal codes usually grant local government a general competence to undertake any service that is not assigned to another level of government or that the local administration is not expressly forbidden to do. This differs sharply from the ultra vires restrictions in some countries (of which Chile is a rare example in Latin America), which limit the municipal mandate to clearly specified competencies. Behind the rhetoric of this general competence, however, lies the all-important legal distinction between so-called discretionary and nondiscretionary functions. The point at which the line is drawn between the two is ultimately determined by central government and reflects the self-imposed limits of that government's encroachment on municipal terrain.

Nondiscretionary functions, those mandated to local government, include few that central government has any interest in undertaking itself. It is these services, and these alone, that the vast majority of municipalities in Latin America actually provide. But they are obligatory in name only, because no mechanism exists to penalize local government if the services are not delivered. These nondiscretionary functions fall into four broad categories:

1. elementary powers of regulation carried out on behalf of central government, such as maintenance of public order, provision of justices of the peace, and civil registration;
2. essential urban services, such as road maintenance, city lighting, street cleaning, solid waste management, and basic land use zoning;
3. essential revenue-generating public services, such as slaughterhouses, cemeteries, public markets, and bus terminals;
4. basic social services, such as public hygiene, granting of commercial and industrial licenses, and weights and measures.

By contrast, discretionary functions are those that central government has an interest in undertaking. Most, if not all, of them were in practice absorbed by central government during the period of demunicipalization. As a result, the role of local government in those functions for which it has been granted a discretionary mandate usually amounts to little more than serving as a junior partner in ongoing central government activities at the local level. In several countries, most notably Brazil, these concurrent powers have led to poor coordination in service delivery between central and local government, producing inefficient duplication in some areas and gaps in others where no tier of government takes responsibility for provision. These discretionary functions fall into three broad categories:

1. public utilities (water, sewerage, and electricity supply);
2. social services (primary health care and basic education);
3. planning (road transport and zoning).

Despite the rhetoric of general competence, Latin American municipalities have rarely taken the initiative to expand their own mandate beyond the nondiscretionary and discretionary services outlined in the municipal code. This may be explained in part by the general financial, technical, and political weakness of local government. Another reason is the highly legalistic system of audit used by central government to review municipal administration. The fear of becoming enmeshed in a complex legal maze over which they have little understanding or control has effectively discouraged most municipalities from extending their mandate.

This unrealistic uniformity in the legal mandate horizontally across municipalities, combined with the blurred allocation of responsibilities vertically between different tiers of government because of the legal ambiguity of discretionary and concurrent powers, has led to a bewildering variety in the range and level of municipalities' service provision within each country. The situation has been succinctly summed up in common parlance as follows: Latin American municipalities can do anything except that which is expressly prohibited; on the other hand, they are not expressly obliged to do anything.

A noticeable feature of the recent strengthening of local government in some countries has been the transfer of core services in the social sector (health and education) from central government to local government in the form of nondiscretionary functions. In almost all cases, the initiative has come from central government. Chile provided the pioneering example, and over the period 1979–1987 the administration of primary health care and primary and secondary education was transferred to local government. In Colombia responsibility for water supply and sewerage, as well as construction and maintenance of schools, health clinics, and roads, was transferred to local government after 1987; this led to the closing of a number of central government agencies that previously administered these services. In 1994 the Bolivian government announced its intention to transfer the administration of health and education services from central to local government.

Since the mid-1980s there has also been a noticeable incursion by municipalities into the field of local economic development in several countries, notably Brazil. This has been motivated primarily by the desire to create local employment opportunities during a period of growing urban poverty brought about by structural adjustment. Such initiatives led to the promotion of small-scale industries through the establishment of low-rent facilities in industrial zones, and they often involved collaboration with nongovernmental organizations (NGOs). In such schemes, municipalities have usually given preference to assisting cooperative forms of industrial ownership, which have been generated as part of a wider policy of encouraging community participation in local government.

However, policing remains one of the most centralized functions of the Latin American state. As a result, municipal police powers are invariably circumscribed to minor matters such as road traffic control and supervision of municipal markets. Despite its centrality to the broader issues of democratization and the fostering of a sense of citizenship, nowhere in the region has policing been devolved to local government to any significant degree since the 1980s. Although they now greatly exceed the military as the main perpetrators of human rights violations in the region, the police are hardly ever accountable to local government (Fox:108). This poses particular problems in rural areas, where most violations occur.

SPECIAL SOCIAL WELFARE PROGRAMS

Since the early 1980s governments in many Latin American countries have created special social welfare programs designed to protect the most vulnerable members of society from the severe drop in living standards brought about by policies of macroeconomic structural adjustment, often imposed by the International Monetary Fund. In several countries—notably Chile, Bolivia, and Mexico—local government has been assigned a major role in administering these programs on the grounds that such a decentralized approach can provide a safety net in a more efficient and transparent manner while also enhancing citizenship through community participation in their implementation. In the early 1980s the Chilean government restructured the existing system of state welfare in order to direct resources more precisely to the poorest. This "top-down" approach emphasized state-directed targeting to the household level. Local government was assigned the key responsibilities of identifying target households through regular and detailed household surveys and administering the ensuing range of benefits. The advent of a democratic government in the 1990s has seen the adoption of a more demand-led and participatory approach with the incorporation of community-based investment projects through the Fondo de Solidaridad e Inversión Social (FOSIS), a social development program (C. Graham:317).

The Bolivian Emergency Social Fund (ESF) was introduced in the wake of a harsh 1985 stabilization plan and has attracted considerable international attention. It represented a very different approach to the Chilean program, targeting its resources at the level of the community rather than that of the individual household. It was also administered differently. From the start, it was independent from the central government bureaucracy, was nonpartisan in nature, and was exclusively demand-led. Local government, often working in association with nongovernmental organizations, played a key role in generating requests for funding from local communities. The ESF also enhanced the capacity of local government through the provision of financial transfers independent of central government (C. Graham:312). Like the ESF, the Mexican Solidarity program, launched in 1988, also sought to relieve poverty in the wake of structural adjustment. However, its operations have been strongly influenced by the parallel objective of propping up the flagging support for the ruling party. This has meant that, although the approach is demand-led, it has failed to develop the nonpartisan features found in Bolivia during 1985–1989. Local government authorities play a key role in the operation of the Solidarity program by controlling the disbursement of federal funds to neighborhood solidarity committees at the submunicipal level.

SERVICE DELIVERY

Municipal services are delivered in one of four main ways in Latin America. First, they may be directly administered through a hierarchy of municipal secretariats and departments that are directly subordinate to the executive. Second, they may be indirectly administered by municipally owned foundations. These foundations remain closely tied to the municipal administration, with their chief executives being nominated by the mayor and their staff employed on basically the same terms as municipal officials. They do, however, allow service deliverers greater budgetary independence. Third, they may be indirectly administered by enterprises that either are wholly owned by municipalities or are joint ventures with the private sector. As private companies, they operate with an even greater degree of flexibility with regard to pay and conditions of service, although their chief executives are still usually nominated by the mayor. Finally, services may be delivered by private companies or voluntary agencies that have gained the concession as a result of a tendering procedure; service delivery is formalized in a contract with the municipality. The contracting out of service delivery to the private sector in this way is a well-established practice throughout Latin America, especially for solid waste disposal and street cleaning. In many municipalities, however, clientelism and nepotism have led to a lack of transparency in tendering procedures for such concessions, as well as inadequate mechanisms for monitoring and regulating the concessionee's performance. In some countries, notably Argentina, political controversy over contracting out has led to severe problems of human resource management and to disruption in service delivery, as municipalities have first contracted out and then annulled contracts in order to provide the service in-house, or vice versa.

5

LOCAL GOVERNMENT FINANCE

The share of local government in total public expenditure within Latin America ranges from a low of only 2 percent in Panama and Paraguay to a high of 18 percent and 24 percent in Brazil and Colombia (see Table 5.1). As in other parts of the world, there is no strong positive correlation between this share and the level of national per capita income (see Figure 5.1). The financial pattern of Latin American local government is similar to that found in many other parts of the world. When measured by their share of gross domestic product, municipalities tend to be more important as providers of public services than as collectors of revenues, and in every country revenue raised by local government from its own sources falls far short of its expenditure obligations. A very small number of larger municipalities rely primarily on own-source revenues to finance their current spending, although the vast majority of smaller municipalities depend heavily upon intergovernmental transfers for their day-to-day operations. Almost all municipalities, large and small, depend primarily upon discretionary central government grants and soft loans in order to finance capital expenditure, and when these transfers are taken into consideration, local government achieves fiscal balance.

OWN REVENUE GENERATION

The major sources of locally raised revenue are taxes, fees, and user charges, although the distinction among them is often blurred in practice. Earnings generated by commercial ventures such as bus terminals and theaters

Table 5.1   Share of Local Government in Total Public Expenditure in Latin America

Country	Percent Share of Local Government in Total Public Expenditure	GNP/Head, 1991 (U.S.$)
Argentina	11 (1988)	2,790
Bolivia	8 (1993)	650
Brazil	18 (1991)	2,940
Chile	11 (1991)	2,160
Colombia	24 (1992)	1,260
Costa Rica	4 (1989)	1,850
Dominican Republic	4 (1986)	940
Ecuador	5 (1992)	1,000
El Salvador	3 (1990)	1,080
Guatemala	14 (1987)	930
Honduras	8 (1984)	580
Mexico	3 (1990)	3,030
Nicaragua	13 (1989)	460
Panama	2 (1991)	2,130
Paraguay	2 (1988)	1,270
Peru	8 (1987)	1,070
Uruguay	4 (1986)	2,840
Venezuela	7 (1989)	2,730

Source: Data from Chapters 10 through 27 of this book and World Bank, pp. 238–239.

usually constitute a very minor source of net revenue because such municipal enterprises rarely operate at a profit. Although the fiscal powers of local government vary considerably from country to country, property taxation, vehicle road taxation, business licenses, and a charge (tax) for public lighting and cleaning typically account for the bulk of local revenue raised by large and medium-size municipalities. The remainder comes from a plethora of minor taxes, fines, and fees for administrative services. Except in Uruguay and Brazil, local tax rates are fixed by higher tiers of government, although municipalities usually retain the power to decide on the level of fees, user charges, and betterment levies. In order to circumvent central government restrictions upon local powers of taxation, municipal authorities often impose obligatory fees that are not directly related to the provision of any specific service. In effect these fees function as taxes.

Taxes

There are three major types of municipal taxes in Latin America: property tax, a vehicle road tax, and a tax on local economic activity (which is usually levied on business turnover). Of these, property tax is the single most important source of locally generated revenue for municipalities throughout the region. The only exceptions are in Argentina (where it is a provincial tax), El Salvador (where it is a central government tax), the Dominican

Figure 5.1   Share of Local Government in Total Public Expenditure in Latin America Versus National Per Capita Income

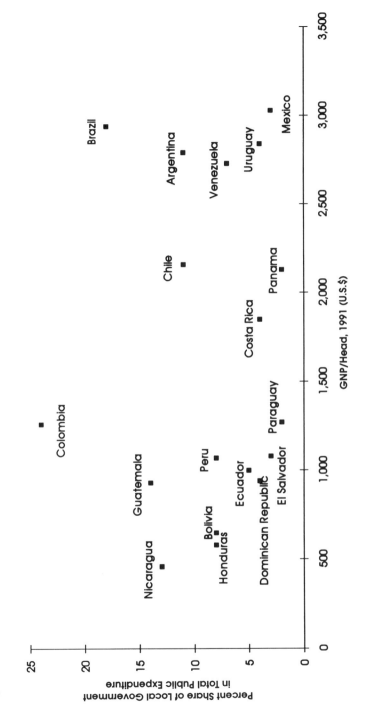

Source: Data from Table 5.1.

Republic (where there is no such tax), and Brazil (where other local taxes are more important). Property tax in Latin America is normally assessed on the basis of improved site value (i.e., land plus buildings), and valuation is based on field measurement of physical characteristics, with desk computation based on unit values for specific zones, land uses, and standards of construction. The tariff rate, expressed as a percentage of the capital value, is usually stipulated by municipal finance laws, and central government allows little discretion for municipalities to vary it.

The institutional arrangements for property taxation vary considerably within the region. In Brazil all major aspects of property taxation—policymaking (tariff setting, exemptions, revaluations, and inflation adjustment) as well as administrative aspects (identification, valuation, billing, and collection)—are the responsibility of local government, although the federal government provides substantial technical assistance to municipalities in all of these areas. By contrast, in Chile and Mexico, all aspects are assigned, respectively, to the central government and to state governments, which then transfer the collected revenue to local government. In most other countries, central government retains control over policymaking, and local government is responsible for most administrative aspects. In a small number of countries, the administration of property taxation is divided between central government, which identifies and values property, and local government, which bills and collects the tax.

There are five reasons the effectiveness of property taxation (i.e., the amount collected in relation to the potential possible at current specified rates) is low in almost all countries. First, valuations are usually grossly underreported because of the system of self-assessment whereby property owners are allowed to complete the forms that determine the declared value of their properties. The widespread use of progressive tariff rates in fixing tax liabilities means that the incentive to underreport is stronger when the property is more valuable. Second, the revaluation of unit values is infrequent, is often postponed by central government decree, and invariably lags well behind the rate of inflation (except in Brazil and Colombia, where indexation is the norm). Third, even in larger municipalities, the haphazard revision of the cadastre fails to record the growth in the number of individual properties and their increasing complexity, especially in the informal housing sector. Fourth, exemptions are rife in many countries. These may include government buildings as well as residential buildings of historical value. Properties occupied by senior citizens also frequently receive substantial discounts. For example, in Chile a 1982 presidential decree exempted properties constructed by public housing programs from property taxation for twenty years. Originally intended as a hidden subsidy to low-income households, a large proportion of these properties—which account for as many as 70 percent of residential properties in some municipalities—were soon occupied by families above the poverty line.

The yield from municipal taxation as a whole often fails to keep pace with the growth in population and real incomes. Taxes lack buoyancy for several reasons: the failure to increase unit values in line with inflation; the ceilings imposed on tariff rates, most of which are fixed by central government; the failure to keep tax registers up to date with population and economic growth; evasion by taxpayers; collusion between taxpayers and tax officials over self-assessment; long delays in payment by taxpayers and ineffective enforcement of sanctions in the form of penalty surcharges; and outright fraud by tax officials. As a result, the payment of municipal taxes often takes on the characteristics of a voluntary contribution rather than a legal obligation, especially in smaller municipalities.

Tax inefficiency (i.e,. the proportion of revenue spent on collecting the tax) is often high because of the costs of administering a myriad of minor taxes. Many of these taxes are levied on a fixed basis (and thus are rapidly eroded by inflation) rather than on a percentage basis, and this reduces tax elasticity. There has been little progress in rationalizing and reducing the number of these taxes in the interests of administrative simplicity.

The overwhelmingly urban nature of local government taxation constitutes a major structural problem for the vast majority of Latin American municipalities, which are rural in character. The absence of any provision in municipal tax codes, except in Uruguay, for the taxation of agricultural activity presents a pressing problem for poor, rural municipalities. The shortage of alternative sources of locally generated revenue in highland Peru is such that a local tax on the transport of cattle is widely levied, despite being expressly forbidden in the 1984 municipal code. Although municipalities are, in most countries, legally empowered to tax rural as well as urban properties, in practice the former are usually exempt. This failure to harness a major potential source of locally generated revenue is a key reason for the weak fiscal performance of the vast majority of small municipalities in the region.

Fees and Charges

In addition to taxation, two other sources of locally generated municipal revenue exist: fixed fees imposed for administrative transactions and user charges for the provision of services. The most common fees are those charged for the granting of building licenses and for the establishment of new businesses. Fees are also charged for the rental of market stalls, for the operation of kiosks in public places, and for street vending. The most common consumption-related user charges are for street cleaning, solid waste management, public lighting, public transport, slaughterhouses, cemeteries, and sporting, cultural, or other recreational facilities. Water supply and electricity remain under local government control in a few countries such as El Salvador and Guatemala, and are almost always charged for on the basis of metered consumption. In larger municipalities, charges for street cleaning, public lighting, and solid waste management are often collected by means of a surcharge on bills issued by state water or electricity corporations. The betterment levy—a charge designed to recover the cost of infrastructure improvement from property owners benefiting from the development— exists in most countries but is rarely a major source of local revenue, except in Colombia.

OTHER SOURCES OF MUNICIPAL FUNDS

Intergovernmental Transfers

Until the 1980s, central government financial transfers to local government in most Latin American countries were on a small-scale, ad hoc basis and were subject to sudden variation. The criteria for allocation among municipalities were shrouded in legal obscurity in order to mask the prevalence of clientelism. As a result, such allocations were regarded more as a gesture of goodwill by central government than as a legal right for local government. This arbitrary arrangement greatly inhibited the orderly planning of local service provision because municipalities had no way of forecasting the total resources at their disposal. In several countries, especially Argentina and Ecuador, these transfers functioned as multipurpose deficit grants that were used to cover municipal budget deficits. More often than not, their exact level was the result of bitter and protracted political negotiation between local and central government involving civic shutdowns (*paros cívicos*).

A transfer system based on the sharing of revenue from centrally collected taxes was already found in some countries before the 1980s. In theory, this arrangement had the advantage that local government was able to obtain access to substantial and elastic revenues without the risk of the arbitrariness associated with grant finance. In practice, though, these transfers were often derived from the sharing of revenues from specific national taxes, the proceeds of which came from volatile primary export products such as petroleum (in Ecuador) and coffee (in El Salvador); the funds were distributed preferentially on the basis of their origin (i.e., to oil-rich or coffee-growing municipalities).

During the 1960s and 1970s, a curious complicity developed between central government and local government that encouraged municipalities' growing dependence on financial transfers from central government.

Despite their rhetorical support for local autonomy, municipal leaders often preferred to appear before their own electorate as redistributors of central government expenditures, bargaining on behalf of citizens for a larger share of the public cake, rather than as collectors and administrators of local taxes (which generated opposition among taxpayers and also encouraged greater citizen interest in monitoring the use of locally collected taxes). Central government leaders also preferred this arrangement because it allowed them to maintain some financial control over local government and to retain the political support of municipal leaders.

Borrowing

With the exception of Brazil, borrowing by Latin American municipalities in order to finance investment projects is less pronounced than in other parts of the world with comparable levels of per capita income. Commercial borrowing is confined to larger municipalities, which typically obtain their funds from international lending agencies such as the World Bank and the Inter-American Development Bank, on-lent through government banking institutions. The availability of soft loan finance for medium-size municipalities is limited to revolving fund programs organized by bilateral aid agencies such as USAID and Gesellschaft für Technische Zusammenarbeit (GTZ) and is channeled through official municipal development banks such as BANMA (Honduras), FUNDACOMUN (Venezuela), IDM (Paraguay), INFOM (Guatemala), and ISDEM (El Salvador).

The loan portfolios of these programs have been criticized for their emphasis on non–self-liquidating projects such as municipal headquarters and multipurpose recreational centers, which are built to standardized and often inappropriate designs. Because these projects are not revenue generating, they often lead to a poor repayment record. In recent years, and under pressure from foreign funding agencies, there has been a noticeable shift in the loan portfolios of such programs toward self-financing projects aimed at strengthening municipal tax collection and at improving administrative efficiency through computerization.

LOCAL FINANCIAL MANAGEMENT

In a small number of the larger municipalities in the region, financial administration is highly efficient, with computerized billing and collection carried out through the commercial banking system. In the vast majority of smaller municipalities, however, it remains notoriously deficient. Common problems include the absence of property cadastres; political corruption, which leads to the granting of exemptions from tax liability; clientelist recruitment policies, which result in a lack of staff with appropriate skills; lack of integration and information pooling between departments collecting different taxes; absence of public relations campaigns designed to increase citizens' awareness of their civic duty to pay taxes; time-consuming payment procedures; discourteous treatment of taxpayers by staff; and weak tax inspectorates (D'Alessandro et al.:42–43).

In the absence of comprehensive planning, budgetary and accounting processes in most municipalities operate less as tools of municipal management and more as instruments of financial control by central government. The absence of program budgeting makes it virtually impossible to relate the budget to service priorities and objectives in any meaningful way, thereby greatly inhibiting municipal planning. Instead, central government requires that budgets are prepared so as to show the functional (personnel, goods and services, transfers, investments) rather than sectoral distribution of municipal expenditure. This does not prevent municipalities from maintaining a separate internal budgetary system related to their departmental or program objectives, but very few municipalities can afford the luxury of two budgetary procedures.

Instead, in the vast majority of municipalities, budgets are still drawn up on the basis of preexisting functional categories. As such they are statements of aspiration rather then expectation; they are ways of avoiding choices rather than making them (Davey:16). Financial management then becomes little more than the monitoring of expenditure and income flows in order to avoid a deficit. Expenditure is controlled in accordance with assigned budgetary limits to ensure that individual items are not overspent. The lack of concern for measuring the impact of municipal expenditure in terms of efficiency and effectiveness is reflected in the absence of any performance targets and indicators, as well as in the lack of cost recovery methods in asset management.

Audit Procedures

With the significant exception of Chile, financial mismanagement and outright corruption have been perennial features of local government throughout Latin America. In many countries, an elected legal officer (síndico) forms part of the municipal council, and in most countries, municipalities above a certain size must appoint an internal auditor. In some countries, this official may be removed from office during the municipal term of office only as a result of legal action. Despite these internal control mechanisms, however, the "strong mayor" tradition has meant that, in practice, such mechanisms have often proved ineffective in dealing with financial impropriety.

For this reason, central government also exercises strict financial supervision over local government, except in Brazil and Argentina, where this function is carried out by state government. Various means are used to achieve this supervision, including the power to withhold discretionary grants, the use of centrally mandated municipal spending requirements, the determination of the scope of the municipal tax base, limits on municipal discretion to vary the rates of local taxes, and the approval of municipal budgets. The prior approval of the detailed schedule of tax rates and charges planned by each municipality during the coming year, known as the *plan de arbitrios,* is a particularly tiresome burden imposed by central governments, especially in Central America.

In most countries this supervision is entrusted to the comptroller-general's office, a kind of national audit office, although in some of the smaller countries it is carried out by the ministry of the interior or the ministry of finance. The comptroller-general's office is invariably a prestigious body, steeped in the Luso-Hispanic tradition of administrative law. As such, its overriding objective is to ensure the legality of municipal revenue generation and expenditure. Hence it evaluates municipal performance in terms of budgetary conformity, financial propriety, and legality. These evaluations take the form of a priori and a posteriori audits of municipal accounts, examining the preparation and execution of budgets as well as the purchase and sale of municipal assets. The comptroller-general's office can independently investigate the finances of a municipality without requiring the invitation of the municipal auditor. Supervision is most detailed in Chile, where the comptroller-general receives monthly budgetary reports from municipal auditors within thirty days of the end of the reporting period, thus enabling close monitoring of the aggregate flow of municipal expenditure against income. Elsewhere in the region, annual reporting is the norm. This form of financial supervision is essentially regulatory rather than supportive in nature, and the audit process rarely involves techniques of management accounting. The comptroller-general's office provides little guidance on management practices, carries out no comparative analysis of municipal expenditure, and thus offers little information on managerial efficiency and effectiveness at the municipal level.

LOCAL FINANCIAL STRENGTHENING

A significant strengthening of local government finances was discernible from the early 1980s as part of the general invigoration of local government in the region. Its magnitude varied considerably from country to country, but in almost all countries municipal expenditure per head grew rapidly in real terms, and the contribution of local government as a part of total public expenditure increased. With the notable exceptions of Paraguay and Costa

Rica, where local government's share stagnated at a derisory 1 percent and 4 percent, respectively, throughout the decade, the share typically rose from around 6 to 10 percent as of 1980–1982 to around 12 to 16 percent by 1988–1990. Exceptions at the other end of the scale included Brazil, where the share jumped from 11 percent to around 18 percent, and Colombia, where it is likely to surpass 30 percent by the end of the century. This rapid growth in municipal expenditure was financed from two principal sources: an increase in the size of transfers coming from higher tiers of government, and the granting of enhanced powers to municipalities for local revenue generation.

Revenue Sharing

In most countries, since the 1980s central governments have placed greater emphasis on strengthening local government finances by enhancing the flow of financial transfers rather than by granting them greater powers of local revenue generation. As a result, the share of transfers in total municipal income rose in most countries, and this phenomenon was especially pronounced in smaller municipalities. With the notable exception of Chile, these increased transfers were not usually designed to finance any significant enlargement of local government's responsibilities. Nor were they usually earmarked for specific sectoral expenditures. Consequently, municipal discretion in the allocation of its financial resources was significantly increased. Although the new transfer systems enhanced the potential for greater municipal accountability to the local electorate by widening the breadth of service provision, their general (rather than specific) nature and their lack of earmarking did little to encourage greater cost-effectiveness in local service provision. Central governments rarely established monitoring systems to ensure that these increased transfers were being used efficiently.

The increased transfers normally took the form of general revenue-sharing agreements, under which local government received a stipulated share of national revenue sources. In addition to the welcome general increase in funds, these agreements had four major advantages from the viewpoint of local government. First, because they were linked to major sources of national taxation, they greatly increased the elasticity of municipal income in relation to the overall growth in gross domestic product. Second, in sharp contrast to the volatility and obscurity of the previous transfer system, their predictability and transparency enabled municipalities to program expenditure over the medium term. Third, transfers were allocated among municipalities based on need rather than on which municipalities generated the most funds (i.e., origin-based criteria). Hence, in practice, they functioned like a central government multipurpose, or block, grant. Fourth, this multipurpose grant system enhanced discretion by enabling municipalities to allocate resources in accordance with local priorities. The only limitation on this discretion was the frequent requirement that a minimum share of the grant should be spent on particular services.

The most far-reaching examples of this new approach were in Brazil and Colombia. In Brazil a wide range of new revenue-sharing agreements with both federal and state government were embodied in the 1988 Constitution. Municipalities henceforth received guaranteed transfers that included stipulated shares of the proceeds from federal taxes on income, industrial production, and rural property, as well as from a state value-added tax and a state tax on vehicle ownership. In Colombia local government finances were also greatly strengthened after 1986 by new revenue-sharing agreements for a value-added tax (VAT). The 1992 Constitution introduced a general agreement for the sharing of national fiscal revenue, with the proportion accruing to local government destined to rise, by stages, to 41 percent by 2001; part of the money is earmarked specifically for health and education.

In Guatemala the 1985 Constitution stipulated that 8 percent of national fiscal revenue would henceforth be transferred to municipalities. In Honduras the 1990 municipal code provided for 5 percent of national fiscal revenue to be transferred to municipalities. In the Dominican Republic, a 1983 law assigned 20 percent of the proceeds from national domestic taxation to local government. In all three countries, the effect was to increase the income of smaller municipalities dramatically, which led to much higher levels of investment in social infrastructure.

In Mexico, under a major general revenue-sharing agreement introduced in 1980, states received a share of federal tax revenue, which rose by stages to 21 percent in 1994. States were required to transfer 20 percent of these proceeds, as well as from a state vehicle road tax, to municipalities. Municipalities also received a direct transfer from the federal government's municipal development fund, equivalent to 1 percent of general federal tax revenue. In Peru an arbitrary system of central government transfers was replaced in 1985 by a tax-sharing agreement whereby local government received the proceeds from a surcharge on the national sales tax, from taxes on the sale of property and on vehicle purchases, and from highway tolls. In Venezuela, as part of a 1989 decentralization law, federal government transfers to local government mediated through state government were substantially increased and made more transparent. If the timetable for the reform is adhered to, by 1999 local government will receive an annual nonconditional grant equivalent to 4 percent of central government's ordinary revenue.

In sharp contrast to this regional preference for general grants and associated municipal discretion, transfers to local government in Chile largely took the form of specific grants for new expenditure responsibilities in education and health, which were assumed during the 1980s as local government undertook an "agency" role for central government ministries. These transfers were based on fixed sums per unit of service (capitation fees in the case of education and consultation fees in the case of health). This system of specific grants was designed to ensure that identifiable services were provided to a specified standard and at a particular cost, although they suffered from the drawback that unit fees were rarely weighted to take into account the enormous regional variation in the cost of service provision; in addition, the fees were inadequately adjusted to keep pace with inflation.

Local Tax Strengthening

In a minority of countries, however, central governments placed greater emphasis on strengthening local government finances by granting them greater powers of local revenue generation rather than by enhancing the flow of financial transfers. This was achieved through various reforms, including the transfer to local government of taxes previously received by central government, the granting of discretion to municipalities to alter rates on taxes they were already legally empowered to collect, and measures to improve local tax collection. Revenue from property taxation, the major source of local fiscal revenue, was passed to local government control in Chile (1979), Mexico (1983), Nicaragua (1991), and Paraguay (1992); in Peru the property tax base was extended in 1983 to include business property. In other countries, such as Costa Rica, billing and collection of property taxation was passed from central to local government control, and in Venezuela municipalities were granted new powers to vary tariff rates. In all cases, the direct administration of the property cadastre was seen by municipalities as a crucial prerequisite for improving the local tax yield.

In Chile, a far-reaching municipal tax reform in 1979 transferred control for three major sources of fiscal revenue to local government: residential property tax, municipal business licenses, and a vehicle road license. In Nicaragua a myriad of separate taxes and charges that had to be approved annually for each municipality were replaced in 1986 by a single sales tax, and a municipal tax register was established to improve collection rates. This led to a rapid growth in municipal own revenue, more than offsetting a rapid decline in transfers, and this was sufficient to maintain tax buoyancy despite a period of hyperinflation between 1987 and 1990. In 1991 finances were further strengthened when responsibility for property taxation, a vehicle road tax, and business licenses was passed to local government. In Venezuela local government was granted additional revenue-raising powers in 1989 to collect a betterment levy, a rural land tax, a tax on commercial advertisements, and a tax on gambling. Municipalities were also given absolute discretion in determining the rates of all local taxes levied in their area of jurisdiction—something unusual for Latin America.

The complex relationship between financial transfers and local revenue generation has hardly been studied in Latin America. The evidence to date for a disincentive effect on local revenue generation as a result of increased transfers is inconclusive, despite the fact that recognition and reward for local tax effort were rarely built into the weighting system for allocating transfers among municipalities. In Mexico increased transfers from revenue sharing and grants were accompanied by a decline in local tax effort, and municipal own income remained static in real terms during the 1980s. This happened despite the fact that Mexico was one of the few countries where the system of matching grants was theoretically designed to encourage local tax effort. In Colombia, conversely, the share of locally generated revenue in total municipal income did not decline, despite growing central government transfers. Local tax buoyancy was maintained as a result of a major upward revision and restructuring of local tax rates in 1983, the transfer of control for property taxation administration, and the granting in 1990 of the right to vary local property tax rates and readjust fiscal values in line with inflation.

Equalization

Because so many local taxes in Latin America tend to be urban based, the scope for municipal revenue mobilization is much greater in urban areas than in rural areas. And within urban areas, the municipalities draw revenue especially from zones in which there is large-scale industrial and commercial development or high-income residential property. As a result, in every country disparities in per capita municipal own revenue receipts are very large by international standards, both between urban and rural municipalities and between neighboring urban municipalities within the same metropolitan area.

Consequently, in those countries that stressed enhanced powers of local revenue generation rather than central government transfers as the primary means of strengthening municipal finances, disparities between richer and poorer municipalities became even more pronounced. This was especially true in Nicaragua, where the virtual disappearance of central government transfers weakened the vast majority of poorer municipalities, which lacked the economic base to generate significant own revenues from taxes (such as property tax, sales tax, and vehicle tax) that were newly devolved to local government.

In those countries where municipal finances were strengthened primarily through new revenue-sharing agreements with central government, considerations of horizontal equity were increasingly incorporated into the formulae for allocating these transfers among municipalities. This reflected a growing central government recognition of the enormous disparities among municipalities in the level of service provision and in the potential for own revenue generation. In a growing number of countries, needs-based criteria replaced origin-based criteria as the basis for the allocation of funds derived from revenue-sharing agreements. The formulae usually incorporated weighted variables of relative need and relative local resource availability. The most common needs-based variable was population size, but this was only rarely modified to incorporate the greater needs of municipalities with low population densities. Invariably, the existing level of municipal per capita own revenue generation was used as a proxy for local revenue potential, despite the inherent disincentive effect this had on local fiscal effort. These needs-based composite weighting systems generally granted larger per capita transfers to smaller municipalities than to larger ones. Insofar as smaller municipalities tended to have a relatively high proportion of poor residents, the new systems of allocation were mildly progressive with regard to interjurisdictional equity.

But central government transfers did not incorporate a formal equalization mechanism designed to ensure a standard level of service provision in all municipalities by "topping up" local revenues in areas of below-average fiscal capacity. Instead, transfer formulae usually included equity considerations as one factor among several in the overall weighting system. As a result, despite their increase in scale and their greater transparency in recent years, transfers have not diminished the enormous disparities in municipal income per head. Furthermore, even the limited improvements in interjurisdictional equity that have taken place in some countries have done little to improve interpersonal equity. This is due to the fact that the beneficiaries from expenditures made by small rural municipalities tend to be highly concentrated among households in mini urban centers.

In some countries, origin-based criteria for allocating revenue-sharing transfers among municipalities were retained, but they came under increasing criticism for the distortions they created in the level of service provision. This was especially so in Bolivia, where a 1986 fiscal reform centralized the collection of taxes formerly collected by local government. The concentration of central government tax offices in major cities led to a fall in the tax yield from outlying areas, which, coupled with the origin-based transfer system, greatly increased disparities in income per head among municipalities.

The municipal equalization fund established in Chile during the 1980s represented the most far-reaching reform for improving interjurisdictional equity in the region; it was a striking departure from the Latin American orthodoxy regarding intergovernmental financial relations. Its resources came from 60 percent of the proceeds of property taxation and 50 percent of proceeds from road vehicle taxation, both of which were devolved to local government just prior to the reform. In addition, the fund received 65 percent and 45 percent, respectively, of the proceeds from business licenses collected by the two wealthiest municipalities in the country. By 1990 fund resources amounted to 30 percent of total municipal revenue in the country. The formula for allocating fund resources among municipalities was highly redistributive, and the fund soon became the main source of income for the vast majority of municipalities, 70 percent of which were net beneficiaries from its operation.

FUTURE CHALLENGES FOR FINANCIAL STRENGTHENING

As its responsibilities increase, local government faces the enormous challenge of strengthening its financial base through transfers from central government as well as through own revenue generation. The negative experience of arbitrary and discriminatory transfers prior to the 1980s gave rise to the distorted idea, in much of Latin America, that such grants served only to maintain central government's hegemonic powers by perpetuating weak and feckless municipalities that were dependent upon central government to bail them out. In turn, this led to the erroneous view that genuine financial autonomy required local government to become completely self-financing (D'Alessandro et al.:8). For this reason, the greater proportion of municipal income derived from central government transfers in recent years has often been interpreted as evidence of the further erosion of municipal autonomy.

Although this view is understandable in light of the historical tradition of Latin American centralism, it is contrary to that held in most other parts of the world. The global trend toward greater dependence on central government transfers is intimately linked to the devolution of service delivery functions to the municipal level. The accompanying increase in financial transfers reflects a recognition by central government of the structural inadequacy of locally raised revenue to finance these new expenditure responsibilities adequately. The lack of direct access to major revenue sources means that local government in Latin America will continue to require transfers from central government, whether in the form of revenue sharing or multipurpose grants. This is also true in the rest of the world. In Europe, for example, extensive local government responsibility for service provision is accompanied by a high financial dependence upon transfers from central government. But municipalities do not perceive this as emasculating their autonomy because they are allowed wide discretion in deciding on their expenditure priorities (Smith:88).

Equity considerations pose a particular challenge to the process of fiscal decentralization in Latin America because of the enormous disparities in expenditure per head among municipalities. The danger exists that fiscal decentralization, if not accompanied by mechanisms for significant inter-municipal redistribution, may generate even greater interjurisdictional inequities between richer and poorer municipalities. The possibility of this occurring is increased by the fact that nowhere in Latin America, not even in Chile, is central government yet committed to the goal of ensuring uniform standards of service provision throughout the country for specified public services such as education, public health, housing, and water supply. Although systems of revenue sharing between central and local government currently almost always incorporate equity considerations in their allocative formulae, central government monitoring of the equity, efficiency, and effectiveness of service provision in different municipalities is still noticeably absent.

Despite the preponderant role that transfers seem destined to play in almost all countries in Latin America, there is still enormous potential for raising municipal own revenue, especially in smaller municipalities. New sources of local revenue can be identified, grants can be mobilized from international sources, and municipal borrowing can prudently be increased. But own revenue gains can be obtained most rapidly by improving the administration of existing local sources of revenue. Techniques designed to ensure that all revenue due is properly collected—such as the introduction of the *ficha única* system (which brings together all of a taxpayer's liabilities in a unified tax roll), as well as municipal surcharging on water or electricity bills—are cheap and easily administered ways to maintain the buoyancy of locally generated revenue.

The benefits to be gained from improved administration are particularly strong in the case of property taxation, the yield from which depends upon a combination of four factors: the completeness of the cadastre, the level and accuracy of valuations, the tax rate and exemption schedule, and the efficiency of collection. Efforts to improve property taxation have tended to emphasize a "technology-led" approach that gives priority to the creation of new nationwide cadastres, using expensive methods of aerial photogrammetry and geographic information systems. Yet newly discovered or newly revalued properties will yield little revenue if collections are poorly enforced. For this reason, there is a strong case for giving priority instead to collection efficiency, through making compliance convenient and noncompliance subject to rapid and costly penalties. This strategy is cost-effective and produces rapid benefits (Dillinger:42).

The transfer of greater fiscal responsibilities to smaller municipalities with weak administrations and poor cadastral services poses a particular challenge because of the danger that this may lead to a decline in the local tax yield. In many smaller municipalities, there are also severe practical limits on the ability of municipal authorities to exercise the new fiscal powers devolved from central government. The deeply ingrained reluctance to pay municipal taxes, evidenced by rampant evasion, can often be explained in part by a long history of grossly inadequate service provision. In this situation, municipal authorities must be able to demonstrate an improvement in service performance before they can generate the political support to raise taxes.

6

THE ELECTORAL SYSTEM
OF LOCAL GOVERNMENT

Through their constitutions and electoral codes, Latin American nations have always paid lip service to the democratic election of local government officers. But in every country, central governments, both civilian and military, have intervened periodically to suspend the electoral process for mayors. They have replaced the elected mayors with appointed executive heads, a practice that was particularly enduring in the case of capital cities. Moreover, in contrast to Africa and Asia, where appointed executive heads have been recruited from a central cadre of career-based public administrators, the overriding criterion for the selection of appointed municipal executive heads in Latin America has invariably been political patronage rather than professional competence.

CHARACTERISTICS OF LOCAL ELECTIONS

Electing the Mayor

The most common practice for electing the Latin American mayor is by way of a separate election, which reflects the growing influence of the U.S. "strong mayor" model of local government (see Table 6.1). Mayors are usually elected by a simple plurality, except in Brazilian municipalities with more than 200,000 people, where candidates must obtain at least 51 percent of the votes cast, by means of a second-round runoff if necessary. The system of separate election has gradually replaced the "integrated" French system of indirect election of mayors from among councillors. This system was

Table 6.1   Features of the Local Government Electoral System in Latin America

	Term of Office (years)	Separate or Integral Election?	Reelection of Mayor?	Number of Councillors	Same Time as National/ State Elections?
Argentina	Four	Separate[a]	Yes	6–60	Yes
Bolivia	Two	Integral	Yes	5–13	No
Brazil	Four	Separate	No	9–55	No
Chile	Four	Hybrid	Yes	6–10	No
Colombia	Three	Separate	No	7–28	No
Costa Rica	Four	—[b]	Yes	5–13	Yes
Dominican Republic	Four	Separate	Yes	5 or more[c]	Yes
Ecuador	Four[d]	—[e]	No	5–15	Yes
El Salvador	Three	Separate	Yes	5–13	Yes
Guatemala	Two[f]	Separate	Yes	8–20	Yes
Honduras	Four	Hybrid	Yes	4–10	Yes
Mexico	Three	Integral	No	5–20	No
Nicaragua	Six	Integral	Yes	5–20	Yes
Panama	Five	Separate	Yes	5–19	Yes
Paraguay	Five	Separate	No	9–24	No
Peru	Three	Hybrid	Yes	5–39	No
Uruguay	Five	Separate	Yes	31	Yes
Venezuela	Three	Separate	Yes	5–17	No

Source: Data from Chapters 10 through 27 of this book.

Notes: a. Except in the Province of Chaco, where the mayor is indirectly elected by the council from among its own members, and in the Province of Entre Ríos, where candidates for council membership are elected independently of party lists, with the post of mayor going to the candidate who receives the most votes.

b. The executive head is a city manager appointed by the municipal council.

c. There are a minimum of five council members. Above that, one council member is elected for every 14,000 inhabitants, except in the National District (one per 25,000) and the Municipality of Santiago (one per 17,000).

d. Depending upon their position in the voting list, council members are elected either for a fixed four-year term or for a two-year term with the possibility of immediate reelection. For example, in the case of a fifteen-member council, the seven members receiving the least votes must stand for reelection after two years, whereas the eight who received the most votes continue until the end of the four-year term.

e. The executive head of municipalities that either have populations of more than 100,000 or are provincial headquarters is a separately elected mayor. Elsewhere the council leader, elected from among council members, carries out this role.

f. Except for the Municipality of Guatemala City, which has a four-year term of office.

once widespread in the region but is now retained only in Bolivia, Mexico, and Nicaragua. The separate election of the mayor has also replaced the practice in smaller municipalities of having the council leader, who was elected by and from among councillors, also fulfill the role of executive head. This procedure is now retained only in Ecuadorean municipalities with populations of fewer than 100,000. Chile and Peru have a hybrid form of mayoral election that spans the separate-integrated divide. Under this arrangement, the candidate heading the winning party list for council membership is automatically selected as the mayor. In the Chilean case, this selection is conditional on that candidate obtaining at least 35 percent of the vote. If he or she does not, the mayor is indirectly elected by the councillors from among themselves.

Electing Councillors

Councillors in Latin America have almost always been directly elected, even when mayors have been appointed by central government. This curious fact has often been interpreted as striking evidence of councillors' lack of political significance. Chile was a rare exception to this electoral norm from 1973 to 1992, during which time the military regime appointed both executive heads and councillors along corporativist lines. The practice of including nominated councillors alongside elected members, which is common in parts of Africa and Asia, is virtually unknown in Latin America. Although there is increasing pressure in Bolivia for such municipal representation for leaders of indigenous communities, the only example in operation in recent years has been the experiment on the Atlantic Coast of Nicaragua aimed at incorporating traditional ethnic community leaders into municipal councils.

Throughout almost all of Latin America, councillors are elected at large—not on a ward basis—and through a system that thereby minimizes territorial representation at the submunicipal level. The only exception is Panama, where the "first past the post," system based on submunicipal electoral wards is practiced. Elsewhere, the D'Hondt system of proportional representation is the preferred electoral method. Under this method, council seats are assigned according to the proportion of the total vote each party obtains in a single electoral circumscription, which covers the entire municipal jurisdiction. Individual councillors are elected by party lists, which are usually closed (i.e., ranked). The system of voting by party lists is also usually blocked (i.e., denying the voter the right to select candidates from more than one list). The only exceptions are in Brazil and Chile, where voters choose a single candidate instead of a list of candidates. In the Brazilian case, votes are recorded for each polling station so that the geographical locus of support for individual councillors is known.

In several countries, notably Peru, the electoral system is not based on full proportional representation, but operates according to the "majority-plus" system, under which the party that wins the most votes is automatically granted a majority of council seats and the remaining seats are distributed among other parties on the basis of proportional representation. In a variant of this system, found elsewhere in the region, council seats are distributed exclusively between the two parties that gain the most votes. For example, in the smaller municipalities of Nicaragua, the party that obtains the largest number of votes automatically receives three council seats, and the two remaining seats go to the party that receives the next largest number. In three Argentine provinces (Neuquén, Misiones, and La Rioja), the winning party receives 75 percent of council seats, irrespective of its share of the total vote, and the party that finishes second automatically receives the remaining 25 percent of seats. In the unique case of El Salvador, the party that wins the most votes obtains all council seats; consequently there is no representation of minority parties.

The Municipal Term of Office

There has been much debate within Latin America over the most appropriate duration of the municipal term of office. At present there is wide variation among countries, ranging from a minimum of two years in Bolivia to a maximum of six years in Nicaragua. Altogether, seven countries (Bolivia, Colombia, El Salvador, Guatemala, Mexico, Peru, and Venezuela) still have terms of three years or less (see Table 6.1). The term of office is the same for all municipalities, except in Guatemala, where the Municipality of Guatemala City has a four-year term and all others have a two-year term. Throughout almost all of Latin America, the term of office of the mayor is concurrent with that of councillors. The only exception is the staggered electoral system found in some Argentine provinces, under which half the number of council seats are up for election every two years. Latin America is divided over the question of the reelection of mayors. This practice is permitted in thirteen countries; in others it is either banned altogether, as in Mexico, or permitted only after an interval of one term, as in Brazil, Colombia, Ecuador, and Paraguay.

CRITICISMS OF THE LOCAL ELECTORAL SYSTEM

The local government electoral system in Latin America has been widely criticized for its lack of accountability to the electorate. Five common features militate against accountability: the high ratio of citizens to councillors, the close linkage with national elections, the closed party list system, the prohibition on mayoral reelection, and the absence of territorial representation. A most striking feature of the electoral system is the very small number of councillors. An extreme case was during the Somoza regime in Nicaragua (1937–1979), when all municipalities had only three councillors. Today the number ranges from a minimum of five in most countries to a maximum of only sixty in the case of the Municipality of Buenos Aires. Although this situation is often the legacy of outdated municipal codes promulgated at a time when urban populations were a fraction of what they are today, it is surprising that this deficit of political representation has not been

Table 6.2   Ratio of Citizens per Councillor for Selected Latin American Municipalities

	Municipal Population	Number of Councillors	Citizens per Councillor
Argentina (1989)			
Buenos Aires	2,900,794	60	48,347
Bolivia (1992)			
La Paz	711,036	13	54,695
Santa Cruz	694,616	13	53,432
Cochabamba	404,102	13	31,085
Brazil (1991)			
São Paolo	9,626,894	53	181,640
Rio de Janeiro	5,473,909	42	130,331
Pôrto Alegre	1,380,000	33	41,818
Recife	1,341,000	41	32,707
Chile (1991)			
La Florida	391,253	10	39,125
Viña del Mar	312,306	10	31,231
Concepción	311,537	10	31,154
Colombia (1994)			
Bogotá	6,314,305	28	225,511
Mexico (1990)			
Guadalajara	1,628,617	20	81,431
Nezahualcoyotl	1,259,543	20	62,977
Ecatepec	1,219,238	20	60,962
Nicaragua (1992)			
Managua	973,759	20	48,688
Paraguay (1992)			
Asunción	502,426	24	20,934
Uruguay (1985)			
Montevideo	1,246,500	31	40,210
Venezuela (1990)			
Libertador	1,824,892	17	107,347

Source: Country population censi and individual country chapters in this book.

corrected through subsequent legislative reforms. As a result, political decisionmaking is highly concentrated, and accountability to the electorate is markedly reduced. The maximum limits placed on the number of councillors has led to gross political underrepresentation, especially in larger municipalities, where the ratio of citizens per councillor is much higher than in smaller municipalities. The number of citizens per councillor in these larger municipalities typically ranges between 20,000 and 80,000 (see Table 6.2). These figures are extremely high by international standards. North American and European municipalities have much lower citizen/councillor ratios (France, 110; Sweden, 270; Germany, 400; United States, 490; Spain, 602; Japan, 1,600; Britain, 1,800). This gives far greater scope than in Latin America for the political representation of a diversity of interest groups (Norton:133, 283, 317, 347, 383, 485).

In ten countries, the term of municipal office is coterminous with that of national political office, and in these cases municipal elections are held concurrently with presidential and congressional elections (see Table 6.1). In Costa Rica, the Dominican Republic, and Uruguay, this linkage is taken a stage further because voters select from among closed party lists of candidates for both national and municipal office on a single ballot paper. Hence there is no opportunity on the ballot paper for voters to select a candidate from one party for national office and from another party for local office. This arrangement virtually destroys minority representation in local government because candidates cannot stand for municipal office unless they are included in the party list of a presidential candidate.

More generally, the linkage between municipal and central government elections means that local government elections are overshadowed in importance by the national elections held at the same time. This distracts voter attention away from local questions and toward a consideration of national issues. It also effectively guarantees that clientelist considerations prevail in the selection of party candidates for municipal office. Selection is often determined by the electoral support that potential municipal officeholders can mobilize for the party's national politicians, rather than by the personal capabilities of the candidates and their fitness for local government office. In exchange for this support, the potential officeholders are "rewarded" with municipal office.

The prevalence of the closed and blocked party list system also reduces political accountability to the electorate. Voters are denied the right to rank candidates from within the party of their choice according to their own personal preference. They are also denied the opportunity to select a mix of candidates from different parties. Both features have served to entrench the power of elites within political parties and have thus contributed indirectly to maintaining centralism within Latin American political culture. The system also ensures that intraparty bickering over position on the party list takes precedence over the cultivation of a strong personal relationship between candidates and the electorate.

In five countries accountability is also reduced by the prohibition on immediate mayoral reelection (see Table 6.1). Mayors who are not eligible for reelection do not have the same incentive to maintain standards of probity in office. The problem of mayoral accountability is compounded by the fact that where the simple plurality voting system operates, mayors may be elected with a relatively small proportion of the total vote.

Finally, accountability is reduced by the fact that, under proportional representation, councillors are elected from the municipality at large. As such, they are not individually accountable to particular territorially defined groups of citizens. This is especially damaging because of the wide gulf that already separates civil society and the local state, as exemplified by the extremely high ratio of citizens per councillor. Although in some countries vigorous neighborhood-based citizen groups partially compensate for this vacuum in geographical representation, these groups lack a clear channel of communication with local government through a representative councillor.

ELECTORAL REFORM

From the early 1980s there was a noticeable strengthening of the political autonomy of local government in Latin America. The long-standing tradition of central government interference through the appointment of executive heads was increasingly replaced by the democratic election of municipal authorities. In Peru (1981), Bolivia (1985), and Chile (1992), local government elections were held for the first time since 1968, 1950, and 1973, respectively. In Colombia (1988), mayors were elected for the first time in over a century, and in Paraguay (1991) they were elected for the first time ever. By May 1994, when Panama finally abolished the practice under which municipal executive heads were appointed by the presidency, the democratic election of mayors had become the norm throughout Latin America. The only exceptions were in Costa Rica, where the executive head was a city manager appointed by the municipal council, as well as in two capital cities—the Municipality of Buenos Aires and the Federal District of Mexico City—which were still directly administered by presidentially appointed executives.

Political autonomy was also strengthened by reforms that fortified accountability to the electorate and correspondingly reduced the clientelist relationship between municipal officeholders and central government. In the Venezuelan municipal elections of 1989 and the Chilean municipal elections of 1992, the closed and blocked electoral system was replaced with a voting system having an open and nonblocked list (*panachage*). This reform was particularly profound in the Venezuelan case, where under the previous system councillors had been elected according to their position on a predetermined party list, without their names even appearing on the ballot paper. The reform revealed public support for increased political accountability through personalized voting behavior.

In several countries (e.g., Venezuela and Colombia) the timing of local government elections was delinked from that of national elections. In others the length of municipal office was increased (e.g., from two to four years in Honduras in 1987). And in an interesting departure from Latin American tradition, Venezuela reformed the party list electoral system for local government in 1992 in order to strengthen voter identification with elected councillors. A mixed system, similar to the German model, was introduced under which two-thirds of councillors were elected on a ward basis and the remaining one-third according to party lists. There was also growing interest in electoral reform in Colombia, where proportional representation was seen as encouraging clientelism by reducing the personal accountability of councillors to the electorate (Rojas et al.:44).

REMAINING CHALLENGES TO ELECTORAL REFORM

Despite recent reforms, outdated municipal electoral systems still pose a major challenge to local government in many parts of Latin America. Despite the introduction of free elections for municipal officeholders throughout almost the whole region by the mid-1990s, the democratic deficit remains substantial at the local level. Many features of the electoral system are still in need of reform. Although voting remains compulsory in most countries, electoral registration is based on the "citizen application" approach, in which the citizen is responsible for registering, rather than the "automatic" system, under which the state assumes responsibility for drawing up an electoral register through a postal census every year or so. In many countries, only registered political parties, not citizen organizations, are allowed to field candidates. By international standards, the ratio of citizens to councillors is extremely high and the period of municipal office quite short. Prohibitions on reelection to municipal office are in force in many countries, and the staggering of municipal elections is extremely rare. Municipal elections and terms of office are often still simultaneous and concurrent with those of central government. Systems of proportional representation are based on either a pure party list system without preference voting or a closed party list system that allows preference voting only for the candidates of one list. The open list system, under which the voter may cast preferences for candidates from any of the competing lists, is still a rarity. In almost all countries, various combinations of these structural features of the electoral system continue to militate against accountability to the electorate and administrative continuity. At the same time they also facilitate clientelist forms of political behavior.

7

THE INTERNAL ORGANIZATION OF LOCAL GOVERNMENT

The organizational culture of most municipalities is still imbued with the centralist legacy of *caudillismo* (political bossism), the pork-barrel political culture of Latin America, which thrives on the absence of job stability and the constant rotation of an underpaid and overstaffed bureaucracy. This has led to a nonrational personnel system under which recruitment and promotion are based on patronage instead of merit. Only a few countries have something approaching a local government career system. And even in these countries the career path is usually truncated at the level of department head because posts above that level are confidence posts.

In contrast to many parts of the world, municipal officeholders in Latin America are normally paid salaries rather than a fixed remuneration for every council meeting they attend. In many countries, financial gain is a major attraction for those seeking municipal office. For this reason, the municipal codes of several countries establish limits on the size of officer remunerations in relation to the total income of the municipality. Nevertheless, such payments are often excessive in smaller municipalities, where they absorb a disproportionate share of total municipal revenue, sometimes even exceeding the total wage bill of municipal employees.

THE EXECUTIVE

The internal organization of local government in Latin America has a marked tendency toward unipersonal leadership, inherited from the colonial era, as well as from the twin influences of caudillismo and clientelism. This tradition was reinforced by U.S. foreign aid programs in the 1950s and 1960s, which transferred to Latin America the system prevalent in U.S. municipalities of having a strong elected mayor and a weak council. Collegiate executive boards have disappeared, and today, throughout the region, executive responsibility for local government is exercised by a unipersonal mayor. The mayor is usually known as the *alcalde,* but is referred to as the *intendente* in Argentina, Paraguay, and Uruguay; as the *síndico* in the Dominican Republic; and as the *presidente municipal* in Mexico. In Brazil the mayor is known as the *prefeito.*

The primary function of the mayor is to act as the chief executive officer responsible for the day-to-day operations of the municipal administration, determining broad policy and the functioning of municipal services and investment projects. The mayor formulates and controls the execution of the budget and usually initiates municipal legislation. The mayor appoints all those who hold confidence posts (senior executive assistants who head secretariats, departments, and dependent agencies) and in most countries also has the authority to recruit, supervise, and dismiss permanent municipal staff, although in some countries such decisions must be endorsed by the council. The mayor also acts as the general agent of central government. This role derives from the delegation of law-and-order functions but is far less pronounced now than in the past. It is still important in countries with a strong authoritarian tradition such as Guatemala and Honduras. Elsewhere, the major responsibility of this role today involves coordinating local projects with agencies of central or regional government. Finally, the mayor acts as the official representative of the municipality (e.g., by signing contracts and loans in its name) and as its ceremonial head (e.g., during visits by national political leaders). In the personalist political culture of Latin America, the high visibility of this role has often encouraged aspiring national politicians to view mayoral office as an important stepping-stone in their careers.

THE LEGISLATURE

The Latin American local government legislature is a directly elected municipal council, most commonly known as the *consejo municipal,* but also as the *corporación municipal* in Guatemala and Honduras, as the *junta municipal* in Paraguay, and as the *câmara de vereadores* in Brazil. The council size is extremely small by international standards. Although its size is often justified on grounds of being more efficient, in reality it is a legacy from a time when municipal populations were a fraction of what they are today. It is normal for councillors to elect a council president from among themselves on an annual basis.

The municipal council has two major functions. One is to enact municipal statutes (*ordenanzas*) and internal administrative regulations (*reglamentos*). These are often proposed by the mayor. The other is to supervise the municipal administration carried out under the executive authority of the mayor. The mayor depends on the council for the approval of key financial decisions over such issues as local taxes and the annual budget and expenditure program. In practice, however, legislative scrutiny on financial matters is greatly limited by the absence, even in the largest municipalities (except in Brazil) of the region, of any technical support team to give advice to the council. Instead, debate is often restricted to consideration of the legality or otherwise of budgetary proposals, leaving detailed financial investigation to the comptroller-general's office.

In the larger municipalities, the small size of councils means that councillors are usually fully occupied on municipal business. A proper committee system is unworkable with so few councillors. Instead, individual councillors often oversee a particular area of the municipal administration. In some countries, notably Mexico, these portfolio responsibilities mean that councillors are partly involved in the executive function. This highly personalized system of supervision, when combined with the tradition of clientelism and nepotism, often gives rise to undue interference by councillors in day-to-day divisional management. The most extreme case is Peru, where under the *inspectoría* system, each councillor supervises one branch of municipal administration. In practice, the distinction between such supervision and actual executive power has been so blurred that councillors have considerable de facto power to recruit, dismiss, promote, and regrade staff.

RELATIONS BETWEEN THE EXECUTIVE AND THE LEGISLATURE

Relations between the executive and the legislature at the municipal level have been strongly influenced by the deep-rooted personalist political culture of Latin America. In most countries, the power of the mayor far outweighs that of the council. This is the case irrespective of the formal division of responsibilities provided for by municipal codes. A telling indication of the relative lack of power of the legislature is that elected councils were allowed to operate in many countries during periods when the municipal executive was appointed by central government. In the past, the power of the executive was such that the mayor often acted as leader of the municipal council and chaired its meetings. Today that practice is increasingly rare, although it is still followed in Chile, Guatemala, Honduras, and Peru. In Bolivia, on the other hand, the mayor neither chairs nor is allowed to vote at council meetings, whereas in Brazil the mayor attends council meetings only at the invitation of councillors.

In practice, the power of the legislature vis-à-vis the executive is limited to that of either ratifying municipal legislation or not. In some countries the council even lacks effective power to reject executive action—the municipal codes of Brazil and Colombia still enable the mayor to veto council opposition to executive action. In others the powers of the legislature are further diminished by the fact that the executive is answerable to the council for some functions only, and to central government for others. This arrangement derives from the long-standing identification of the municipal executive as the local representative of the president of the republic. Legal imprecision in the respective attributions of the council and the mayor has often given rise to time-consuming delays in municipal administration as expert (and costly) legal advice is sought in order to resolve conflicts.

In very many municipalities, the power of the legislature is so weak that the council is often confined to surprisingly trivial matters, such as deciding on street names and authorizing the rental of municipal property. Meanwhile important strategic issues regarding the municipality are left exclusively in the hands of the mayor. This has contributed to the generally poor public image of the councillor compared with that of the mayor. The unequal power relationship between the executive and the legislature is reflected in the behavior of individual councillors. Given the relative weakness of the council and the prevalence of clientelism, the power of councillors often derives primarily from their role as a "broker" between interest groups and the mayor. Their prestige depends on their ability to act as a conduit for such groups to the mayor, as well as on their ability to obtain favors from the mayor.

The personalist political culture, which is especially strong in smaller, rural municipalities, affects the relationship between the executive and the legislature. Although the mayor is usually the party leader at the local level, factional opposition to this leadership usually gels around councillors belonging to the same party. This factionalism often galvanizes council opposition to the mayor and expresses itself by the refusal of the council to sanction executive proposals. Such blocking behavior, which is motivated by intraparty bickering rather than by the merits of the case, is a major reason for the inertia in municipal decisionmaking that is common throughout the region.

MUNICIPAL MANAGEMENT

Municipal codes throughout Latin America almost always impose a uniform organizational structure on local government; this uniformity does not take into consideration the enormous variation in the sizes of the local populations. For the vast majority of small municipalities, each with fewer than twenty staff members, this structure invariably proves to be unrealistically elaborate. Implementation of the required number of departments presupposes a much larger staff, which most municipalities simply cannot afford to recruit. In practice, these organizational norms are ignored, the administrative structure remains very simple, and the mayor makes virtually all decisions. The most senior administrative officer, usually known as the *secretario municipal,* remains neglected in terms of formal responsibilities, status, and training.

Even in the larger municipalities of the region, management tends to be highly personalized in the figure of the mayor. This style of management is reflected in the de facto nature of the organizational structure, which bears little relation to its de jure design as laid out in organizational charts and accompanying job descriptions. The lack of effective organizational norms and responsibilities means that functional delegation of authority is not complied with. Instead, there is a concentration of decisionmaking at the highest level and a corresponding lack of it at other levels. This produces a general confusion in operational responsibilities, leading to duplication and disagreement. Because delegation of responsibility is so limited, a corporate management ethos is generally absent. Instead decisions are made on the basis of "orders" from the mayor, which in the absence of any strategic plan fluctuate wildly in response to the pressures of competing political interests. This in turn breeds a lack of initiative within functional departments because these departments lack any long-term plan of activities.

When combined with the absence of a career-based senior administrative cadre and several common features of the electoral system (the prohibition on mayoral reelection, the relatively short term of office, and the absence of staggered elections for councillors), this highly personalized management style also contributes to a serious problem of administrative discontinuity. A major feature of this discontinuity is the tendency for incoming mayors to embark on new, often prestigious projects and to reject the continuation of programs initiated by their predecessors, simply in order to stamp their own character on the municipal government.

Lack of continuity in policymaking between successive administrations, which is common even when successors belong to the same political party, hinders strategic direction in municipal management. On the contrary, by making detailed expenditure planning virtually impossible, it encourages an extreme "short-termism" in local government and a "crisis management" approach to day-to-day decisionmaking. Quick-yield projects are given priority because they are capable of delivering rapid political dividends by bolstering the immediate popularity of the mayor. In a typical three-year term of office, mayors are reputed to spend the first year trying to understand the administration and municipal problems, the second year beginning to tackle these problems, and the third year becoming involved in the forthcoming election campaigns for their successors. Consequently, productive work is reduced to only one year out of the three-year cycle.

The invigoration of local government in recent years has produced few attempts to address the need for the reform of municipal management structures. The striking exception is Chile, where the 1992 municipal code introduced the novel post of municipal administrator. Candidates for this post, who are selected by open competition, must fulfill basic criteria by holding professional qualifications. Standing outside the ranks of both the permanent staff of the municipality and the confidence appointments of the mayor, the administrator reports directly to the mayor. Under this arrangement, the administrator has responsibility for the overall administration of the municipality, although the management of political interests is retained by the mayor. The post is completely new in Latin America and may be likened to that of a town manager in the United States or that of a chief executive in the United Kingdom. There is no evidence that it is being replicated in other countries in the region. The municipal director found in Peru bears some similarities, although this position is essentially a confidence post.

Human Resource Management

There are some 2,700,000 municipal employees throughout Latin America, and they account for approximately 14 percent of total public sector employment in the region. By far the largest number of these workers are employed in Brazil, where they account for 26 percent of total public sector employment (see Table 7.1). By contrast, the 113,000 municipal employees in Mexico account for only 3 percent of total public sector employment in the country. In most Latin American countries administrative statutes and regulations provide the core ingredients of a municipal career system, such as a competitive system of recruitment, a position classification system, and a pay-and-reward system. In practice, these legal provisions for transparent and accountable personnel systems are rarely enforced because of the widespread prevalence of clientelism. Under clientelism, municipal employment is not viewed as an input required in order to produce outputs for the local community in the form of service provision. On the contrary, it is viewed as an output in its own right—a just reward for favors rendered or to be rendered.

Clientelism ensures that local government personnel systems remain weak and highly fragmented throughout the region. As a result, the absence of any proper career system is a striking feature of local government in Latin America and one that distinguishes it from its counterparts in many other parts of the world. There is no vertical integration between the personnel systems of central and local government. Nor is the local government system unified horizontally among municipalities. Instead each municipality

Table 7.1   **Employment in Latin American Municipalities**

Country	Number of Municipal Employees	Total Number of Public Sector Employees	Municipal Share of Employment (percent)
Argentina	253,000 (1986)	1,946,000	13
Bolivia	11,500 (1993)	230,000	5
Brazil	2,000,000 (1994)	7,692,000	26
Chile	94,503 (1992)[a]	269,503	35
Colombia	75,738 (1992)	860,659	9
Costa Rica	6,470 (1987)	159,411	4
Dominican Republic	19,346 (1994)	250,000	8
Ecuador	15,000 (1994)	300,000	5
El Salvador	10,924 (1994)	122,881	9
Guatemala	14,133 (1989)	176,662	8
Honduras	5,900 (1994)	85,507	7
Mexico	113,000 (1991)	4,346,154[b]	3
Nicaragua	6,754 (1994)	73,505	9
Panama	5,061 (1989)	64,000	8
Paraguay	5,245 (1989)	120,000	4
Peru	38,745 (1987)	824,362	5
Uruguay	34,956 (1993)	275,244	13
Venezuela	26,400 (1988)	1,200,000	2
Latin America	2,736,675	18,995,888	14

Source: Data from Chapters 10 through 27 of this book.
Notes: a. Includes education and health workers.
b. Includes workers in state corporations and the social security system.

has its own separate personnel system. The absence of any vertical or horizontal integration greatly inhibits the mobility of local government personnel and is a major factor obstructing the introduction of a career system.

Lack of integration is also found within the personnel system of each municipality, where employees are divided into two categories: those occupying confidence posts and those occupying permanent posts. Staff occupying confidence posts do so at the request of the mayor; they are required to offer their resignation when a new administration takes office. Consequently, they have no security of tenure. Confidence posts usually include all senior staff involved in policymaking or the handling of money, such as department heads, as well as personal staff such as private secretaries. Staff with professional or graduate qualifications fill most confidence posts, and relatively few are found among permanent post holders.

The system of confidence posts has been widely criticized for the discontinuity and loss of "institutional memory" it creates within local government management, as well as for the highly visible form of clientelism from which it is derived. Nevertheless, the practice has some positive features that are often overlooked.

First, in contrast to the rigidity of permanent appointments, appointment to a post of confidence is extremely flexible, and poor performers are easily dismissed by the mayor. Although not appointed overtly by merit, in the larger municipalities of the region those who hold confidence posts must perform well or else risk losing the support of their patron.

Second, the "merry-go-round" created as senior officials move back and forth between municipal posts of confidence and other posts in the public and private sectors is increasingly common in Mexico, Brazil, and Argentina, although it is still unusual in the smaller countries of the region. As staff are removed from confidence posts by incoming mayors, they are replaced by experienced professionals from other public sector organizations. This "circulation of elites" does much to reduce the loss of managerial talent in local government. It also has the advantage of reducing the insularity of local government management by exposing it to fresh ideas from outside.

Third, incoming administrations in the larger municipalities of Brazil and Mexico do not necessarily replace the people occupying posts of confidence. Staff in technical posts are often requested to continue in post. This growing tendency to retain technical staff from one administration to the next is a sign of the gradual introduction of job stability for the senior professional staff of local government. As municipal administration becomes more complex, this trend is likely to increase.

Fourth, in some countries there is considerable interchange between the two kinds of municipal staff, with more senior permanent staff being temporarily promoted to posts of confidence, with the right of reversion to their former posts. This helps to overcome the loss of institutional memory associated with the system of confidence posts and serves as an integrating factor within the bifurcated personnel system.

Confidence posts typically account for no more than 5 percent of total municipal employment. The vast majority of municipal employees are permanent and occupy what are called career posts, although their prospects of promotion are truncated by the confidence-post system. Except in the smaller Central American countries, these posts usually carry a surprisingly high degree of job security, either under general labor laws or as a result of contracts with trade unions representing municipal workers. Clientelism also pervades the management of permanent employees, as can be appreciated by examining practices of recruitment and promotion, the level of staffing, and municipal training.

Recruitment and Promotion

Despite the legal provision for a merit-based system of recruitment, as well as the requirement in some countries that municipal councils must endorse new appointments, familial and political ties retain a major influence over the selection of all grades of staff, especially in smaller municipalities. Posts are rarely advertised, and attempts to introduce recruitment by competitive examination have often been thwarted by the recruitment of "temporary" staff who are subsequently transferred onto the permanent register. Even when recruitment is by open competition, clientelist considerations often continue to play a role in the final decision, thereby concealing the continuation of traditional practices of clientelism.

The subtle manipulation of merit-based practices in order to disguise clientelism is also found in the case of promotion. Criteria for promotion are usually rigidly defined and are based primarily on length of service and educational qualifications rather than on job performance. Although elementary forms of regular staff appraisal have been introduced in larger municipalities, the patron-client relationship between the staff member who writes the appraisal and the staff member about whom it is written usually inhibits any meaningful performance assessment.

Staffing Levels

Overstaffing is a major consequence of clientelism in local government. Even in the larger municipalities of the region, staffing levels are high by international standards, especially considering the relatively limited range of services the municipalities currently provide. The Brazilian municipalities of Pôrto Alegre and Recife had ratios of sixty-four and sixty-seven inhabitants per municipal employee, respectively, in 1991; municipalities within the Metropolitan Zone of Buenos Aires had ratios of 280 inhabitants per municipal employee in 1988. Chile is the only country in the region where limits are placed on municipal staffing levels in relation to population size—currently at one employee per 500 inhabitants.

In the small and medium-sized municipalities of the region, especially in Argentina, Mexico, and Peru, wage costs typically absorb over 80 percent of total expenditure, leaving very little for operational costs and virtually nothing for capital expenditure. The accepted norm in many countries is that locally raised revenue is earmarked exclusively for the payment of salaries, leaving capital expenditure entirely dependent upon transfers from higher tiers of government. Nevertheless, in some countries attempts are made to control overstaffing through financial ratios. In Brazil the share of salaries must not exceed 65 percent of total municipal expenditure. The ratio of minimum to maximum salary levels is also fixed by law, and no employee may earn more than the mayor. In Chile no municipality may spend more than 35 percent of its own income on payments to staff (excluding teachers and health workers). Although the municipal code in Bolivia states that salaries should not exceed half of total municipal income, this rule is invariably broken.

Training

The prevalence of clientelism and the absence of a professional local government service have had a strong influence on the nature of municipal training and on attitudes toward training among local government employees. The form that training takes contributes little to the professionalization of local government. There are no local government professional bodies (in law, accountancy, engineering, and management) offering qualifications that are recognized as a basis for recruitment and salary grading. Much municipal training has served a primarily political purpose as a symbolic exercise in "modern" personnel management and is divorced from personnel departments, which remain weak and overwhelmingly geared toward payroll matters rather than staff development. Training is primarily concerned with the capabilities, skills, motivations, and prospects of individual municipal employees. It typically involves standardized courses for particular groups within the municipal service (accountants, secretaries, etc.). A systems development approach under which training content is designed in response to the needs of specific organizations is a rarity.

Training resources have been concentrated on the highest staff levels, and the beneficiaries have overwhelmingly been those politically appointed officers who occupy confidence posts. Training for these staff positions usually takes place under the auspices of central government public administration institutes. Training content reflects the career aspirations of such advisory staff, who tend to spend only a relatively short part of their career within local government. This training focuses on updating participants on fashionable intellectual issues, which range from the reform of the state to the changing nature of the global economy; the content of this training is divorced from the stark reality of municipal administration and is of little direct relevance to local government. Reflecting the sensibilities of such staff, programs are invariably referred to as seminars, workshops, or colloquia rather than as training courses. They also tend to be extremely short in duration (one or two days).

By contrast, few resources are devoted to the job-related training of junior and middle-level staff, even in larger municipalities. In the absence of career development and because promotion is rarely related to actual job performance, such lower-grade permanent staff often form negative attitudes toward training because it is correctly perceived as having marginal impact upon their promotion prospects. The limited training that takes place for these grades is usually carried out by central-government-funded municipal training bodies, often with the support of foreign donor agencies. This training tends to be highly mechanical. It is usually confined to teaching municipal law (i.e., how to follow the rules embodied in municipal codes) and explaining central government reporting procedures that must be followed by local government, especially in the field of municipal accounting and budget preparation. Training methods are highly traditional and class-room-based, with little opportunity for participation. There is a noticeable absence of training based on the identification and resolution of real prob-lems faced by municipalities, and case study material derived from the actu-al operation of local government is rarely used. Trainers are drawn primari-ly from central government and often have little practical experience with local government. Training events are usually very short, with little planning and no follow-up. Often a series of standardized courses is repeated throughout the country with no variation to reflect local priorities.

An exception to this rule is the prestigious Brazilian municipal training institute, Instituto Brasileiro de Administração Municipal (IBAM), which has been a pioneer in the field of local government training since its estab-lishment in 1952 and has developed as a center of excellence in the delivery and dissemination of relevant training methods to municipalities in Brazil and elsewhere in Latin America. Unlike its counterparts in the rest of the region, IBAM receives hardly any core funding from central government; instead it sells its services to individual municipalities on request. This mar-ket approach has ensured that its training product has reflected the needs of municipalities.

THE CHALLENGE OF
HUMAN RESOURCE MANAGEMENT

The issue of human resource development is surprisingly absent from the debate on strengthening local government in Latin America. It is often por-trayed as a purely technical issue that will somehow sort itself out as both decentralization and community participation gain momentum. Yet the transfer of new competencies and financial resources to municipalities will not guarantee an increase in either the efficiency or the efficacy of local ser-vice provision if existing administrative practices are continued. On the con-trary, given the already overstaffed and inefficient nature of municipal administration, it may simply create more problems than it will solve, and it runs the risk of discrediting the whole decentralization process. Nonethe-less, the rate of return from investment in municipal management training will remain uneconomic until the countries of the region move toward fully integrated national municipal career systems.

The invigoration of local government in the 1980s led to a concern to improve the managerial and administrative competence of municipalities in Latin America. This concern was primarily expressed by renewed efforts to support official institutions responsible for the training of local government officers (see Table 7.2). Many of these institutions had been founded in the 1950s and 1960s as the technical arm of municipal development banks

Table 7.2   Official Municipal Training Institutions in Latin America

Country	National Institution and Year Founded
Argentina	None
Bolivia	Servicio Nacional de Desarrollo Urbano (SENDU), 1972 (closed down in 1986)
Brazil	Instituto Brasileiro de Administração Municipal (IBAM), 1952
Chile	None
Colombia	Escuela Superior de Administración Pública (ESAP), 1958
Costa Rica	Instituto de Fomento y Asesoría Municipal (IFAM), 1971
Dominican Republic	None
Ecuador	Instituto Nacional de Fomento y Desarrollo Municipal (INFODEM), 1987
El Salvador	Instituto Salvadoreño de Desarrollo Municipal (ISDEM), 1987
Guatemala	Instituto de Fomento Municipal (INFOM), 1957
Honduras	Banco Municipal Autónomo (BANMA), 1961
Mexico	Centro Nacional de Estudios Municipales (CNEM), 1984
Nicaragua	Instituto Nicaragüense de Fomento Municipal (INIFOM), 1990
Panama	None
Paraguay	Instituto de Desarrollo Municipal (IDM), 1971
Peru	Instituto Nacional de Fomento Municipal (INFOM), 1983 (closed down in 1992)
Uruguay	None
Venezuela	Fundación para el Desarrollo de la Comunidad y Fomento Municipal (FUNDACOMUN), 1962

financed by foreign aid, but most of them had rapidly ossified. A study of these institutions carried out in the late 1970s revealed a dismal scenario. Most training programs were still using traditional lecture methods, and very few were experimenting with innovative training methods. In very few cases were courses linked to a career system, and none of the institutions were carrying out any evaluation and follow-up of their own programs (Jickling:61–62).

During the 1980s, these training institutions began to receive a boost to their operations by way of increased funding from central government and foreign aid agencies. One notable source of such help from within the region itself was IBAM. By the mid-1990s, IBAM was providing technical assistance to almost all other Latin American countries through a program of consultancies and scholarships.

Two regional initiatives also made a significant contribution to strengthening national training institutions. In 1981 a Latin American chapter of the International Union of Local Authorities (IULA) was established in Quito, Ecuador, with financial support from the Dutch aid program. Through its training arm, the Latin American Center for Training and Development of Local Government (CELCADEL), it has undertaken an extensive program of region-wide courses, workshops, and seminars, backed up by a linked publication program, designed primarily to introduce participatory training methods into the curricula of national municipal training bodies. With funding from the World Bank, the United Nations Centre for Human Settlements (HABITAT), and the Inter-American Development Bank, IULA-CEL-CADEL has sponsored an experimental program since 1989, known as SACDEL, which has pioneered an action-oriented approach to the "training of trainers," including both municipal officers and staff of nongovernmental organizations, through a network of municipal institutions in the region.

The 1980s also saw increased activity in support of local government by the Centro Latinoamericano de Administración para el Desarrollo (CLAD), a regional organization comprising twenty-one member nations in Latin America and the Caribbean, which was established in Caracas in 1972 with financial support from Spain and the United Nations Development Programme (UNDP). Although its brief covers public sector management training in general, CLAD began to emphasize local government training as part of its technical assistance program for reform of the state, thus reflecting the regional trend toward decentralization.

In several countries where official training bodies were either weak or nonexistent, intermediary NGOs were established in the 1980s to support local government, with financial backing from German foundations. The Konrad Adenauer Foundation of Germany helped to establish such bodies in Panama (IPADEM), El Salvador (ISAM), Bolivia (INIDEM), and Peru (INICAM), and the Friedrich Ebert Foundation provided financial support for INIFOM (Nicaragua).

8

CITIZEN PARTICIPATION IN LOCAL GOVERNMENT

Latin American societies have historically been very exclusionary, and the poor have rarely been allowed to participate in governmental decisions affecting their lives. Despite this fact, in many parts of the region, forms of community participation are widely practiced in everyday life. This is especially so in those countries, such as Guatemala and Bolivia, where pre-Columban cultural traditions remain strongest. Yet, paradoxically, it is precisely in these countries where institutionalized racism has ensured that social exclusion from the political process has been greatest. One of the most common expressions of this exclusion has been the refusal by governments to permit citizen participation in local government. This refusal has taken various forms, ranging from the denial of official recognition for citizen organizations to the physical elimination of community leaders. Instead, the poor have often become enmeshed in a subordinated relationship with local political elites through a political control mechanism known as clientelism.

Clientelism poses a major obstacle to the process of democratization in contemporary Latin America; it may be defined as a form of patron-client exchange in which the client bargains for resources in exchange for favors provided to the patron. Efforts by underprivileged groups to introduce their demands within the decisionmaking process of the state have usually been expressed through these kinds of exchanges (Herzer and Pírez:86). Clientelism acts as a form of political integration and co-option through which the representation of the interests of lower-income groups in the arena of political decisionmaking is controlled.

The recent invigoration of local government has affected the exclusionary nature of Latin American society, although the impact has been complex, and there has been enormous variation of experience both among and within countries. The extent to which it will either reduce or strengthen clientelism at the local level is the subject of much controversy. Two particularly significant features of this invigoration—the greater access of local government to financial transfers from central government and the greater citizen participation in local government—are likely to influence the outcome strongly.

INTERGOVERNMENTAL TRANSFERS AND CLIENTELISM

Until the 1980s, the arbitrary and erratic system of financial transfers from central to local government played a key role in "greasing the wheels" of clientelism at the municipal level. In particular, preferential access to central government grants was often conditional upon the local mobilization of votes for national political leaders. This system has largely been replaced by new transparent and stable revenue-sharing formulae under which the allocation of central government grants among municipalities is determined by objective criteria.

It has been argued that this reduction of discretionary financial transfers, coupled with greater political accountability through electoral reform, will undermine the basis on which clientelism thrived. Instead, under a decentralized system of government, political elites will be measured by their success in service delivery because they are now accountable to the electorate. A contrary view, however, asserts that the growth in central government transfers will unwittingly bolster clientelism and encourage corruption at the local level. According to this view, transferring financial power to local government may simply shift the canker of clientelism from the national to the local arena, where it will be even harder to control because of the absence of the strong countervailing regional and sectional interests found at the national political level. Where the municipal system is already subordinated to the logic of intraparty factionalism and is not accountable to the electorate, enhanced financial transfers could simply encourage the existing "short-termism" of municipal management styles, leading to even poorer selection of investment projects and even greater inefficiency of service provision.

There are several reasons for believing that the recent financial strengthening of local government has given municipal officeholders even greater opportunities for practicing clientelism. First, the sheer volume of financial transfers received from central government is growing fast. Second, because these funds are not usually earmarked, mayors retain considerable flexibility in deciding on their use. Third, because these transfers do not directly raise the burden on local taxpayers, there is less pressure for accountability to the electorate over their use. Fourth, central governments have failed to put in place nationwide structures for monitoring standards of local service provision, which would expose the deficiencies in resource allocation caused by clientelism. Finally, it may be argued, the increased level of transfers has invariably altered the balance of power within local government by enhancing the relative strength of the mayor vis-à-vis that of the municipal council. By thus reinforcing the strong mayor model, financial decentralization has in the process contributed to the unipersonal concentration of political power upon which clientelism depends.

CITIZEN PARTICIPATION AND CLIENTELISM

The exclusionary style of development has been a major underlying cause of social conflict in Latin America, and opposition to authoritarian rule in the 1970s and 1980s was often expressed through vigorous community organizations that emerged during this period. These organizations sought to serve as a counterweight to the centralist tradition by making both national political elites and their clientelist counterparts at the municipal level more accountable to the local electorate.

These organizations reflected widespread popular frustration with the ossified structures of representative democracy, especially with the gross deficiencies in the local electoral system. The newly established democratic governments of the region sought to channel this community mobilization by encouraging greater citizen participation in their own decisionmaking processes, and this was a major factor in the invigoration of local government in the region. The creation of participatory mechanisms for dialogue and consensus building at the municipal level became essential ingredients for strengthening the long-term prospects of democracy and for containing social tensions. Citizen participation was also seen as a way of introducing greater rationality into municipal resource allocation so as to reflect the broad interests of the population. This participation would confront the social problems generated by the exclusionary nature of the development process, in particular the poor access to health care, education, and land for housing.

Efforts to encourage citizen participation were carried out primarily through revisions to municipal legislation that encouraged municipalities to grant official recognition to community organizations. Municipalities were obliged to consult with citizen organizations and the general public through periodic cabildos abiertos, and legal provision was made for municipalities to undertake local referendums and plebiscites and to accept popular initiatives and the recall of officeholders (Cunill:110–140). The electoral monopoly of political parties was abolished, and citizen organizations were allowed to present independent candidates for municipal office. It was hoped that the promotion of citizen participation in policymaking at the local level would overcome the arrogant technobureaucratic tradition whereby the vast majority of citizens were not consulted over matters affecting their lives. A more radical interpretation assumed that community demands presented in the form of civic movements and protest marches would bypass typical patron-client networks. This would ensure that municipal officeholders would be more accountable to electorates, thereby reducing the prevalence of clientelism and corruption in the longer term—the so-called goldfish-bowl argument.

Citizen participation was also viewed as a way of improving municipal service provision by helping to overcome critical local deficiencies in finance, know-how, and management. Voluntary contributions of labor and materials for municipal investment programs could harness the energy of self-help organizations to offset shortages of municipal finance. The involvement of more citizens in decisionmaking could also help to redress the shortage of qualified staff and so raise overall efficiency through improved project formulation and implementation. In many countries, this represented a tacit recognition by government that, for decades, virtually all public investment of direct benefit to the poor (primary schools, health clinics, and the extension of water mains and electricity connections) had been carried out by community (rather than local government) initiative. There was also a new willingness by municipal authorities to accept assistance from NGOs in helping to promote citizen participation in local government; this was particularly noticeable in Bolivia and Peru. Finally, citizen participation was seen as a way of tackling the inefficiency in municipal service provision caused by clientelism. Mayors often preferred to treat problems and issues in isolation from one another because doing so enhanced the mayors' own decisionmaking power by tying citizens to the mayors in relationships of personal subordination. To the extent that it required common problems to be tackled in a structured and accountable manner, citizen participation countered clientelism and diluted the personal influence of the mayor.

In the larger cities of the region, democratization saw the introduction of mechanisms for citizen consultation at the submunicipal level. The local administrative boards established in Colombia in 1986, the network of local area boards established throughout the Municipality of São Paolo in the late 1980s, and the neighborhood councils set up in Montevideo in 1993 were notable examples. Such mechanisms are often projected as political initiatives designed to strengthen citizen involvement in local government. In theory, local area offices can make the municipality more accessible to citizens and more responsive to their needs; in addition, local area committees can serve to strengthen citizen participation in local government (Lowndes:54–58). In Latin America, as elsewhere, however, these initiatives were motivated primarily by managerial considerations. As such, they sought to ensure a more effective delivery of municipal services through deconcentrated structures. The submunicipal committees were usually limited to an advisory role, with only limited policymaking powers, and they rarely operated with their own budgets.

BASISMO

In many parts of Latin America the community participation movement came under the influence of radical intellectuals who questioned the capacity of community participation to counter clientelism in local government. One particularly influential line of thought was *basismo* (grassroots autonomy), which emerged among left-wing circles in Latin America during the 1970s. The point of departure of basismo was a critique of the different forms of citizen participation in local government that were emerging at this time. These forms included the following: consultative mechanisms that channeled citizen demands and information to and from municipal authorities; an audit role in checking on the probity and efficiency of municipal action; direct community involvement in municipal investment programs, usually in the form of voluntary labor contributions; and direct powers over municipal decisionmaking.

Basismo criticized the first three of these on the grounds that they constituted either subordinated participation, whereby community organizations existed primarily as support mechanisms for plans previously decided on by municipal authorities, or collaborative participation, whereby municipal plans and objectives were simply communicated to existing community organizations in order to obtain a political consensus. All three forms of participation were regarded as concessions granted by local government, rather than rights obtained by community organizations, and were seen as linked to a style of local government that concerned itself primarily with service provision. This was regarded by basismo as little more than charity (*asistencialismo*) and was contrasted unfavorably with the higher goal of self-government. According to basismo, only the fourth form of participation, whereby community organizations assumed an executive role over municipal decisionmaking, constituted genuine participation (Chirinos:89–94).

At the heart of this interpretation of community participation lay a rejection of the highly inadequate workings of representative democracy in Latin America in favor of an ill-defined ideal of direct democracy. This utopian stance was often bolstered by tacit support from dogmatic Marxist groups. These groups took a purely negative view of local government, which they perceived simply as the last bastion of officialdom on the line dividing civil society and the state. Therefore local government had to be destroyed as part of a wider struggle against the state. This view was strongly contested by advocates of citizen participation in local government. They argued that, although local government was part of officialdom, it nevertheless operated in an ambiguous frontier zone between the state and civil society. Though not denying the power of dominant and clientelist interests at the municipal level, they believed that local government retained an independent legitimacy as the natural representative of broader community interests.

Basismo encouraged community organizations to reject any form of activity that was channeled through the existing structures of local government. As such, it was responsible for a strong anti-institutional stance found to varying degrees within urban social movements during the 1980s; this viewpoint expressed itself through a tendency to give priority to confrontation rather than negotiation with local government. The experience of community participation in Peru, the country where basismo was strongest during the 1980s, is instructive. Throughout the 1980s, direct democracy was widely advocated by community leaders in the poorer district municipalities of Lima and elsewhere. The corollary was that representative democracy was denigrated. This extreme stance tended to be overly critical of municipal authorities but did not pose alternative solutions to urban problems. This stance quickly lost electoral support, however, when it was incapable of delivering concrete improvements in service provision during a time of severe economic crisis. Ironically, in its place, a strategy that stressed managerial efficiency rather than citizen participation as a rapid route to better service provision proved surprisingly effective as a vote winner. By the mid-1990s, left-wing parties had themselves adopted such a strategy.

The extreme form of direct democracy that basismo advocated posed a real threat to citizen participation in local government. It was impossible to translate the mechanisms of direct democracy, which were feasible in small groups and were based on the equality and shared interests of members, to the wider municipal arena, where divergent interest groups coexisted. Unlike in the small-group scenario, where consensus and lack of delegation was accepted as the norm, delegation and representation became necessary in the larger context, as did compromise through negotiation.

Nevertheless, basismo did have the virture of alerting community organizations to the alternative danger of falling into the trap of a neutered form of participation that simply reinforced clientelism. In this respect, the experience of Brazil is equally instructive and suggests that community organizations can often be manipulated and accommodated within clientelist styles of municipal management. In Brazil, as in Peru, citizen participation in local government was weakly institutionalized, but for very different reasons. Most examples of participation appear to have taken place at the personal initiative of the mayor, whose role as facilitator had many drawbacks. This arrangement encouraged a network of individual relationships between local neighborhood leaders and the mayor, marginalizing both councillors and the wider membership of community groups in the process. These initiatives were rarely institutionalized, as shown by the fact that existing administrative processes and forms of decisionmaking were not modified. Their extreme dependence upon political support from above made their continuity highly problematic. Because they depended on the goodwill of the mayor, the prohibition on mayoral reelection meant that initiatives invariably collapsed when this support was removed.

In parts of Brazil, the ideological momentum of basismo was sustained from the mid-1980s by the victory of radical municipal administrations belonging to the left-wing Partido do Trabalhadores (PT). However, the high initial expectations about the role of neighborhood associations, and the "popular councils" they spawned, in reshaping urban policies were rapidly moderated. The relationship between these new participatory channels and the orthodox executive and legislative institutions at the municipal level had not been clarified, and the confrontationalist discourse of PT militants soon clashed with that of municipal executives from their own party. This contributed to the split between twelve out of thirty-six PT mayors and the party itself between 1988 and 1992. Efforts to grant a deliberative role to community organizations in the key executive function of municipal budgeting failed, even in major PT-controlled municipalities such as São Paulo and Pôrto Alegre. The popular councils, whose own credentials of being genuinely representative were questionable, were eventually relegated to a consultative role (Assies:49–54). Nevertheless, by 1995 the popular council in Pôrto Alegre had begun to play a major role in municipal budget preparation. In particular, participation introduced a more rational criteria for the selection of investment projects.

PROSPECTS FOR COMMUNITY PARTICIPATION

The relationship between civil society and the local state throughout Latin America varies between two ideal types. On the one hand is the independent mobilization of the population as citizens who will make demands upon municipal authorities; on the other is the integration of the population into a subordinate relationship based on clientelism, through which material favors are exchanged for political support by means of a network of highly personalized and unequal but reciprocal patron-client relations. Two fundamental conditions appear to be necessary for community participation to flourish in Latin American local government. Municipal authorities must be favorably disposed toward the idea of community participation in the first place, and existing citizen organizations must already have developed a certain presence at the local level (Herzer and Pírez:91).

Some of the best examples of community participation have taken place when communities mobilize in opposition to the state, and by their nature these efforts are likely to be short-lived if successful. This general rule is applicable to Latin America, where the upsurge of community organization in the 1970s and 1980s was intimately linked to the demise of military rule. As the 1980s wore on, a wide gulf emerged between the rhetoric and reality of citizen participation in Latin American local government, and the real level of participation was usually no higher than that found in other countries of comparable living standards. Lack of continuity became a notable feature of community participation throughout the region. Mobilization was built around specific demands (*revindicaciones*), and once these were realized, participation tended to diminish.

For this reason, the recent pressure for citizen participation in local government may simply have been a conjunctural phenomenon associated with the transition to democracy in the region. If this proves to be the case, the high levels of citizen participation will gradually wither away after having fulfilled an indispensable but essentially catalytic role in erecting a more genuinely representative form of democracy at the local government level.

9

INTERMUNICIPAL RELATIONS

Intermunicipal cooperation in Latin America takes three forms: (1) local-level collaboration among neighboring municipalities for joint service provision through the common ownership of expensive assets; (2) national associations for the purpose of lobbying central government, usually on financial matters; and (3) international cooperation within the region. Local-level cooperation among municipalities is generally weak. In rural areas, the joint pooling of equipment for building and maintaining roads is increasingly common, although the sharing of skilled human resources (engineers, surveyors, and accountants) is rare except in Brazil. In metropolitan areas, intermunicipal cooperation is often restrained by territorial rivalries and is usually limited in practice to joint disposal of solid waste.

Cooperation at the national level is stronger, and intermunicipal associations now exist in all countries except Mexico, Nicaragua, Panama, and Uruguay (see Table 9.1). National associations were formed as far back as 1939 in the Dominican Republic, 1954 in Paraguay, and 1967 in Venezuela. These early initiatives invariably remained ineffectual because of their extreme political dependence on central government. In other countries, they were banned altogether during periods of authoritarian rule. In Brazil the Associação Brasileira de Municípios, founded in 1948, collapsed in the late 1960s under military rule, and the Chilean Confederación Nacional de Municipalidades, founded in the early 1950s, was banned by the military government in 1973.

Until recently the capacity of these national municipal associations to express the collective aspirations of local government was dulled by the strong control exercised by central government over their operations. This often took the form of central government appointment of the chief executive (as in Costa Rica and Paraguay), heavy financial dependence of the association on central government grants for its operational expenditure, and obligatory membership for municipalities.

Table 9.1   National Intermunicipal Associations in Latin America

Country	Association and Year Founded
Argentina	Asociación de Municipios Argentinos (AMA), 1991
Bolivia	Asociación de Gobiernos Municipales Autónomos de Bolivia (AGMAB), 1989; Asociación Boliviana de Municipalidades (ASBOMUN), 1990
Brazil	Confederação Nacional de Municipios (CNM), 1979
Chile	Asociación Chilena de Municipalidades (ACM), 1993
Colombia	Federación Colombiana de Municipios (FCM), 1989
Costa Rica	Unión Nacional de Gobiernos Locales (UNGL), 1976
Dominican Republic	Liga Municipal Dominicana (LMD), 1939
Ecuador	Asociación de Municipalidades Ecuatorianas (AME), 1968
El Salvador	Corporación de Municipalidades de la República de El Salvador (COMURES), 1992
Guatemala	Asociación Nacional de Municipalidades (ANAM), 1965
Honduras	Asociación de Municipios de Honduras (AMHON), 1960
Mexico	None
Nicaragua	None
Panama	None
Paraguay	Organización Paraguaya de Cooperación Intermunicipal (OPACI), 1954
Peru	Asociación de Municipalidades del Peru (AMPE), 1982
Uruguay	None
Venezuela	Asociación Venezolana de Cooperación Intermunicipal (AVECI), 1967

In many countries the electoral system also discouraged intermunicipal cooperation, at both a local and a national level. The short term of office and the prohibition on reelection encouraged mayors to emphasize projects to produce results that were both rapid and clearly attributable to their own administration. These considerations meant that priority was not given to the kind of long-term collaboration between adjoining municipalities in which political benefits would have to be shared with others and might not even be realized until long after the mayor left office. Similarly, the practice of linking local and central government elections through concurrent terms of office and single-list voting systems also discouraged the development of a cross-party consensus that was required if national municipal associations were to operate as an effective counterweight to central government.

The emergence of a new breed of national municipal association during the 1980s was an important by-product of the invigoration of local government. New associations were established in Peru (1982), Bolivia (1989), Colombia (1989), Argentina (1991), El Salvador (1992), and Chile (1993). The structure of these new municipal associations reflected the greater political autonomy of local government. In sharp contrast to their previously established counterparts, membership was voluntary, they did not depend upon central government for financial support, they stressed political pluralism rather than sectarianism in their mode of operation, they granted equal voting rights to all municipalities irrespective of size, and their leadership was freely elected and not imposed by central government. These national associations soon became an influential mouthpiece of local government and a powerful lobby in favor of greater decentralization.

Intermunicipal cooperation at the international level within Latin America dates back to the first congress of an inter-American municipal association known as Organización Interamericana de Cooperación Municipal, held in Cuba in 1938. More recently regional cooperation has depended heavily upon support from foreign governments, notably from the Spanish government through the Organización Iberoamericana de Cooperación Intermunicipal (OICI), founded in 1955; from the Dutch government through the Latin American chapter of the International Union of Local Authorities (IULA-AL), established in Quito in 1981; and from the U.S. government through the Federation of Municipalities from the Central American Isthmus (FEMICA), established in 1991. Such organizations have provided a forum for the exchange of experiences among municipal specialists from within the region, although they have been less effective in developing technical cooperation programs among member nations. Recent official declarations by members of IULA-AL (see Appendix 1) and FEMICA (see Appendix 2) demonstrate the growing assertiveness of the Latin American municipal movement toward the central governments of the region.

PART 2

COUNTRY PROFILES

10

ARGENTINA

Argentina is a federal nation comprising twenty-three provinces and the Federal Capital (Capital Federal) of Buenos Aires, which is surrounded by the Province of Buenos Aires. Below the province level, the country is covered by more than 1,100 municipalities. Both provinces and municipalities have elected governments. The structure of government at the subprovincial level varies according to the respective provincial constitution. In some provinces (e.g., La Rioja), municipal jurisdiction coincides with the subprovincial administrative structure, thereby incorporating both urban settlements and rural hinterlands. In most other provinces (e.g., Córdoba), municipal jurisdiction is confined to specific urban settlements, with large parts of the rural hinterland bereft of any structure of local government at all, a factor that strengthens the political affinity between rural citizens and the provincial government.

The Federal Capital, with a population of 2.9 million in 1989 equivalent to 9 percent of the national total, has municipal status and is known as the Municipality of the City of Buenos Aires (MCBA). The MCBA lacks the political autonomy of other municipalities in the country. Its executive head is appointed by the president, and its sixty-member elected deliberative council receives its delegated powers from the National Congress. The Metropolitan Zone of Buenos Aires (Zona Metropolitana de Buenos Aires), comprising the MCBA and nineteen municipalities (*partidos*) within the surrounding Province of Buenos Aires, has a combined population of eleven million, equivalent to 33 percent of the national population. There is no metropolitan government, and the metropolitan zone also lacks any practical significance for urban planning (Pírez, 1991c:45). Because of the enormous concentration of population in the Buenos Aires area, most municipalities are very thinly populated, with over half having fewer than 2,000 inhabitants and fewer than 10 percent having more than 10,000 inhabitants.

HISTORICAL DEVELOPMENT

The 1853 Federal Constitution, still in force today, does not include any national municipal legislation and makes no reference to municipal autonomy. Instead, it empowers each province to approve its own constitution and to establish norms for the municipalities within its own jurisdiction. Hence, municipalities were organized as part of each province's system of government. For over a century thereafter, provincial constitutions reflected the prevailing view that municipalities were mere administrative dependencies of provincial government. In the 1850s and 1860s, the leading intellectuals of the day, Juan Bautista Alberdi and Domingo Sarmiento, debated the merits of local government. This polemic petered out in the 1880s, when, at a time of burgeoning European immigration, the latter revised his earlier support for municipal autonomy in favor of Alberdi's oligarchic views. Support for these views was most clearly demonstrated by the widespread introduction of the property vote (Ternavasio:67).

During the 1950s, this highly restrictive view began to be replaced by a broader definition of municipal autonomy, as illustrated by the promulgation of modern provincial constitutions in Chubut, Río Negro, Neuquén, Misiones, Formosa, and Santiago de Estero. During the military governments of 1966–1973 and 1976–1983, however, local government elections were abolished, and municipalities were once again reduced to mere administrative units of central government. With the return to civilian rule in 1983, a new impetus toward greater municipal autonomy was reflected in the reform of provincial constitutions in Córdoba, La Rioja, and Salta.

As a result of these historical circumstances, the extent of local government autonomy within Argentina today varies to a much greater degree than elsewhere in Latin America—from the Province of Buenos Aires, where municipalities are little more than deconcentrated administrative units of the provincial government, to the Provinces of Córdoba and La Rioja, where they enjoy a significant degree of political autonomy. In some provinces, comprehensive municipal laws are sanctioned only by the provincial legislature, whereas in others, notably Córdoba, individual municipal charters may be drafted by a local citizens' convention.

ORGANIZATIONAL STRUCTURE

Argentinean local government comprises a unipersonal executive head, or mayor (intendente) and a legislature (concejo deliberante). The mayor and councillors (concejales) are usually elected for four years in separate elections, except in the Province of Chaco, where the mayor is indirectly elected by the council from among its own members. In a unique departure from

Latin American tradition, in some provinces municipal elections are staggered, with half the council seats renewed every two years. The number of councillors is determined by provincial law. In the Province of Buenos Aires it ranges between six in municipalities with fewer than 5,000 inhabitants and twenty-four in municipalities with more than 200,000 inhabitants. The MCBA has the largest council in the country, with sixty members.

In almost all provinces, at the same time as council elections, direct elections are also held for membership of municipal school councils (*consejos escolares*), each of which in the Province of Buenos Aires has six members. These advisory bodies at the municipal level liaise with the provincial government over the administration of primary and secondary education.

There is a diversity of electoral systems for local government. Proportional representation based on a closed party list system is the most common practice. In several provinces such as Neuquén, Misiones, and La Rioja, however, council seats are distributed exclusively between the two political parties gaining the most votes. The winning party receives 75 percent of council seats irrespective of its share of the total vote, and the party that comes second automatically receives the remaining 25 percent of the seats. In the Province of Entre Ríos councillors are elected independently of party lists, with the post of mayor going to the candidate who receives the most votes. In most provinces, mayors may stand for reelection on expiry of their terms of office.

FUNCTIONAL RESPONSIBILITIES

The division of responsibility for service delivery among federal, provincial, and local government varies considerably among and within provinces, and widespread overlapping of functions among the three levels of government greatly restricts the rational allocation of resources (Herzer, 1992a:27). In general, federal and provincial government have concurrent responsibility for higher education, preventive health care, major bus terminals, housing, electricity, and gas supply, whereas provincial and municipal governments have concurrent responsibility for primary education, primary health care, water and sewerage, and regional highways. In 1994 responsibility for secondary education was in the process of being transferred from federal to provincial government.

Local government has sole responsibility for a diverse range of activities including solid waste collection and disposal, road building and maintenance, sewerage and drainage, parks, markets, cemeteries, land use zoning, building regulation, public hygiene, public lighting, traffic control, and regulation of public transportation. Although provincial government has prime responsibility for education and health, in practice municipalities are responsible for the maintenance of school buildings, and many municipalities operate their own hospitals, which often represent a considerable drain on their finances. The contracting out of municipal service provision to the private sector is a well-established practice in many provinces. Municipal supervision of contractor compliance is often minimal (Pírez and Gamallo:19).

PERSONNEL SYSTEM

In 1986 there were 253,000 municipal employees, accounting for 13 percent of all public sector employment in the country. Gross overstaffing has been a major feature of local government in Argentina. As a result, personnel costs absorb the lion's share of recurrent expenditure, thereby greatly constraining the growth of capital expenditure. This overstaffing is a product of the clientelist political culture, which subordinates both provincial and local government to short-term party interests. The mayor is usually assisted by four confidence-post secretaries (for intergovernmental relations, finance, public works, and social work) as well as subsecretaries. In contrast, the posts of municipal accountant, treasurer, and head of purchasing are held by officials appointed by the council at the suggestion of the mayor. There has been a long-standing conflict between permanent municipal staff and those appointed under confidence posts. This has often led to lack of cooperation by career staff (García and Garay:21).

Municipal employment rose rapidly during the 1980s, primarily as a welfare mechanism to offset the increase in unemployment brought about by the impact of IMF structural adjustment policies. Given that the share of local government in gross domestic product did not rise during the period, employment growth was made possible only by a significant decline in the real income of municipal employees. This led to declining skill levels and higher rates of absenteeism. These factors combined with an increase in unnecessary bureaucracy to produce a marked deterioration in the public image of local government (Herzer, 1992a:20). In 1988 municipalities within the Metropolitan Zone of Buenos Aires employed an average of one person per 280 inhabitants, and by 1993 municipal employment figures had become a closely guarded secret.

FINANCIAL STRUCTURE

As in much of Latin America, the limited capacity of Argentine local government to carry out the responsibilities assigned to it is largely explained by the lack of financial resources. Historically, local government has accounted for a small share of total public expenditure. During the period 1960–1985, local government (excluding the MCBA) accounted for 9.5 percent of total public expenditure, compared with 51.9 percent for central government and 38.6 percent for the MCBA and provincial governments combined (Pírez, 1991b:329). By 1988 this figure had risen to 11 percent (FIEL:14–17). There is an enormous disparity among municipalities in terms of expenditure per head. In 1994 the MCBA had a budgeted expenditure per head of U.S.$1,155 for its population of three million, although the neighboring Municipality of La Matanza had only U.S.$30 per head for its population of one million.

In recent years there has been a noticeable shift in the financing of local government toward a greater reliance on transfers (*coparticipaciones*) from provincial government. In 1970 transfers from provincial government represented only 25.2 percent of total municipal financial resources, rising steadily to 48.2 percent by 1985, while the contribution of locally generated revenue fell correspondingly (Pírez, 1991b:330). Financial transfers to local government have two sources: a share of the funds received by the province from central government, and funds derived from the sharing of taxes directly collected by the province (income tax, property tax, and road vehicle tax). Municipalities play no part in decisions regarding the size and manner of these transfers, which are exclusively determined by negotiation between central and provincial government.

Although three factors—population size, local revenue yield, and equal shares—are found in most formulae, the actual criteria for the allocation of financial transfers to municipalities varies considerably among provinces. In the Province of Buenos Aires, 8.6 percent of total provincial income (locally generated revenue and transfers from central government) is distributed to municipalities according to the following criteria: 65 percent in direct proportion to their population size; 25 percent in inverse proportion to their fiscal capacity; and 10 percent in direct proportion to their geographical area.

In the Province of La Rioja, municipalities receive 10 percent of all provincial incomes received from the federal government. Of this, 60 percent is automatically transferred, and 40 percent is destined as a contribution toward a municipal development fund to finance public works. The 60 percent share is distributed to municipalities according to the following criteria: 85 percent in direct proportion to their population size; 10 percent in inverse proportion to their population size; and 5 percent in direct proportion to the value of their locally generated revenue. In addition, municipalities receive a 20 percent share of the proceeds collected from income tax and a 50 percent share of the vehicle road tax, both of which are distributed according to the above-mentioned 60-40 criteria. Municipalities also receive 8 percent of the provincial housing tax.

In addition to these nondiscretionary transfers, there are two significant discretionary financial transfers from provincial to local government. First, provincial governments often provide arbitrary subsidies, usually decided on the basis of clientelist considerations, in order to cover the deficits of individual municipalities. Second, it is common practice for provincial governments to provide regular transfers, known as *convenios,* which are earmarked for the maintenance of schools and hospitals administered by municipalities.

The major source of locally generated revenue, typically accounting for half of the total, is a composite charge *(tasa de alumbrado, barrido, y limpieza,* or ABL) levied for the provision of public lighting, street cleaning, and solid waste management. In effect, the ABL is often a tax when it is levied as a surcharge on provincial property taxation and is thus unrelated to the actual cost of service provision. Other important sources of locally generated revenue are a public health and environmental fee levied on industry and business and a road maintenance fee levied on rural property owners. A betterment levy is designed to recoup part of the increase in property values occasioned by infrastructure improvements. In practice it is used to finance the improvements. Property taxation is usually a provincial tax and is a major source of locally generated revenue only in the MCBA and in the municipalities of more recently created provinces. By 1990 municipal assessments of property values in the MCBA had fallen to only 4 percent of their market values. The widespread evasion of municipal taxes and fees of all kinds is a major explanation for the declining contribution of locally generated revenue to total municipal income (Pírez, 1991a:46, 88).

INTERMUNICIPAL COOPERATION

The development of intermunicipal associations has been weak in Argentina because of the pervasive influence of clientelist political structures at the local level that bear primary allegiance to provincial party bosses *(caudillos).* In fact, until recently the few examples of such associations were usually promoted by provincial governments themselves as a means of consolidating their authority over local government. A notable exception, however, is the mayors' forum (Foro de Intendentes) in the Province of Córdoba. A first national meeting of municipalities took place in Buenos Aires on 6–7 December 1990, which gave birth the following year to a national municipal association, Asociación de Municipios Argentinos (AMA). The AMA has not prospered, mainly because the initiative was orchestrated by the federal government.

SUPPORT SERVICES

Reflecting the clientelist nature of local government, there is no national training body for local government, nor do such bodies exist at the provincial level. The national public sector training institute, Instituto Nacional de la Administración Pública (INAP), carries out piecemeal training for local government employees, and some universities and political parties do likewise.

CITIZEN PARTICIPATION

The municipal codes of most provinces do not refer specifically to citizen participation, but instead confine citizen involvement in local government to the right to vote. There are an estimated 687 administrative bodies at the submunicipal level. These fall within the jurisdiction of a formally constituted municipality, but they often have delegated powers, their own resources, and in some cases their own elected council. Some municipal codes provide for deconcentrated administrative units (*delegaciones municipales*) for service provision at the submunicipal level, with their authorities appointed by the mayor. The provincial constitutions of Córdoba and La Rioja provide mechanisms that facilitate a high degree of citizen involvement in municipal affairs. Among these mechanisms are referendums; citizen initiatives that oblige the council to consider any issue; and a system of popular recall, under which an elected official may be removed from office before his or her term of office ends.

The MCBA has developed a system of submunicipal citizen representation in local government that is unique in Argentina; this system has evolved in part in order to counterbalance the democratic deficit caused by the non-elected nature of the MCBA's executive head. The municipality is divided for administrative purposes into fourteen districts, each of which has a neighborhood council (*consejo vecinal*) composed of nine members (*consejeros*), who are directly elected by proportional representation according to party lists and who serve a four-year term of office. The main functions of the neighborhood council are to promote citizen participation in local policymaking and to act as a channel of communication between the municipal executive and local citizens. In particular, the councils liaise with citizen associations (*sociedades de fomento*) that have arisen in connection with the struggle for land titling and the provision of basic infrastructure services.

Nevertheless, given the clientelist political culture, the vast majority of these citizen associations, rather than representing the local citizenry as a whole, are closely identified with a political party. As such, they exert influence through personal contacts with leading municipal authorities, usually the mayor, rather than through the formal institutions of local government. Recent evidence from the Municipalities of Resistencia (Pírez, 1991a:121–146) and Neuquén (Herzer and Pírez:95–121), however, points to the emergence of more independent citizen associations that may represent a rejection of the clientelist relationship with local government authorities.

PROSPECTS FOR LOCAL GOVERNMENT

In August 1989, prompted by a severe fiscal crisis leading to hyperinflation, the federal government initiated a major reform of the state designed to reduce radically the public sector borrowing requirement through a sweeping privatization program. Although the major impact by far has been the transfer of federally owned companies to the private sector, local government has been encouraged to extend the practice of contracting out service provision to the private sector.

A study of the Municipality of Córdoba, where virtually all basic urban services (street cleaning, solid waste collection, traffic lights, car parks, parks and gardens, and public lighting) have been contracted out, has highlighted two serious administrative deficiencies found throughout the country in the wake of privatization. One is the lack of impact evaluation of municipal investment projects and the absence of any structure to monitor contract compliance and service quality by private contractors responsible for the delivery of municipal services. The other is the absence of any overall sectoral coordination of municipal activities (Herzer, 1992c:47).

With the focus of the reform program concentrated on redrawing the boundary between the public and private sectors of the economy, little attention was paid to decentralization of functions within the public sector itself. Nevertheless, several provincial governments, notably that of Córdoba, have used the state reform program to legitimize their ongoing programs for the devolution of responsibility for social services (education, health, and social welfare) to municipalities in their jurisdiction. A sharp reduction in the level of federal government transfers occasioned by the severe fiscal crisis has seriously limited the capacity of provincial governments to provide municipalities with extra finance in order to match newly devolved responsibilities. In turn, this fiscal austerity has dampened the enthusiasm of local government toward the assumption of new responsibilities (Díaz de Landa:320). The transfer of property tax to municipal control would be a positive step in helping to overcome this fiscal problem.

With the notable exception of municipalities in the Province of Córdoba, local government in Argentina generally has a more limited degree of autonomy from higher levels of government than elsewhere in Latin America. The tremendous diversity in attributions of municipalities has led to much legal uncertainty, which in practice has been used to reduce municipal autonomy. There is a strong case for advocating greater homogeneity in municipal legislation, although with the need to respect provincial autonomy.

11

BOLIVIA

Bolivia is a unitary nation divided into four subnational administrative tiers of government. At the regional level there are nine departments, each governed by a prefect appointed by the president of the republic. The departments are subdivided into 112 provinces, headed by subprefects appointed by the departmental prefect. At the subprovincial level there are 301 subprovinces (*secciones de provincias*) and 1,408 cantons headed by government officials known as corregidores.

A multitier local government system consisting of 296 municipalities follows this administrative subdivision at the departmental, provincial, subprovincial, and canton levels. However, its territorial jurisdiction is confined to recognized urban areas only (a unique situation in Latin America). This means that the rural population, who are mainly of indigenous ethnic origin, have no local government representation.

There is enormous variation in municipal size. In 1992 only three municipalities (La Paz, Santa Cruz, and Cochabamba) had populations greater than 400,000. Another five had populations between 90,000 and 400,000, thirteen between 15,000 and 90,000, and sixty-five between 3,000 and 15,000. The remaining 137 municipalities, equivalent to 61 percent of the total, each had fewer than 3,000 inhabitants.

HISTORICAL DEVELOPMENT

Since gaining independence in 1825, Bolivia has lost over half of its original territory—on the Pacific coast to Chile, in the Chaco to Paraguay, and in Acre to Brazil. This territorial dismemberment (*desmembración territorial*) is deeply rooted in the national psyche and is a major factor explaining the highly centralized system of government. The first major municipal code was not enacted until 1942. It replaced legislation dating from 1878 under which mayors were appointed by the president from among candidates nominated by directly elected councillors. The limited degree of municipal autonomy granted by the 1942 code was soon removed by central government. From 1949 to 1987 no local government elections took place, municipal councils were abolished altogether, and mayors were once again appointed by central government.

The 1952 revolution led to a rapid increase in central government intervention in urban policy. A far-reaching urban land reform allowed for expropriation of all urban properties in excess of 10,000 square meters, with owners retaining control of only 1,000 square meters. Although it lasted only two years (1954–1956), during this time 20,000 people in La Paz, the capital city, were beneficiaries. Nevertheless, the prevailing centralist views of the revolutionary government meant that local government was not strengthened during this period (Finot:23).

The introduction of military rule in 1964 led to a further decline in the powers of local government and a corresponding increase in the role of central government and the private sector. In 1973 responsibility for public housing and urban planning (including cadastres, land use zoning, and the issuing of building permits) passed from municipal control to the Ministry of Housing and Urban Affairs. By the mid-1970s five separate central government bodies (the Ministry of the Interior, the Ministry of Housing and Urban Affairs, the Ministry of Finance, the comptroller-general's office, and the Subsecretariat for Administrative Reform of the Planning Council) were overseeing the activities of local government. But each of these bodies dealt independently with municipalities. The absence of any coordination among them reflected the lack of any national strategy for municipal development (Jickling:38).

By the early 1970s, the central governments of most Latin American countries had already taken over basic service provision at the local level. In Bolivia, by contrast, water supply, sewerage, and electricity remained under nominal municipal control, although the actual extent of service provision was very limited. In 1972 the military government set up regional development corporations (*corporaciones de desarrollo departamental,* or CDDs) at the departmental level, which were financed by a mix of direct central government transfers and royalties on regionally produced minerals and petroleum. The CDDs represented the first serious move toward deconcentration of central government activities in Bolivia. Led by the CDD of the Department of Santa Cruz, the corporations rapidly absorbed basic local service provision from municipalities, starting off in the departmental capitals and subsequently broadening their remit throughout the region. In pursuit of this objective, they attached minimal importance to strengthening local government (Rondinelli and Evans:35).

As elsewhere in Latin America, the return to civilian rule that occurred in Bolivia starting in the early 1980s was accompanied by renewed pressure for decentralization. Three additional factors made this pressure particularly strong in the case of Bolivia. First, the traditional centers of economic and political power (La Paz and the mining towns) had begun to decline in relative importance as a result of the emergence of the Department of Santa Cruz and the eastern agricultural frontier as a new regional growth pole. Second, the centralist Bolivian state failed dismally to confront a severe economic crisis in 1982–1984. Third, the historically powerful trade union movement and left-wing political parties, whose programs had hitherto been built upon a centralist approach to development, faced a major crisis when their economic base in the tin-mining industry collapsed (Boye:220).

Local government lacked the capacity, however, to channel this clamor for change to its own advantage. The general public already held an extremely low opinion of local government, based on its perceived ineffectiveness during decades of military rule. Furthermore, democratization starkly revealed local government's major deficiencies: a legacy of dependence on central government and a highly bureaucratic mentality among its staff. Instead, regional civic committees (*comités cívicos departamentales,* or CCDs) emerged in each department to spearhead the decentralization process, led by the committee in the Department of Santa Cruz, which had been formed as far back as 1951. Government decentralization policy in recent years has been more a response to pressure from these CCDs than to pressure from local government.

A new municipal code, Ley Orgánica de Municipalidades No. 696, was passed in 1985, and although it recognized the autonomy of local government, it surprisingly did not incorporate rural hinterlands within municipal boundaries. For the first time in decades, municipal elections were held in December 1987, although the low turnout (43 percent) reflected the legacy of popular apathy toward local government.

Meanwhile, the CCDs pressed for the implementation of Article 110 of the 1967 Constitution, which had made provision for an elected regional tier of government in the form of directly elected departmental councils. Between 1983 and 1989 no fewer than eighteen different decentralization bills were presented to Congress (Oporto:48). Yet by 1994 a decentralization law had still not been passed because of continuing fears among the political elite that this might lead to the balkanization of Bolivia.

ORGANIZATIONAL STRUCTURE

Bolivian local government comprises a unipersonal executive head, or mayor (alcalde), and a legislature (known as the consejo municipal in the case of departmental capitals and as the junta municipal in provincial capitals). The only exception is at the lowest level, that of the canton, where there is no legislature and where power resides exclusively in the hands of the elected mayor, known as the *agente cantonal*. The mayor is indirectly elected from among councillors (*consejales*), except in the canton, where the mayor is directly elected. The mayor neither chairs nor is allowed to vote at council meetings.

Although the attributes of the municipal legislature are uniform throughout the country, the council size varies according to the status, as well as the population size, of the municipality. The nine municipalities that either are departmental capitals or have a population greater than 100,000 have thirteen councillors; municipalities that are provincial capitals or have populations greater than 10,000 have seven councillors (known as *munícipes*); the remaining municipalities representing urban areas at the subprovincial level have only five councillors. Because this system of classification does not fully reflect the distribution of population, several municipalities that are provincial capitals have fewer councillors than some municipalities that have smaller populations but are departmental capitals.

In all cases, the mayor and councillors are elected for two years, the shortest municipal term of office in Latin America. Officeholders are eligible for immediate reelection on expiry of their terms of office. The short term of office and indirect election of the mayor, as well as the power of the council to revoke the mandate of the mayor, have led to widespread administrative discontinuity.

A relationship of supervision and subordination exists among individual municipalities, which reflects the highly centralized political system in Bolivia. Mayors and councils of municipalities that are departmental capitals have the authority to supervise the activities of their counterparts in the capitals of that department's provinces. Similarly, mayors of provincial municipalities supervise the activities of the agentes in the cantons under their jurisdiction. In practice this means that smaller municipalities must strive to counter not only the encroachment of central government bodies at the local level, but also the interference by the municipal authorities of their departmental capital. In particular, this subordination makes the smaller municipalities vulnerable to the willingness of larger municipalities to pass on financial transfers to which the former are legally entitled under revenue-sharing agreements with central government.

FUNCTIONAL RESPONSIBILITIES

Following the gradual assumption of powers by central government agencies, by the 1980s there was a widespread lack of clarity over the respective responsibilities of departmental prefects, departmental development corporations, and municipalities. The 1985 municipal code granted the following functions to local government: urban land use planning, land titling, development and maintenance of the cadastre, public hygiene, water, sewerage and storm drainage, solid waste management, public lighting, and public transportation. In practice, however, in the larger departmental capitals, municipal functions have been greatly reduced by the activities of central government agencies, and such municipalities now exert minimal control over urban growth and land use planning. Conversely, in the smaller provincial headquarters, where central government agencies have not extended their reach to the same extent, in 1989 municipalities still displayed significant responsibility for water supply (31 percent), solid waste management (26 percent), and electricity and public lighting (19 percent). A combination of remoteness and lack of income meant that 4 percent of such municipalities carried out no service delivery functions at all (Ardaya:128).

In 1986 the central government proposed to decentralize primary health care and education to municipalities. Because the proposal was not accompanied by corresponding measures to strengthen municipal administrative and financial capacity, most CCDs and municipalities expressed their opposition, and the proposal was dropped.

PERSONNEL SYSTEM

In 1993 there were 11,500 municipal employees, accounting for 5 percent of total public sector employment in the country. The thirty-eight largest municipalities employed around 80 percent of the total, although at the other end of the scale, over 56 percent of provincial municipalities had fewer than six employees each (Ardaya:127). In the same year, there was considerable variation among the largest municipalities in the number of inhabitants per employee, ranging from 260 in La Paz and Cochabamba to 688 in the case of Santa Cruz.

The municipal code states that all local government employees are covered by the national labor law and are granted career service benefits by the municipal employee statute. In practice, however, a municipal career system does not exist. Nepotism and clientelism, as well as graft and corruption, were identified as major problems of municipal personnel management as far back as the 1960s (Jickling:36; Aron-Schaar:497). Yet since the return to democracy in the mid-1980s, appointments have continued to be made on the basis of personal and political loyalties, and recruitment by open competition remains extremely rare. Privileged access to building plots for house construction remains a special benefit for municipal employees, although this also depends on favoritism.

Municipal administration remains highly centralized and personalized in the mayor. Proper organizational structures are rarely adhered to, and lines of command and the functional division of labor are blurred. The limited political horizon imposed by the two-year term of office leads to a lack of any systematic and strategic approach to decisionmaking, which is dominated by short-term considerations. This ad hoc management is exacerbated by the absence of regular municipal monitoring of the efficiency of the service delivery under their control (Araujo and Gamarra:37–42).

FINANCIAL STRUCTURE

Municipal finance is extremely weak in Bolivia, even by the standards of Latin America. In 1993 local government accounted for around 8 percent of public sector expenditure. There are enormous disparities among municipalities in revenue generation. In 1991 the ten largest municipalities accounted for 94 percent of total municipal income, with an average income per head of U.S.$14.60 compared with U.S.$0.54 in the remaining 213 municipalities (Ramírez:73).

Until recently municipalities relied heavily on locally raised sources of revenue. In 1986 a major tax reform (Law 843), part of an IMF-imposed structural adjustment program, centralized the collection of major municipal taxes in the hands of central government, including urban property taxation, the vehicle road license, and taxes on the sale of property and vehicles. Ambiguity regarding what taxing powers remained with municipalities led many to stop collecting taxes altogether for fear of double taxation. As a result, smaller municipalities have experienced a dramatic decline in their local revenue. The local tax base of provincial municipalities was particularly affected by the 1986 reform, and by 1989 the main sources of revenue for those municipalities had been reduced to licenses (29 percent), market fees (25 percent), a cowhide tax (20 percent), and a tax on a fermented maize drink known as *chicha* (5 percent) (Ardaya:128). The system of revenue sharing that was established as part of the 1986 centralization of tax collection had the following highly inequitable distribution: central government, 75 percent; departmental corporations, 10 percent; municipalities, 10 percent; and state universities in each department, 5 percent. The distribution of the municipal share was exclusively origin-based, i.e., in proportion to the amount of tax revenue generated within each municipality. As a result, in 1989 the three largest municipalities (La Paz, Santa Cruz, and Cochabamba), which together made up only a quarter of the national population, received 83 percent of the total allocation to municipalities (Araujo:12).

These disparities were especially pronounced within metropolitan areas because of the close relationship between municipal spending needs and population size. The tendency for people to commute across municipal boundaries in search of work meant that revenues tended to accrue in those municipalities where people worked and not where they lived. For example, in 1989 the Municipality of La Paz received revenue-sharing receipts fourteen times larger on a per head basis than in the neighboring Municipality of El Alto. The latter is a dormitory town for workers in the informal sector, an estimated 100,000 of whom commute daily to La Paz in search of work. The effect was a highly visible difference in the relative quality of service provision between the two municipalities (Araujo and Gamarra:28).

In the absence of any equalization mechanism, the vast majority of smaller and poorer municipalities received virtually no central government transfers under this arrangement. This was partially offset by their preferential access to investment grants from the Emergency Social Fund, a government program in operation from 1985 to 1989 that was designed to alleviate extreme poverty during structural adjustment (Graham:1241).

INTERMUNICIPAL COOPERATION

Intermunicipal cooperation is weak in Bolivia. In the 1970s, the military government encouraged the establishment of municipal associations at the departmental level, but no national association was permitted (Jickling:40). From time to time, smaller municipalities have formed their own associations in order to lobby larger municipalities and central government over financial transfers from revenue sharing. In 1986 a regional association of provincial municipalities was formed in the Department of Cochabamba in order to challenge the Municipality of Cochabamba, the departmental capital, over the assignment of taxation responsibilities. Subsequently, regional associations of provincial municipalities were formed in the Departments of Santa Cruz, La Paz, Potosí, and Oruro.

The legal relationship of subordination between municipalities that are departmental headquarters and those that are provincial headquarters has hindered the establishment of a single national municipal association. Instead, two separate associations currently exist that pursue broadly similar objectives: the Asociación de Gobiernos Municipales Autónomos de Bolivia (AGMAB), founded in 1989, which comprises departmental headquarters, and the Asociación Boliviana de Municipalidades (ASBOMUN), founded in 1990, which comprises provincial headquarters. Because of its stronger financial basis, the AGMAB is the more significant association.

SUPPORT SERVICES

There is no official municipal training body in Bolivia. In 1970 the Institute of Public Administration of New York carried out a major study of Bolivian local government, which highlighted its weakness in terms of human resources. As a result, the Servicio Nacional de Desarrollo Urbano (SENDU) was established in 1972 as a semiautonomous agency within the Ministry of Housing and Urban Affairs in order to provide training, technical assistance, and soft loan finance to municipalities. SENDU was heavily criticized for its failure to incorporate municipal repayment capacity into its lending policy, and it was eventually abolished in 1986 as part of the IMF-imposed structural adjustment program. In 1987 the Instituto de Investigación y Desarrollo Municipal (INIDEM) was established as an NGO with funding from the Konrad Adenauer Foundation of Germany in order to provide training, technical assistance, and consultancy services to local government. In the same year, a training institute, the Instituto de Capacitación Municipal (ICAM), was established within the Municipality of La Paz with financial support from the French government.

CITIZEN PARTICIPATION

Citizen participation in Bolivian local government is noticeably weak in comparison with the rest of Latin America. Liberal reformers, nationalist revolutionaries, leftist political parties, trade unions, and nongovernmental organizations have all sought to introduce an individualistic concept of citizenship that undermines indigenous social organization and political practice based on communal decisionmaking. As a result, the representative political model of local government has simply ignored those territorial areas where indigenous forms of direct democracy have survived (S. Rivera:116). This long tradition of an exclusionary state has meant that deep-rooted community organizations among the indigenous peoples of rural areas (*ayllus, sindicatos agrarios,* and *comunidades*) and their counterparts (*juntas de vecinos*) in the urban fringes where migrants are concentrated, continue to be denied legal recognition. Nor are these organizations allowed to contest municipal elections, which remain the exclusive preserve of political parties. This thinly disguised racism continues to provide municipalities with a convenient pretext to grant minimal support and encouragement to community organizations. As a result, citizens perceive that municipalities are incapable of assisting them in the attainment of their basic needs, and self-help has become the accepted norm. A rare exception is the Municipality of Sucre, which pioneered community-based urban planning workshops at the submunicipal level from 1988 to 1991 with the aim of involving neighborhood associations in the selection, implementation, and supervision of local investment projects (Tellería: 29).

Unlike elsewhere in Latin America, the typical land settlement process is carried out largely without any municipal involvement. In the face of municipal apathy, the urban poor have learned to solve their problems by their own means. Unlike in many other Latin American countries, urban squatting in Bolivia normally takes an individualistic form, and mass invasions are relatively rare. This, in turn, has reduced the pressure for municipal improvement from community organizations (A. Rivera:121).

Institutionalized mechanisms for citizen participation in local government are limited. Successive administrations have established their own ad hoc mechanisms, each of which has become identified with a political party or faction within the party. As a result, the opportunity for constructing independent and self-sustaining citizen participation over the longer term has been restricted. Nevertheless, heavy NGO involvement in the Emergency Social Fund from 1985 to 1989 helped to establish new links between community organizations and local government, especially in smaller municipalities (Graham:1243).

PROSPECTS FOR LOCAL GOVERNMENT

The colonial structure of government has survived longer in Bolivia than anywhere else in Latin America (Finot:24). Deep ethnic discrimination underlies urban-rural inequalities in Bolivian society, and this is reflected in the fact that the vast majority of indigenous citizens living in rural areas are effectively denied local government representation. Although rural peasants are legally obliged to vote in cantonal elections for the agente, they receive virtually no benefits in the form of municipal service provision. A surprisingly high proportion of municipalities still fulfill a purely ceremonial role, receiving no income, employing no staff, and carrying out no service delivery activities.

The debate in Bolivia over decentralization and the reform of the state has largely ignored this fundamental injustice and has focused instead upon the need to introduce an elected regional tier of government at the departmental level. This has given rise to justified fears that the existing unitary system of government might be threatened by the emergence of a quasi-federal system that could simply exacerbate the extreme regional inequalities within the country and replicate a new centralization at the level of each departmental headquarters.

Very little attention has been attached in the decentralization debate to the need to proceed beyond the departmental level in order to strengthen the role of local government (Oporto:52). The most urgent priority for municipal reform is to redesign the revenue-sharing formula between central and local government in a manner that reduces the share that departmental capitals receive and distributes it more equitably among municipalities. Other priorities include the redrawing of municipal boundaries to incorporate surrounding rural areas; the legal recognition of traditional systems of local government among peasant communities; the abolition of the supervisory-subordinate relationship between municipalities; the separate election of the mayor from that of the council; a lengthening of the short two-year municipal term of office; and an end to the prohibition on independent candidates for local government election. If these reforms are not carried through, the introduction of regional government may simply further weaken local government, which is already extremely frail by comparison with the rest of Latin America.

12

BRAZIL

Brazil is a federal nation comprising twenty-six states and the Federal District of Brasília, the capital city. Below the state level, the country is covered by a total of 4,974 municipalities. These are divided for purely administrative purposes into over 8,130 districts. Both states and municipalities have elected governments, and those districts that are not municipal headquarters may have deconcentrated administrative offices (*subprefeituras*). The Federal District of Brasília has a unique form of government, with its own directly elected governor and district assembly and with the combined fiscal powers of both state and municipal government.

In 1973 and 1974 nine metropolitan regions were established (in Rio de Janeiro, São Paulo, Belo Horizonte, Pôrto Alegre, Recife, Salvador, Curitiba, Belém, and Fortaleza). Metropolitan authorities were established in these regions, which made up 32 percent of the national population by the mid-1980s. They functioned as deconcentrated planning and coordinating agencies of state government, and their major impact was in infrastructure development and planning regulation (de Souza, 1985:106–109). But there was no metropolitan government. The metropolitan authorities were abolished by the 1988 Constitution, which gave state governments the power to reestablish them, but only in a form which did not contravene municipal autonomy.

Brazil has the largest disparity in municipal population size in Latin America. In 1994 only 460 municipalities, 9 percent of the total, had more than 50,000 inhabitants, but together they accounted for over 60 percent of the national population. Eleven municipalities each had more than one million inhabitants. The largest of these, the Municipality of São Paulo, had over 9.6 million inhabitants, with the fourth largest budget in the country, after the federal budget and those of the States of São Paulo and Minas

Gerais. By contrast, 3,611 rural municipalities, equivalent to 73 percent of the total, each had fewer than 20,000 inhabitants.

HISTORICAL DEVELOPMENT

The Portuguese introduced a system of local government that had evolved in their own much smaller country with a very different economic profile from that of Brazil. Municipalities were established in those urban areas that were granted the title of town (*vila*). Although their attributions were extremely limited in scope, they were nevertheless wider in scope than their Spanish equivalent elsewhere in Latin America. Conversely, large rural areas under plantation agriculture operated as semiautonomous fiefdoms beyond the effective control of local government. This legacy of the colonial period—a tradition of relatively greater municipal autonomy on the one hand, and a relatively greater neglect of rural areas on the other—still distinguishes the Brazilian local government system from its counterparts elsewhere in Latin America.

The centralizing Napoleonic model of government was influential during the period of the Brazilian Empire (1822–1889). The local government executive was subordinated to higher authority through a prefectoral system, and provincial assemblies retained the right to legislate on all matters relating to municipal affairs. The overthrow of the monarchy in 1889 and its replacement by a republican form of government saw the introduction of a highly decentralized form of federalism that was modeled on the U.S. presidential system and the separation of powers. The Napoleonic model was abolished by the 1891 Constitution, which enshrined the concept of municipal autonomy. States were granted the right to promulgate their own municipal codes, but one state, Rio Grande do Sul, even granted municipalities the right to approve their own codes. Between 1891 and 1926 local government became a concern primarily of state government, with minimal interference by the federal government.

The legacy of the colonial patrimonial state, in which powerful private interests had shared authority with public bodies, continued in the structures of *coronelismo,* the peculiar expression of clientelism in rural Brazil. Although it is often portrayed purely as a relationship of municipal subordination to state-level oligarchies, the control that local political bosses (*coroneles*) exercised over voting behavior gave them considerable bargaining powers in their dealings with state government (Grossi:82–83).

The short-lived 1934 Constitution introduced a more transparent system of intergovernmental financial relations that considerably strengthened municipal autonomy in relation to state government. Municipalities were granted the right to levy their own taxes, administer their own affairs, organize their services, and elect all officeholders. A state tax on industry and professions was henceforth shared equally with municipalities. This greater autonomy was, however, eliminated during the Vargas dictatorship (1937–1945), when all municipal councils were abolished and executives were appointed by state intervenors. Nevertheless, the Vargas period did see the first attempts to modernize local government, notably through the introduction of recruitment on a merit basis.

With the return of democracy, the promulgation of the "municipalist" 1946 Constitution gave local government more powers than ever before. The revenue-sharing system was extended, and its own tax base was expanded. The number of municipalities grew rapidly, from 1,668 in 1946 to 4,114 in 1964, as local political elites vied for the federal income tax transfers to which new municipalities now became automatically entitled.

The bureaucratic-authoritarian military regime that ruled the country from 1964 to 1985 used the rhetoric of local government autonomy and decentralization as part of its strategy of harnessing the public administration system more closely to its own designs. The formalities of municipal autonomy were largely preserved, and local government elections were retained, with the exception of 201 municipalities that were either state capitals, national security zones, or mineral-producing areas, where executive heads were appointed by the military. Nevertheless, effective autonomy was greatly reduced. Municipalities were converted into deconcentrated units of central government by being integrated as implementing agents at the bottom of a sophisticated administrative hierarchy, through which increased centrally allocated resources were channeled (Batley, 1984:66).

The reduction of the financial power of local government was a key element in this strategy. Municipal participation in the revenue sharing of the two most important federal taxes was abruptly halved, the collection of rural property tax was transferred to federal government, and other taxes were simply withdrawn altogether from local government control. At the same time, local government discretion in spending was drastically curtailed by tight earmarking of federal transfers and by strict federal audits.

The process of political liberalization from 1975 onward led to a gradual restoration of municipal financial powers. The earmarking of shared taxes was abolished in 1981, and municipal participation in the two major federal taxes soon surpassed the level prior to 1968, reaching 16 percent by 1983. The 1988 Constitution granted an unparalleled degree of autonomy to local government within a federal system of government. For the first time municipalities were defined as autonomous (not subordinate) members of the union, free to organize their activities so long as they did not infringe on competencies reserved by the Constitution to other tiers of government. It also granted them the freedom to adopt their own organic law, tantamount to a municipal constitution. Municipal laws no longer required approval by any other authority and could be contested only in the courts. This legislative autonomy was bolstered by increased financial resources. New constitutionally defined transfers also limited the discretionary power of federal government patronage over local government.

ORGANIZATIONAL STRUCTURE

Brazilian local government comprises a unipersonal executive head, or mayor (prefeito), and a legislature (câmara de vereadores). Mayors are separately elected under a simple plurality ("first past the post") system, except in municipalities with more than 200,000 inhabitants, where they must obtain at least 51 percent of the votes cast, if necessary by means of a French-style run-off. The number of councillors (vereadores) varies according to the population of the municipality. According to the 1988 Constitution, municipalities with fewer than one million inhabitants may have a minimum of nine and a maximum of twenty-one councillors. Those with populations between one million and five million may have a minimum of thirty-three and a maximum of forty-one councillors, whereas those with more than five million inhabitants may have a minimum of forty-two and a maximum of fifty-five councillors. Municipalities may decide their own number of councillors within these constitutionally defined limits (an unusual feature in Latin America). Councillors are elected by a party list system of proportional representation on a city-wide basis. Voters select a single candidate from a party list. Seats are distributed among parties in proportion to their candidates' aggregate share of the overall vote, and parties' seats are then allocated in rank order to their highest-scoring candidates. All municipal officers are elected for a four-year term of office. Councillors, but not mayors, may stand for immediate reelection.

Brazilian local government is based on a presidential model derived from the United States. The separation of powers is so pronounced that the mayor does not even attend council sessions (a unique situation in Latin America). The mayor may hire and fire municipal staff, a power that has increased greatly with the gradual demise of the merit system since the 1960s. Executive domination is strengthened by the fact that, in practice, the council cannot reject the budget proposed by the mayor nor alter it in such a way as to increase total expenditure. The mayor can veto bills passed by the council, although such action may be overruled by a two-thirds majority of the council.

The power of the mayor is strengthened by his or her role as a broker in negotiations with higher tiers of government, especially in order to access federal and state grants for municipal investment. When these grants are jeopardized by conflict between political leadership at the local and state levels, the mayor can play a crucial role in breaking the logjam. The political fortunes of the mayor often depend on the ability to negotiate successfully for federal and state investment programs to improve local service delivery.

The council has traditionally played a relatively minor role in municipal affairs, serving primarily as an important channel for the expression of sectional interests (Lordello de Mello, 1991:161). In recent years, there has been a growing tendency for councillors also to represent territorial interests within the municipality. This has increased the dependence of individual councillors upon obtaining "favors" from the mayor in order to enhance their own prestige (Grossi:98). However, the 1988 Constitution strengthened the council vis-à-vis the mayor by granting it new powers over the design of policies and the planning and approval of the municipal budget. The hyperinflation of recent years, by making frequent revisions of the annual budget necessary, has provided new opportunities for councillors to challenge the power of the mayor. Councillors may also impeach and remove the mayor by a two-thirds majority on grounds of administrative misconduct, and this has become a surprisingly common practice since 1988.

FUNCTIONAL RESPONSIBILITIES

The Brazilian system of local government has a uniformity that contrasts sharply with other federal nations of Latin America. Municipal elections, for example, take place at the same time throughout the federation. Individual states are responsible for creating municipalities in accordance with their own legislation. But the municipalities must conform with broad principles established in the federal constitution. As a result, there is no categorization of municipalities by economic structure or population size, and all have the same powers. Thus, even the smallest municipalities are granted concurrent powers for service delivery with higher tiers of government (Lordello de Mello, 1980:474). The respective competencies of different tiers of government are notoriously ill defined, even by the standards of Latin America, and the prevalence of concurrent powers among federal, state, and local government remains a significant feature of Brazilian local government (Batley, 1992:4). This has resulted in a notorious lack of coordination, leading to duplication of service provision in some places and its complete absence elsewhere, especially in the case of education. The practice of granting concurrent powers has the added drawback that no one tier of government can then be held accountable when the service in question is not delivered (de Souza, 1989:16).

In the past, this ambiguity in municipal attributions served as a convenient pretext for intervention in municipal affairs by higher tiers of government. Under the "rationalization" of service delivery carried out by the military regime (1964–1985), federal and state grants were earmarked in such a way that municipalities were squeezed out of infrastructure activities and into social services, especially primary education, as well as town planning and general maintenance functions.

Clarity in the allocation of responsibility for service provision among local and other tiers of government was blurred by two distinct but complementary trends: the invasion of the municipal sphere by federal and state government, and the de facto renunciation of functions by municipalities themselves. For example, small municipalities often allowed the state highway department to assume responsibility for local road construction, in return for which they forfeited a share of the federal fuel and lubricants tax. As a result, federal agencies now provide many basic services such as telecommunications and electricity, whereas states provide most water and sewerage services.

Surprisingly, the 1988 Constitution did not produce a clearer allocation of responsibilities. The federal government was the only tier to be assigned a significant number of exclusive functions, whereas state and municipal government were each assigned only one exclusive function: piped gas and urban public transportation, respectively. On the other hand, concurrent powers for some thirty different functions were granted to all three tiers. In theory this meant that municipalities have a general competence to perform any function "of local interest" not denied them by the Constitution.

Concurrent functions that were defined as "primarily" of municipal competence included preschool and primary education, primary health care, recreation and sport, culture, and tourism. Within the general field of urban development, itself defined as a concurrent activity, municipalities were given prime responsibility for land use zoning, building inspection, and the licensing of industrial and commercial activities. Municipalities have jealously guarded these powers, emasculating attempts at metropolitan planning. Municipalities with populations of more than 20,000 were also required to draw up urban development plans with the force of law in terms of land use zoning.

The outcome of this complex legal arrangement is that there is almost no service uniformly offered by all municipalities, and very few in which the state may not be an alternative provider or regulator. Urban municipalities are likely to undertake or regulate the following activities: urban planning, land acquisition, public transportation, preschool and primary education, primary health care, cultural activities, local road construction, public lighting and street cleaning, solid waste management, municipal markets and slaughterhouses, basic welfare provision for children and handicapped persons, recreation, and squatter settlement upgrading. Public housing, secondary education, and water supply are more often administered by state government (Batley, 1992:13).

In spite of the opaqueness in responsibility for service delivery among different tiers of government, the Municipality of Curitiba, the capital of the State of Paraná, presents a striking example of the potential role of local government in the Brazilian development process. In the late 1960s the municipality established the Instituto de Planeação e Pesquisa de Curitiba (IPPUC), a cross between a think tank and a planning department, under the charismatic leadership of Jaime Lerner, who has served three separate terms as mayor. Curitiba soon developed an international reputation for coherent urban planning based around a cheap and highly efficient bus-centered public transport system.

The core of the strategy has been the location of commercial and industrial development along four corridors radiating outward from the central area. These corridors have been developed along major routes that contain a divided roadway for high-speed traffic, inner lanes for slower local traffic, and a central lane for an express bus system. The system, including the fare structure, is managed by the city, although it is operated by private bus companies. Prior to implementation, the municipality purchased undeveloped land, which enabled it to provide lower-income housing areas near public transport. Implementation has been assisted by very strict enforcement of zoning laws, as well as incentives to compliance—in particular a computerized supply of information about the legal requirements for planning consent, as well as a fast-track system for planning approval (Davey, 1993:159–160). Other initiatives to improve the quality of life include the recycling of solid waste, preservation of the architectural heritage, expansion of green areas, and a mass environmental education program (Rabinovitch:63).

PERSONNEL SYSTEM

In 1994 there were an estimated two million municipal employees in Brazil, equivalent to 26 percent of total public sector employment. Local government employment increased by 77 percent between 1985 and 1991 as a result of the rapid growth in municipal income. The share of labor costs in total municipal expenditure rose from 15 percent to 23 percent during the same period. A constitutional provision limits salary costs to a maximum of 65 percent of municipal income.

In contrast to much of Latin America, job security and immobility are striking features of Brazilian local government. The 1967 Constitution required open selection of municipal staff under the statutory (*estatutário*) system of recruitment. In practice, however, this was circumvented, for the purposes of political patronage, by the establishment of a special category of employment that was regulated by the private sector labor code, the Consolidação das Leis do Trabalho (CLT). In practice, staff recruited during the military regime under the CLT enjoyed the same job security as statutory employees.

Following the return to civilian rule, municipalities inherited a staff characterized by poor qualifications and low motivation. There was both an absence of staff discipline and extreme overstaffing. The 1988 Constitution sought to resolve these problems by requiring municipalities to choose a single employment system for all staff (except those occupying confidence posts), with future recruitment exclusively on a merit basis and with provision for career development. The Constitution empowers each municipality to enact its own labor code, organize its own personnel system, and establish pay scales and conditions of service. These features must conform with certain principles established for all federal, state, and municipal personnel: a merit system of appointment for all posts except confidence posts; guaranteed tenure after two years; an inflation-proof pension at full pay after thirty-five years of service for men (after thirty years for women); trade union rights, including the right to strike; and a proper dismissal procedure with the right to appeal. The freedom of each municipality to establish its own separate service conditions has reduced horizontal mobility between municipalities, thereby hampering the development of a nationwide career system in local government.

Despite these successive constitutional provisions and the high degree of job stability, attempts to introduce a merit-based personnel system, which date back to the 1940s, have largely failed in the face of clientelist practices (*empreguismo*) (de Barros Loyola:14–15). By 1991 promotion by merit still hardly existed (Batley, 1992:43). As in the past, there is no assurance that legislative measures alone will eradicate the deep-rooted exercise of patronage in personnel matters.

Confidence posts (*cargos de confianca*) represent a third form of municipal employment that falls outside the constitutional requirements covering permanent staff. These senior posts, the incumbents for which are selected by the mayor, are more widespread than in most of Latin America. They extend from secretariat heads to departmental and even divisional chiefs. These appointments may be made from outside or within the statutory system, although the 1988 Constitution does encourage internal appointments.

FINANCIAL STRUCTURE

Brazilian local government finances have been greatly strengthened in recent years and now account for a far higher proportion of public sector expenditure than in any other country in Latin America. This share rose gradually from 11 percent in 1987 to 18 percent by 1991, by which time it was comparable to that found in many European countries (Villela:182).

The 1967 Constitution significantly diminished municipal financial autonomy by reducing municipalities' powers of direct taxation in exchange for a larger share of federal and state taxation, which was transferred by means of an ambitious revenue-sharing agreement. This arrangement was accompanied by extensive control through the earmarking of transfers. The 1988 Constitution strengthened this revenue-sharing arrangement, increased the number of taxes that municipalities could exploit directly, and limited the earmarking of transfers from revenue sharing to the requirement that at least 22 percent of municipal income should be spent on education. These measures more than compensated municipalities for the losses they had incurred as a result of the 1967 fiscal reform.

As a result of the new powers of taxation granted by the 1988 Constitution, the fifty or so largest municipalities now obtain more than half of their total income from own revenue sources, of which the major ones are as follows: a tax levied on over 100 different services (ISS); an urban land and property tax (IPTU); the property sales tax (ITIBI); a retail sales tax on gasoline and other fuels (IVVC); a betterment tax; and a range of fees (for building licenses, advertising, etc.) and user charges (for solid waste management, public lighting, etc.).

But the vast majority of municipalities still receive most of their income in the form of transfers deriving from five constitutionally defined revenue-sharing agreements with both federal and state government. The Fundo do Participação Municipal (FPM), a municipal participation fund, is the most important and is derived from 22.5 percent of the proceeds of federal taxes on income and on industrial products (IPI). Its allocation among municipalities is highly redistributive. Ten percent of the municipal share is distributed among state capitals according to population but weighted inversely to regional domestic product. The remaining 90 percent is distributed among other municipalities according to inversely weighted population size. As a result, a municipality with a population of 5,000 receives four times as much per head as one with a population of 100,000 (Davey, 1989:30). In 1990 the FPM guaranteed a minimum transfer of U.S.$260,000 to every municipality, and its deliberate poverty weighting greatly benefits the vast majority of small municipalities in the country. It is the main source of income for the poorest half of all municipalities. In the impoverished northeastern part of Brazil, two-thirds of all municipalities depend on the FPM for over 60 percent of their income (Batley, 1984:62).

The second major source of municipal income from revenue sharing derives from 25 percent of the proceeds of the state value-added tax (ICMS). Three-quarters of this municipal share is distributed on an origin basis, although states have discretion to distribute the remainder according to an equity-based formula. It is the largest tax in Brazil and is the major source of income for the more populated and more developed municipalities.

The third major source of municipal income from revenue sharing derives from the federal tax on industrial products (IPI). Ten percent of the proceeds is transferred to states and to the Federal District in proportion to the value of the exported portion of their industrial production. Out of the amount received, states must distribute 25 percent to municipalities, two-thirds on an origin basis and one-third at the discretion of each state.

Local government derives income from two other revenue-sharing agreements: the state tax on vehicle ownership and the federal tax on rural property; for both, 50 percent of the proceeds is distributed among municipalities on an origin basis. Municipalities also retain all federal income tax paid by their own employees.

In addition to these nondiscretionary transfers, municipalities also receive discretionary earmarked grants for capital investment from seventeen separate federal programs and a wide range of state sources. These grants have traditionally served as a crucial mechanism for exercising political patronage by ensuring the allegiance of municipal bosses to national political leaders. In so doing, they have encouraged a clientelist style of politics that has undermined the integrity, efficiency, and continuity of administration at all levels (Davey, 1989:33).

Municipalities are allowed by law to borrow from commercial banks for short-term cash flow purposes only. Long-term borrowing from federal and state development banks is limited by the rules that debt must not exceed 70 percent of net revenue in the previous year, that the annual increase must not exceed 20 percent, and that debt service payments must not exceed 15 percent of net revenue. Because of the extensive range of federal grants available to local government, as well as the highly volatile nature of financial markets, the scale of borrowing by municipalities is low compared with borrowing by states. Nevertheless, at the end of 1991, the municipalities that are state capitals together had outstanding debts of U.S.$2 billion.

Expenditure per head varies considerably among municipalities, reflecting the enormous geographical differences in income and wealth within Brazil. Nevertheless, these disparities are much less pronounced than anywhere else in Latin America. In 1984 average municipal expenditure per head in the richest region, the Southeast, was only 4.8 times greater than in the poorest region, the North (Davey, 1989:23). Disparities are likely to be further reduced by the reform of revenue sharing introduced by the 1988 Constitution. The highly redistributive FPM strongly favors the smaller and poorer municipalities, and this effect more than compensates for the regressive effect of the origin-based industrial and commercial taxes (ICMS and

ISS), which are the most important sources of revenue for prosperous municipalities in the South and Southeast.

In contrast to other Latin American countries, where a comptroller-general's office audits municipal accounts, the high degree of legal autonomy enjoyed by Brazilian local government means that this function is carried out by the council itself, with supervision from the state tribunal of accounts. The state tribunals impose strict control, and it is not uncommon for mayors to be dismissed for financial impropriety. The only exceptions to this arrangement are the Municipalities of São Paulo and Rio de Janeiro, which have their own tribunals.

INTERMUNICIPAL COOPERATION

Brazil has the strongest tradition of intermunicipal cooperation in Latin America. The Associação Brasileira de Municipios was founded in 1948 as the mouthpiece of the municipal movement (*movimento municipalista*), which campaigned in favor of decentralization. It organized a number of national municipal congresses, the first of which was held in 1950 (Lordello de Mello, 1958:39). In 1964 it was abolished by the military regime but was reestablished in 1979 as the Confederação Nacional de Municipios (CNM). In 1983 the nationwide municipal movement was recreated as the Frente Municipalista Nacional, which played a major part in the successful lobbying for greater financial autonomy for local government in the 1988 Constitution.

The State of Santa Catarina is a pioneer in intermunicipal cooperation. By 1982 all of its 197 municipalities belonged to one or another of the eighteen intermunicipal associations within the state (Velloso da Silva:59). By 1994 there were more than 150 municipal associations, including five national associations, plus one in each of the twenty-six states. The 120 regional associations at the substate level carried out joint activities with pooled funds. Among the important services they provide to their members are: representing local interests to state government; employing specialists such as surveyors, engineers, and accountants; providing consultancy assistance; and operating road machinery pools (Davey, 1989:4).

SUPPORT SERVICES

The Instituto Brasileiro de Administração Municipal (IBAM), founded in 1952, is the most well established and prestigious municipal training institution in Latin America. It differs from its counterparts elsewhere in the region in two important ways that are clues to its success. First, IBAM is self-financing and does not depend on a core grant from central government. This financial independence has contributed greatly to its institutional stability and protection from the kind of government interference that has hindered the development of similar institutions in the rest of Latin America. Second, affiliation with IBAM is not compulsory for Brazilian municipalities—by 1993, 55 percent of all municipalities were affiliated. This ensures that the content of the courses IBAM offers reflects the training priorities of the municipalities that purchase its services. IBAM offers an extremely comprehensive range of courses, from general administrative functions such as budgeting, revenue collection, cadastre, and supplies management, to specific technical subjects such as public lighting, road maintenance, construction of public markets, and even cemeteries.

Over 90 percent of IBAM income derives from municipal membership fees and charges for consultancy, training, and research, which are carried out for local government by the institute's 150 permanent staff and fifty outside consultants. By 1987 over 40,000 municipal employees had attended its courses, and another 120,000 had taken part in its correspondence training program (Lordello de Mello, 1987:8). IBAM also provides technical assistance to many other Latin America countries, as well as to countries in sub-Saharan Africa.

CITIZEN PARTICIPATION

The protest movement that from 1975 on spearheaded the return to democracy was linked to a rapid growth in citizen organization, especially in the poorer suburbs of the large industrial cities in the South. This process was encouraged by the grassroots movement of ecclesiastical communities (*comunidades eclesias de base*), supported by the Catholic Church and a new left-wing political party, Partido do Trabalhadores. However, many analyses have tended to exaggerate the strength and autonomy of such grassroots movements. Only a tiny minority (3 percent) of the population ever participated in the Movimento de Amigos do Bairro (MAB) in Nova Iguaçu near Rio de Janeiro, one of the best-organized neighborhood associations in Brazil from 1974 to 1985 (Mainwaring:178, 194). In three of the most frequently cited examples of citizen participation in local government during this period—Lages in the State of Santa Catarina, Boa Esperança in the State of Espíritu Santo, and Piracicaba in the State of São Paulo—the municipal legislature was completely excluded as a channel for participation. Initiatives here lacked continuity and remained extremely fragile because of their dependence upon the goodwill of individual mayors (Grossi:117–121).

Nevertheless, the political strength of these movements was reflected in the 1988 Constitution, which introduced several legislative innovations to promote citizen participation in municipal affairs. Among these are plebiscites and referenda; the popular tribunal (*tribuna popular*), whereby citizens can participate in the discussion of bills during full council; and the popular initiative (*inititiva popular*) whereby legislation may be proposed at the request of at least 5 percent of the electorate.

The Constitution also requires participation by "representative bodies" in the planning of municipal activities, and this takes three major forms: (1) the municipal councils (*conselhos municipais*), committees of interested organizations that may be designated by municipal law to supervise and advise the municipality on issues relating to specific functional sectors; (2) the popular councils (*conselhos populares*), territorial groupings of interested organizations that may comment and advise on local priorities, issues, and problems; and (3) the neighborhood associations (*associaçãos de moradores*), which often collaborate with the municipality in small-scale community investment projects by providing voluntary labor. In the Municipality of São Paulo alone there were 1,600 neighborhood associations in 1989.

Despite these reforms, clientelism remained a deeply ingrained feature of the political culture of Brazil as the coronelismo prevalent in rural areas was transferred into an urban setting. The explosion of citizen participation since 1975 may be signaling the decline of paternalism as citizens exert their democratic rights in municipal affairs. This is supported by evidence from the Municipality of Cambé in the State of Paraná (Ferguson:21). Conflicting evidence from the State of Minas Gerais, however, suggests that the clientelist relationship between citizens and the state may simply be replicating itself through the new structures established under the 1988 Constitution (Alencar et al.:11). The decentralization of primary health care to the municipal level has exposed the difficulties of developing mechanisms that guarantee effective citizen participation while avoiding a situation in which participation is used simply to manipulate communities in the interest of local elites (Filho:128–129). A study of the Vila Brasil slum near Rio de Janeiro suggests that, in such an unequal society as Brazil, clientelism continues to represent an attractive means to extract community benefits (Gay:664–665).

PROSPECTS FOR LOCAL GOVERNMENT

Brazilian local government has long enjoyed a high degree of legislative autonomy on matters over which it has exclusive competence. Since the promulgation of the 1988 Constitution, this legislative autonomy has been combined with a degree of genuine political and financial autonomy that far surpasses that of any other country in Latin America. But the 1988 reforms have given rise to two problems. First, none of the constitutionally defined revenue-sharing agreements with federal government are designed to reward local tax effort. As a result, there is little incentive for elected officeholders in the vast majority of smaller municipalities to risk the political unpopularity of increasing the yield from locally collected revenue sources. As a result, these municipalities are becoming increasingly dependent upon transfers. Second, although the proportion of federal revenue transferred to state and municipal government has greatly increased, there has been no corresponding reallocation of responsibilities for service provision among different tiers of government. As a result, although the federal share of total tax revenue fell, there was no corresponding decrease in the scale of its expenditure obligations, especially in the fields of education and health care.

By 1993 this radical fiscal decentralization had become a significant factor contributing to macroeconomic instability in Brazil. Relations among tiers of government and even among municipalities in the same region have become highly unstable. There is growing pressure to replace the ambiguity of concurrent powers with clear functional boundaries between municipalities and other tiers of government, especially within metropolitan areas, both to correct the growing fiscal imbalance and to ensure greater efficiency and equity in service delivery. The federal government may claw back some fiscal transfers so that municipalities will assume more responsibility for local revenue generation. This would encourage a process whereby fiscal resources become more clearly related to expenditure responsibilities (Shah:99–102).

13

CHILE

Chile is a unitary nation divided for administrative purposes into thirteen regions, including the metropolitan region of Santiago. Each region is headed by a centrally appointed official (intendente). The regions are divided into fifty-one provinces, each headed by an appointed governor. Below the province level, the country is covered by a total of 335 communes (*comunas*), all but one of which has municipal status.

The population is highly concentrated in the capital city of Santiago (population 4.5 million), which accounts for 34 percent of the national total. The Province of Santiago comprises thirty-two municipalities in and around the city. These include the Municipality of Santiago (population 148,000), which covers only the central business district. Santiago has no metropolitan government, although growing problems of air pollution and public transport disorder are increasing the pressure in this direction.

There is an enormous difference in population size among municipalities. In 1991, 197 municipalities, equivalent to 59 percent of the total, each had fewer than 20,000 inhabitants and together formed only 15 percent of the total population. Of these, fifty-three municipalities had populations of fewer than 5,000, fifty-five had between 5,000 and 10,000, and eighty-nine had between 10,000 and 20,000 (Garay et al.:21–92). Only forty municipalities, equivalent to 12 percent of the total, had more than 100,000 inhabitants, but together they accounted for 57 percent of the total population.

HISTORICAL DEVELOPMENT

Chile has a strong history of centralism and lacks any ingrained municipal tradition (Rosenfeld et al.:222). Since the 1833 Constitution (the country's first), local government has acted largely as an agent of central government.

The only exception was a radical devolution of political power to the communes from 1891 to 1920. But this experience proved extremely negative, serving only to foment clientelism and rampant local corruption. Centralization was reasserted under the 1925 Constitution and reflected in subsequent municipal codes enacted in 1931 and 1955. The executive heads of the largest municipalities (Santiago, Valparaíso, Concepción, and Viña del Mar) were appointed by the president of the republic, whereas the remaining municipalities operated under the close prefectoral supervision of presidentially appointed provincial officers. The system of indirect and annual election of the mayor from among councillors, who in turn were elected on the basis of ever-shifting pacts between party factions, led to political anarchy and administrative chaos (Etchepare:24). By the 1970s, there was general agreement that local government faced a crisis of identity. Its functions were reduced to a minimum, and personnel costs absorbed the bulk of its expenditure (Tomic and González:66, 89). Nor did the electoral victory of a Marxist coalition led by President Salvador Allende (1970–1973) alter this situation because his government adhered to the prevailing socialist dogma in favor of centralism.

Under the military regime of General Augusto Pinochet (1973–1990), local government was radically reformed. The limited degree of local democracy was completely abolished. Elected mayors were replaced by government-appointed executive heads, and elected councils were replaced by corporativist bodies known as *consejos de desarrollo comunal* (CODECOs), which comprised approved business and professional interests. The entire public administration was integrated even more closely into a vertical command structure, and central government control over municipal affairs was intensified through a 1975 municipal code. Paradoxically, however, during this period of military rule, a significant reorganization and deconcentration of service delivery responsibilities took place, with far-reaching and lasting consequences for local government. A new administrative hierarchy comprising regions, provinces, and communes was created by the 1980 Constitution. The executive heads of each tier were appointed by central government, and their functional responsibilities were more clearly defined. Under this new arrangement, local government became primarily responsible for social expenditure (primary health care, basic education, and social welfare). In order to finance these new responsibilities, municipalities were assigned new sources of local revenue, provided with earmarked transfers; a mechanism for redistributing financial resources from richer to poorer municipalities was also introduced. These changes were incorporated in a new municipal code passed in 1986.

The redrawing of local government boundaries formed an integral part of a strategy of social control pursued by the military regime. For example, during the 1980s, the number of municipalities within the Province of

Santiago was doubled from sixteen to thirty-two by a redrawing of existing boundaries. In combination with the forced resettlement of squatter groups, this change served to consolidate legally the spatial segregation of different social classes through the formation of socially homogeneous municipalities. This social polarization was highlighted by the growing disparities in the expenditure per head of different municipalities within the Santiago conurbation (Portes:23).

Ironically, the military regime laid the foundations for the subsequent revitalization of local government (Espinoza et al.:131). Hence, though accepting many of the regime's reforms, the civilian government of President Patricio Aylwin (1989–1993) sought to democratize the system of local administration inherited from his military predecessors. A constitutional reform passed in November 1991 granted legal autonomy to local government for the first time in Chilean history. This reform was incorporated in a new municipal code, Ley Orgánica Constitucional de Municipalidades No. 19130, on 19 March 1992, after which the first democratic elections of municipal officers for twenty years were held in June 1992. In October 1992 a structure of regional government was introduced, with powers to coordinate the regional operations of line ministries and to manage a regional investment fund. Each regional government comprises the presidentially appointed intendente and a regional council whose members are elected by municipal councillors.

ORGANIZATIONAL STRUCTURE

Chilean local government comprises a unipersonal executive head, or mayor (alcalde), and a legislature (concejo municipal). All municipal officers are elected for a four-year term with the possibility of immediate reelection. Unlike the procedure of most other Latin American countries, the mayor is not separately elected but usually heads the list of the winning party for council seats. If the top candidate gains a minimum of 35 percent of the vote, he or she is directly elected as mayor. If the top candidate gains less than 35 percent of the vote, the mayor is elected indirectly by councillors (concejales) from among themselves. In the 1992 municipal elections, fifty mayors were directly elected.

Chile has for long been characterized by a strong mayor system of local government. Prior to 1973, intense intra- and interparty rivalry for the position of mayor proved as great an obstacle for collaboration in project planning and implementation as did the shortage of funds and legal competencies (A. Valenzuela:53). The strong mayor system continued during the military regime and has been strengthened by the current municipal code (Raczynski and Serrano, 1987:131–134). Under this arrangement, the executive and legislature are connected in a manner somewhat distinct from the rest of Latin America. The mayor convenes and presides over council meetings, although several key official posts (municipal secretary, secretary of planning and coordination, and community development secretary) are legally required to service both the council and the mayor.

The reemergence of intense party competition at the local level and the continuing dominant position of the mayor raised the specter of a return to the administrative disorder of the pre-1973 period. For this reason, the 1992 municipal code made possible the appointment of an administrator by municipalities. Standing outside the ranks both of the municipality's permanent staff and of the confidence staff named by the mayor, the administrator would hold professional qualifications and would be selected by open competition. Although reporting to the mayor, the administrator would be concerned with the overall administration of the municipality and would separate this duty from the political interests of the mayor. The post of municipal administrator is new in Chile and in Latin America as a whole, although it was tried unsuccessfully in Venezuela from 1978 to 1988. The role may be likened to that of a town manager in the United States or that of chief executive in the United Kingdom.

Councillors are elected according to an open party list system under which, as in Brazil, voters select a single candidate. Their number is extremely small, even by Latin American standards, ranging between a minimum of six and a maximum of only ten. Five municipalities, each with more than 150,000 electors (Valparaíso, Viña del Mar, Santiago, La Florida, and Concepción) elect ten councillors; twenty-nine municipalities, each with between 70,000 and 150,000 electors, elect eight councillors; and the remaining 300 municipalities, each with fewer than 70,000 electors, elect six councillors.

FUNCTIONAL RESPONSIBILITIES

Chilean municipalities are granted no general competence; they operate instead under the ultra vires principle, which restricts their activities to what they are statutorily permitted. In practice this greatly restricts their legally autonomous status (with regard to their organization and functioning), even though that status is enshrined in the 1991 constitutional reform. The exclusive functions of local government include urban transportation and planning regulation, supervision of building construction, public lighting, drainage, parks, solid waste management, community development, and cemeteries. Municipally owned markets and slaughterhouses are less common than elsewhere in Latin America. The contracting out of municipal services (especially solid waste collection) to the private sector is much more common than elsewhere in Latin America, although the internal procedures for monitoring their efficiency and effectiveness remain weak.

Municipalities share the following functions with central government institutions: social welfare, public health, environmental protection, education, sports, tourism, road construction, low-cost housing, and disaster prevention. During the 1980s responsibility for primary and secondary education and basic health care was transferred to municipalities. By 1992, 59 percent of all school pupils were enrolled in municipal schools (SUBDERE:96). As a result, Chilean local government has formal responsibility for a much wider range of services than anywhere else in Latin America, although central government continues to exert control over the way municipalities organize education and health services. These two services must accord with standards set by the respective ministries; nationally established salaries must be paid, and the number of teachers employed must match that established before the services were transferred to municipal control.

Since the 1980s, municipalities have also been given the task of regularly identifying the poorest households through testing that uses a fourteen-point questionnaire known as the Ficha CAS. The municipal social welfare department is charged with collecting and processing this data, as well as with arranging payment of a range of state welfare payments, including old-age pensions, child benefits, housing benefits, maternity benefits, single mother benefits, subsidies for water and sewerage bills, and unemployment benefits.

Although central-local relations are in transition from the earlier more centralized system, municipalities still remain subordinate to several hierarchies of control. Formally they relate to the central government through the Ministry of the Interior, which has broad responsibility for public administration and specifically for local government. Besides its general supervisory and guardian role, this ministry controls the redistribution of municipal funds and the allocation of regional funds. Municipalities are also supervised by two agents of the president at the local level: the regional intendente and the provincial governor.

Line ministries and other public service agencies are required to allocate a proportion of their budgets for regional expenditure and to maintain regional offices (SEREMIS), which are coordinated by the intendente in the form of a regional cabinet. The SEREMIS also have a supervisory and guiding role over municipalities in their sector. Intendentes are advised in relation to planning and the distribution of regional investment funds by regional secretariats of planning and coordination (SERPLACs), which at the same time retain a relationship of accountability to the central planning ministry. The SERPLAC acts for municipalities as the gatekeeper for the funding of local investment projects.

PERSONNEL SYSTEM

In 1992 there were 94,503 municipal employees, accounting for 35 percent of total public sector employment in the country—the largest such share in Latin America. Of these, 58 percent were education staff, 23 percent were permanent administrative staff, 9 percent were health staff, 7 percent were unclassified, and 3 percent were temporary administrative staff. The approximately 22,000 permanent municipal staff are regulated by a 1989 administrative statute. This guarantees them almost total job security and puts them into one of eight ranks (ranging from auxiliary to mayor) and one of twenty salary grades. Salaries are determined nationally, with some variation to cover higher costs in some regions. Promotions between grades and ranks has depended largely on the existence of vacancies, and selection is based on length of service and formal qualifications. A system of annual performance assessment has been introduced and is intended to influence employees' positions within any salary grade. Teachers and health workers, who became municipal employees during the 1980s, are not covered by the 1989 statute. Teachers' pay and conditions are covered by a teachers' statute, although by 1994 there was still no similar arrangement for health workers.

A large proportion of municipal employees were recruited during the military regime from 1973 to 1989. The previous administrative statute governing conditions of appointment was suspended by decree in 1980, and this allowed the military-appointed mayors to make a clean sweep of staff. Job stability was removed, and mayors had complete freedom to hire, promote, and fire at will (Rosenfeld et al.:206). Prior to relinquishing office, the military regime approved the above-mentioned 1989 administrative statute to ensure job security under the incoming democratic government for the poorly qualified staff recruited during the military regime.

Municipalities are closely regulated, with regard to both staff levels and staff structure. The municipal code limits overall numbers in three ways, and these limits are strictly policed by the comptroller-general's office, to which any new appointment must be reported. First, no municipality may spend more than 35 percent of its own income on payments to staff (excluding teachers and health workers). Second, each municipality has a fixed permitted limit on its permanent staff level. Permitted staffing levels, at one permanent employee per 500 inhabitants, are very small even by Latin American standards. Some municipalities have fewer than ten permanent staff, few have more than 200, and only the Municipality of Santiago has more than 1,000. Third, only three posts are designated as confidence posts: the head of the planning and coordination secretariat, the chief legal advisor, and the head of the community development department. This greatly reduces the ability of the mayor to recruit and dismiss at will. One way municipalities avoid the restriction on staff numbers (but not the 35 percent rule) is to recruit honorary professional staff on short-term contracts. In practice this amounts to a reinvention of confidence posts.

Although the mayor is, in principle, free to establish the internal organization of the municipality subject to council approval, the municipal code requires municipalities to conform to a standard organizational structure. Municipalities with populations of more than 100,000 must have a secretariat of planning and coordination, as well as directorates of community development, municipal works, parks and cleaning, public transportation and traffic, administration and finance, legal advice, and audit. Although smaller municipalities are allowed to group these functions into a reduced number of posts, this elaborate organizational structure is still far too complex for them.

Frequently cited personnel problems include inadequate job descriptions, an inability to recruit except at the bottom of the pay scale (because first preference for vacancies must be given to existing staff), low pay at the point of entry (and therefore difficulty in recruiting qualified staff), low permitted staff numbers in small municipalities (and therefore few professional staff), a lack of opportunities for promotion, and a lack of qualified staff able to generate applications for investment funding. There is also resentment by teachers and health workers at having been drawn into the municipal service (because of its poorer terms of employment), although the teachers' statute passed in 1992 did guarantee a national minimum wage to all teachers.

FINANCIAL STRUCTURE

The financial strength of Chilean local government has increased considerably as a result of the reforms carried out by the military regime. The share of local government expenditure in total public expenditure rose from an average of 2.8 percent during the period 1977–1979 (Tomic and González:88) to 7.3 percent during the period 1987–1991 (Contraloría:65). In 1991 this share was 8.0 percent, and 11.3 percent if health and educational expenditures are included. By comparison with the rest of Latin America, a high proportion of local government income is locally generated, accounting for 89 percent of the total during 1985–1991. The reasons for this can be traced back to a far-reaching municipal tax reform carried out by the military regime in 1979 as a prelude to the transfer of responsibility for health and education from central to local government. This tax reform granted to municipalities the total proceeds from three major sources of locally generated revenue:

1. a residential property tax, levied at 2 percent of the fiscal value of property. Maintenance of the cadastral register and collection of the tax are both handled by the national tax authorities on behalf of local government. Delay in registering new properties and late notification of changes in land use result in widespread underpayment, over which municipalities have little control.
2. a series of municipal licenses for exercising professional, industrial, and commercial activities, which are levied at 0.5 percent of the declared value of assets. Liability for large companies is based on the geographic location of their permanent labor force. This greatly favors the wealthy Municipalities of Santiago and Providencia, where the headquarters of large industrial, commercial, and retailing companies are concentrated. Conversely, municipalities with large-scale mining or hydroelectric operations that employ little labor, or with fruit-packing installations that employ large numbers of temporary workers, suffer under this arrangement.
3. a vehicle road license that is charged at much lower rates for commercial vehicles (taxis, trucks, and buses) than for passenger vehicles. Vehicle owners are not obliged to pay the tax in the municipality where they reside (an unusual feature). This has led to intense competition by municipalities in tax collection.

Other revenue sources include a charge for solid waste management, which is collected together with the property tax in the case of households and with the municipal license in the case of businesses, as well as taxes on the modification of residential property, on local advertising, and on the sale of vehicles.

The major source of local government income, however, is a municipal equalization fund (Fondo Común Municipal, or FCM) administered by the Ministry of the Interior. It derives its resources from several sources: 60 percent of the proceeds from property taxation; 50 percent of the proceeds from the vehicle license; and 65 percent of the proceeds from municipal licenses collected by the wealthy Municipalities of Providencia and Las Condes, as well as 45 percent of the proceeds collected by the Municipality of Santiago. In 1992 the origins of total FCM resources were as follows: property taxation, 70 percent; vehicle tax, 20 percent; municipal licenses, 5 percent; and a central government grant, 5 percent.

By the late 1980s, 30 percent of total municipal revenue was subject to redistribution through the FCM (SUBDERE:52). The bulk (90 percent) of the FCM is distributed among municipalities according to the following significantly redistributive formula: 10 percent in equal parts among all municipalities; 20 percent in proportion to the total population of each municipality; 30 percent in proportion to the number of properties exempt from taxation in each municipality; and 40 percent in inverse proportion to the locally generated revenue per head of each municipality. In addition, an annual amount equivalent to no more than 10 percent is distributed on a discretionary basis to selected municipalities in order to cover recurrent deficits. The FCM is the main source of income for the vast majority of municipalities, 70 percent of which are net beneficiaries from its operation. Its overall impact is substantially redistributive. For example, in fiscal year 1985/86 its effect was to decrease income per head by 7–14 percent in the three richest municipalities within the metropolitan region of Santiago and to increase revenue per head by 35–50 percent in the three poorest municipalities. This narrowed the ratio between expenditure per head of the three richest and three poorest municipalities from 10:1 to 5:1 (Raczynski and Cabezas:57).

Unlike in much of Latin America, central government transfers (excluding education and health) play a relatively small role in Chilean local government, accounting for 11 percent of total municipal income during 1985–1991. Nevertheless, only a few very large municipalities have significant resources for investment, and most others rely heavily on access to centrally controlled grants that are earmarked for specific investment purposes. Small municipalities experience considerable problems in the preparation of applications for such funding, in matching their own investment priorities with those for which funding is offered, and in obtaining guidance during project implementation. These investment grants are channeled through the Ministry of the Interior and regional governments. The most significant programs are the Programa de Mejoramiento de Barrios (PMB), an urban improvement program; the Programa de Mejoramiento Urbano y Equipamiento Comunal (PMU), a community development program mobilizing voluntary labor organized by neighborhood groups; the Fondo Nacional de Desarrollo Regional (FNDR), a regional development program; the Fondo Social Presidente de la República, a special presidential fund for the eradication of extreme poverty; and the Fondo de Solidaridad e Inversión Social (FOSIS), a social development program administered by the Ministry of Planning. Several of these programs are funded by Inter-American Development Bank loans, but repayment obligations are assumed by the national government.

Municipalities also receive specific earmarked transfers from central government in order to meet new expenditures associated with the transfer of responsibility for primary and secondary education and primary health care. In the case of primary and secondary education, the responsibility for which was gradually passed to local government between 1979 and 1986, the earmarked transfers are based on a capitation fee, the Unidad de Subvención Educacional (USE), which varies according to the level of education. In 1991, 85 percent of municipal spending on education derived from these central government transfers, and 12 percent was paid for out of general municipal revenue. In the case of primary health care, the responsibility for which was gradually passed to local government between 1981 and 1987, the earmarked transfers are calculated on the basis of a maximum number of treatments given; this number is established for each municipality and is known as the *techo fapem* (TP), which was introduced in 1986 by the Ministry of Health. In 1991, 69 percent of municipal spending on health care derived from the TP, and 25 percent was paid for out of general municipal revenue.

The financial transfers from the ministries have proved inadequate to cover the costs of administering and providing these new services. As a result, the financial situation of local government deteriorated sharply starting in the mid-1980s, primarily because of the fall in the real value of transfers earmarked for education and health (E. Valenzuela:127). By 1992 the deficit had reached 26 percent of total health and educational expenditure. This growing shortfall has been covered by municipalities' own income, thereby reducing the availability of funds for investment purposes. This has been only partially compensated for by ad hoc disbursements from the regional investment fund, FNDR, mainly for urgent repairs to schools and health clinics. These growing financial difficulties have put increasing strain on the municipal equalization fund, obliging central government to boost it with discretionary grants in order to cover municipal indebtedness, a procedure that in practice amounts to a central government transfer to local government.

Municipalities have limited financial autonomy. They may not borrow in their own right, and they cannot create new taxes without central government approval. The comptroller-general's office exercises a strict supervision of municipal administration with regard both to its general legal propriety and to the fulfillment of its budgetary obligations (Baeza:6). Municipalities must keep separate budgets for education and health, and all accounts have to be submitted to the comptroller-general's office on a quarterly basis. If municipalities were to introduce new charges not foreseen under the municipal code, this would be identified by the legal audit carried out by the comptroller-general's office, and the proceeds would be confiscated by central government. Nevertheless, one positive feature of this intense central government supervision is that the rate of nonpayment of municipal taxes is extremely low by comparison with the rest of Latin America.

INTERMUNICIPAL COOPERATION

A national municipal association was first established in the 1950s. The Confederación Nacional de Municipalidades (CNM) received initial support from the Municipality of Santiago and was financed through a 1 percent levy on municipal income. Although membership was voluntary, all municipalities soon joined the CNM. The extreme polarization of political opinions during the Allende government (1970–1973) led to a crisis within the CNM and its eventual division into two competing bodies. After the military coup of 1973, the CNM was dissolved and no further municipal association was permitted.

Following the return to democracy, plans were made to set up another municipal organization, the Asociación Chilena de Municipalidades (ACM). With the support of the Friedrich Ebert Foundation and an NGO known as Cordillera, a working group formulated the basic principles of voluntary membership and a decentralized structure upon which the association would be based. It also identified staff training as a priority function for the new association (Martelli:3–37). These proposals were endorsed by a preparatory meeting in November 1992 attended by thirty mayors (Sassenfeld:143–154). The formal launching of the ACM took place at the first national congress of mayors, held in Viña del Mar in May 1993.

SUPPORT SERVICES

Surprisingly, Chile has no tradition of local government training and only a very diffuse structure of public administration training in general. During the military regime, in-house training by government agencies was ruled out by the ideological argument that this was a private sector activity. There is no national local government training body, and the provision of training for municipalities is scattered among a range of governmental bodies (comptroller-general's office, Ministry of the Interior, etc.), several universities, and NGOs, almost all of which are located in Santiago. As a result, training is carried out in a piecemeal fashion with little overall coordination or strategic direction. This has led to duplication of activities, a striking example of which was the publication, within weeks of each other in 1992, of municipal management manuals for nationwide distribution by both the Ministry of the Interior and the Ministry of Planning.

Municipalities are empowered by the 1992 municipal code to offer and pay for their own basic training or to organize it by agreement with outside bodies. But this is effectively ruled out for the vast majority of smaller municipalities because of a combination of small budgets, low staff numbers, and the limited promotion prospects (which reduce staff motivation for training). With high levels of staff turnover there is also the danger that training may simply accelerate the loss of staff. Besides, for those municipalities wishing to train staff there is no systematic information on the programs available, and few of the programs that are available relate specifically to the realities of municipal life.

CITIZEN PARTICIPATION

In a pioneering move in Latin America, neighborhood associations (juntas de vecinos) were granted legal recognition by the government of President Frei in 1968. During the subsequent left-wing government of President Allende (1970–1973), citizen participation in development was actively encouraged. Both neighborhood associations and cooperatives flourished on a scale unparalleled in the postwar history of Latin America, but they were strongly subjected to clientelist forms of control by competing parties within the government coalition. Because of the weakness of local government, the groups developed much closer links with central government institutions responsible for local service delivery than with municipalities.

During the military regime from 1973 to 1989, citizens were afraid to join independent neighborhood associations because of violent repression of any opposition by the state. Interestingly, the 1968 law that officially recognized neighborhood associations was not abolished. Instead, the military regime retained the law in order to manipulate citizen participation. This was graphically demonstrated by an official circular (known as K-23) in 1977 stating that henceforth the leadership of all neighborhood associations would be chosen by the governor from a list of nine candidates proposed by the mayor (Rosenfeld:45). Although there was a resurgence of citizen participation during the last years of the Pinochet regime, much of this evaporated after the restoration of democratic rule. Nevertheless in 1992 there were an estimated 27,400 citizen organizations nationwide, with a combined membership of over 2.7 million (SUBDERE:115).

The 1992 municipal code aimed to democratize the corporativist form of citizen participation that had been propagated by the military regime through the CODECOs. It promoted the role of neighborhood associations, although avoiding the politically divisive form that they had assumed during the Allende government. In addition to an elected council, each municipality has an economic and social community council (*consejo económico y social comunal,* or CESC) composed of representatives of neighborhood associations (40 percent); special interest groups such as educational, cultural, professional, trade union, and sports groups (30 percent); and business associations (30 percent). Having between ten and thirty members, depending on the number of inhabitants, these community councils are chaired by the mayor and fulfill an advisory role. They have the right to be consulted on municipal accounts and local development plans. Each municipal administration also has a community development division whose prime function is to promote centrally financed community projects in liaison with the CESC and regional authorities. The municipal code also makes provision for citizen consultation through plebiscites, which may decide on the merits of specific investment projects at the request of either the mayor or 15 percent of the electorate. The result of a plebiscite is binding only if more than 50 percent of the electorate vote.

PROSPECTS FOR LOCAL GOVERNMENT

Chilean local government now displays some of the most innovative features within Latin America: the creation of the municipal administrator, the municipal equalization fund, and the devolution of responsibility for education and health. Nevertheless it remains weak in terms of its resources and powers, and it is very dependent on higher levels of government. The transition from the deconcentrated system of local administration established by the military regime to a more devolved structure of local government faces resistance from entrenched political interests, from a deeply ingrained tradition of administrative centralism, and from a legacy of mistrust felt by citizens toward municipal authorities (inherited from the military period).

The structural deficit caused by local government's growing responsibilities for health and education, as well as the associated dependence on ad hoc transfers, have highlighted the need for a municipal financial reform in order to strengthen the resource base of local government. The capacity of municipalities to contribute toward solving their own financial problems is limited by the close control exercised over them by central government and by the fact that they have minimal involvement in the administration and collection of their main source of income, property taxation. As these financial difficulties deepen, especially among smaller municipalities, the pressure for reform of the FCM will intensify, both to include a larger central government grant element and to incorporate a "quality of life" indicator in the allocation formula so as to strengthen its redistributive impact.

.

14

COLOMBIA

Colombia is a unitary nation comprising thirty-two departments and the Capital District (Distrito Capital) of Bogotá, which has the same attributions as a department. The historic cities of Cartagena and Santa Marta have the status of special districts. Below the department level, the country is covered by 1,034 municipalities. Both departments and municipalities have democratically elected governments. Metropolitan areas were created in 1979 in five conurbations: Medellín, Barranquilla, Pereira, Bucaramanga, and Cali, although there is no structure of metropolitan government.

The disparities in population size among municipalities, although pronounced, are less than in much of Latin America. In 1988, five municipalities had more than 500,000 inhabitants, twenty-six had between 100,000 and 500,000, thirty-nine had between 50,000 and 100,000, 417 had between 12,000 and 50,000, 328 had between 6,000 and 12,000, and 194 had fewer than 6,000.

HISTORICAL DEVELOPMENT

Following its independence from Spain in 1810, Colombia experimented with a federal system of government. A reaction against the unlimited autonomy this system granted to municipalities resulted in a unitary constitution in 1886. This ushered in a century of extreme political centralization, and the first major municipal legislation was not enacted until 1913. During this period, departments were headed by presidentially appointed governors, who in turn appointed municipal executive heads (except in Bogotá, where this person was appointed directly by the president). These centrally appointed officials exercised effective control over directly elected departmental assemblies and municipal councils. An electoral system based on closed party lists strengthened national party control over the selection of local political leaders, and it simultaneously loosened the accountability of the latter to the local electorate. This hierarchical arrangement strengthened clientelism at the local level because the criteria for distributing financial support to municipalities were based primarily on the need to secure political allegiance among client groups.

From the 1970s onward uncontrolled urbanization, woefully inadequate public service provision, and a marked increase in regional income disparities led to a gradual decline in the political legitimacy of the elites who dominated the highly centralized political system. The absence of opportunities for citizen participation contributed to widespread political alienation, as manifested by rising levels of electoral apathy and a growing culture of political violence. The municipality became emasculated to such an extent that it was reduced to a purely territorial concept, devoid of any semblance of local government (Viviescas:54).

The emerging gulf between the state and civil society was highlighted by the spread of over 200 civic strikes (paros cívicos) between 1970 and 1986. These were organized by local citizens' groups protesting the poor service provision and the concentration of government expenditure in the largest cities. In 1979 the three largest municipalities together absorbed 72 percent of total local government expenditure, and their expenditures per head were six times larger than those of smaller municipalities (Uribe-Echevarría:15). These movements had important consequences for local government. On the one hand, they represented a challenge to the clientelist political culture at the municipal level. On the other hand, both appointed mayors and elected councillors were obliged to offer the movements tacit support for fear of further reducing their own extremely limited legitimacy (Collins, 1988:430).

In response to growing social unrest, which threatened the stability of the entire political system, modernizing factions within the ruling Conservative and Liberal parties began to reform the Colombian state. Jaime Castro, former minister of government and pioneer of the reform movement, mapped out five key elements that were incorporated in 1986 legislation: (1) direct election of mayors, (2) introduction of local referendums, (3) fiscal strengthening of local government—continuing a process that had already begun in 1983, (4) administrative decentralization, and (5) citizen participation in municipal affairs. The reforms were subsequently incorporated in a new municipal code, Código de Régimen Municipal No. 1333, on 25 April 1986, which replaced the outdated 1913 municipal legislation. Thanks to these reforms, in March 1988 the first direct election of mayors in over a century took place.

Following a public campaign spearheaded by university students, a new constitution was promulgated in 1991. Its overriding concerns were to build a participatory democracy by opening up the political system to include former guerrilla groups, to decentralize political power, to reduce bureaucratic controls, and to give the executive more direct control of the administrative structure. The 1991 Constitution defined the Colombian nation as "decentralized," and several articles granted a new degree of political and financial autonomy to local government. The term of municipal office was lengthened, and the total number of councillors was changed to an uneven number. The discretionary system of central government transfers to local government was replaced by one based on constitutional guarantee, and the level of such funding was significantly increased.

ORGANIZATIONAL STRUCTURE

Colombian local government comprises a unipersonal executive head, or mayor (alcalde), and a legislature (concejo municipal). The number of councillors (consejales) varies between a minimum of seven in municipalities with populations of fewer than 5,000 and twenty-one in those with populations of more than one million. Bogotá is a special case, with one councillor for every 150,000 inhabitants. In 1994 it had twenty-eight councillors. The municipal term of office is three years, with immediate reelection prohibited for both mayors and councillors.

The 1886 Constitution had introduced the dichotomous system known as "political centralization with administrative decentralization," in which the mayor fulfilled a triple function as representative of the departmental governor, head of the municipal administration, and chief of police. As such, the mayor's role was primarily to ensure the implementation of national policies at the municipal level. Under this arrangement, the council was granted a degree of coparticipation in the executive function, mainly through the powers of three senior administrative officers it selected: the municipal attorney (*personero*), with powers akin to the European ombudsman; the municipal auditor (*contralor*), with audit powers over the operations of central government at the local level; and the treasurer (*tesorero*). The mayor remained an employee of the departmental government, whose governor retained the legal right to veto decisions taken by the municipal council. This division of executive responsibility, combined with tension between centrally appointed officials and locally elected officeholders, led to constant conflict between mayors and councils.

The 1986 reforms clarified the respective roles of the executive and legislature. The fragmentation of executive responsibility was significantly reduced. This power was now concentrated in the hands of the elected mayor, who ceased to be a departmental employee and became a municipal employee. The treasurer was henceforth appointed by the mayor.

FUNCTIONAL RESPONSIBILITIES

The 1913 municipal code empowered municipalities to carry out any services not expressly reserved by law to other levels of government. This breadth of responsibility, however, was not accompanied by adequate financial provision, and until very recently local government actually provided relatively few services. In common with much of Latin America, a process of demunicipalization took place starting in the 1960s, and a system of concurrent powers was instituted that reflected widespread central government intervention in service delivery at the local level. Responsibility for education and health services was transferred to central government, cadastral surveying was transferred to a central government agency, and urban transportation and public housing were taken over by autonomous state agencies. Some large municipalities, however, set up their own semiautonomous authorities, administered by boards, for the provision of electricity and water supply. By 1981 services provided by most municipalities were confined to road maintenance, slaughterhouses, markets, and solid waste management (Uribe-Echevarría:13).

Starting in 1987, responsibility for major functions was gradually devolved to local government as part of the municipal reform program. This included responsibility for water supply and sewerage, environmental health, construction and maintenance of schools, health clinics and roads, low-cost housing, agricultural extension, urban transportation, and cadastral surveying. This decision led to the closure of a number of ministerial departments and autonomous agencies of central government such as the municipal development institute, Instituto de Fomento Municipal, which had previously taken overall responsibility for school building, water supply, and environmental health (Rodríguez:22). The overly hasty closure of the state water corporation, INSFOPAL, however, led to considerable disruption in water supplies because of the unpreparedness of municipalities to assume this new responsibility.

Responsibility for education and primary health care was gradually devolved from central government starting in the late 1980s, supported by corresponding transfers to departmental and local governments of financial resources earmarked for the payment of salaries and for investment. Although priority was granted to municipalities with populations of more than 100,000, by 1994 there remained considerable ambiguity in the allocation of responsibilities between departments and municipalities in both sectors.

PERSONNEL SYSTEM

In 1992 there were 75,738 municipal employees in Colombia, equivalent to 8.8 percent of total public sector employment (Cifuentes:117–118). Beginning in 1938, many attempts have been made to introduce a merit-based career system in local as well as central government, but little progress has been made (Mendoza:19). Following a period of intense political violence (1948–1953), the settlement negotiated in 1958 and known as Frente Nacional provided that the two major political parties would alternate in government every four years for sixteen years (until 1974) and that they would divide public appointments equally at all levels. This system of parity (*paridad*) had the effect of institutionalizing political clientelism throughout local government on a scale unparalleled in the rest of Latin America. Although each municipal council had the power to establish its own position classification system and salary scale, the parity system effectively blocked the development of a career system at the local government level. The 1991 Constitution made provision for a civil service career throughout the public sector, including all local government staff except those holding confidence posts; the necessary enabling legislation was approved in 1992.

FINANCIAL STRUCTURE

For several decades, municipal finances in Colombia were stronger than the average in Latin America, and they have been further strengthened by recent fiscal reforms. The share of local government in total public expenditure, which was already 17 percent in 1973 (Linn:7), rose to 24 percent in 1992. In the late 1970s, a major World Bank study into central-local financial relations, known as the Bird-Wiesner report, drew attention to a growing fiscal crisis in local government, which had been brought about by the heavy dependence on financial transfers from central government. The problem was compounded by the growing fiscal deficits of semiautonomous municipal enterprises operating at the local level. For example, by the mid-1980s, the Bogotá Electricity Corporation alone had a foreign debt of U.S.$1.5 billion, equivalent to 15 percent of the foreign debt of Colombia and 76 percent of the foreign debt originating from the Capital District of Bogotá (Díaz Arbelaez:131, 139).

The study provided the baseline for the significant municipal fiscal reforms of the 1980s, starting with a major upward revision and restructuring of local tax rates in 1983. This was followed in 1986 by the introduction of a revenue-sharing agreement for a value-added tax under which the share of total VAT proceeds accruing to municipalities rose gradually from a base of 25.8 percent in 1986 to a maximum of 50 percent by 1992. Although the

VAT transfer was divided among municipalities primarily according to relative population size, the allocation formula was mildly redistributive. Municipalities with populations of fewer than 100,000 received a proportionately greater share than larger ones. In the case of municipalities with more than 100,000 inhabitants, central government retained between 30 and 50 percent of VAT proceeds for a regional educational fund. Although 75 percent of the proceeds were earmarked for municipal investment, in practice most of the transfers received by smaller municipalities were spent on recurrent expenditure.

During the 1980s, the growth in own revenue generation by local government kept pace with that of transfers received from central government. Three major sources—a tax on industry and commerce, urban and rural property taxation, and a vehicle road license—typically accounted for over 90 percent of locally generated revenue. In addition, and unique for Latin America, some of the larger Colombian cities have raised substantial resources from a betterment levy. A series of municipal tax reforms enabled locally generated income to rise by 65 percent in real terms between 1980 and 1987 (Gaitán et al.:165). In 1983 property tax administration was passed from a centralized national agency to the municipalities. In 1985 municipalities were empowered to levy property taxes on both joint ventures and enterprises wholly owned by the public sector. In 1990 they were granted the freedom to vary the property tax rate between 0.01 and 0.16 percent of the fiscal value and to readjust fiscal values in line with the annual consumer price index. And the 1991 Constitution granted municipalities the exclusive right to levy both urban and rural property taxation.

By 1990 a marked difference in income sources had emerged between large and small municipalities. The main source for municipalities with more than 500,000 inhabitants was the industry and commerce tax, followed by property taxation, with VAT transfers from central government in third place. The situation for the vast majority of municipalities with fewer than 100,000 inhabitants was the reverse. VAT transfers represented between 60 and 80 percent of total income and property tax between 7 and 10 percent, with industry and commerce tax accounting for less than 5 percent.

Law 60 of 1993 provided the enabling legislation for the radical reallocation of competencies among different tiers of government, as envisaged in the 1991 Constitution. This further deepened the process of financial decentralization in two ways. First, municipalities and departments began to receive a new central government transfer, known as the *situado fiscal,* which arose from the devolution of responsibilities for health care and education. In 1994 this accounted for 23 percent of national fiscal revenue, and it is scheduled to rise to 24.5 percent in 1996. The situado is earmarked specifically for paying the salaries of health and education workers and is distributed according to a complex formula that combines considerations of equity and local tax effort (Santana, 1993:66). Second, the VAT transfer was replaced by a general revenue-sharing agreement known as the *transferencia,* under which the share of national fiscal revenue transferred to municipalities will rise gradually from 14 percent in 1993 to 22 percent by 2001. The proceeds are distributed among municipalities according to a complex formula combining redistribution and incentives for own revenue generation (Santana, 1993:70). The transferencia is earmarked for social investment. A minimum of 80 percent of the total received by each municipality must be spent on education (which gets at least 30 percent), health (25 percent), water supply (20 percent), and recreation and culture (5 percent).

INTERMUNICIPAL COOPERATION

A national municipal association, the Federación Colombiana de Municipios (FCM), was founded only after the first democratic elections for mayors in 1988. The statutes for the new body were approved at its inaugural congress, held in Cartagena in February 1989 and attended by 147 mayors. Membership is voluntary, and by 1992 over 300 municipalities, equivalent to 30 percent of the national total, were affiliated with the FCM. All municipalities have equal voting rights, which ensures that the interests of the vast majority of smaller municipalities predominate. In 1993 the FCM was granted a 0.01 percent share of the transfers (*participaciones*) received by municipalities, and it now has representation in some central government bodies, notably the national housing institute (INURBE) and the state investment fund (FONADE). Currently the role of the FCM is confined to lobbying on behalf of local government, and it does not provide technical assistance for its members. In its submission to the Constituent Assembly prior to the 1991 constitutional reform, the FCM proposed the uninominal system of election for councillors on a ward basis (Rojas et al.:76).

SUPPORT SERVICES

Training and technical assistance for municipalities depend heavily on the Escuela Superior de Administración Pública (ESAP). This public sector institute, founded in 1958, had a combined teaching and research staff of 189 in 1993. It offers a wide range of undergraduate, postgraduate, and in-service programs in urban and regional administration. These programs are designed primarily for the staffs of smaller municipalities and are conducted by fourteen regional centers that participants travel to or correspond with. ESAP also uses distance learning for specialized noncertificated training for municipal professionals, such as treasurers and personnel officers, who are within reach of its regional centers and fifty-two subregional units. In addition, it provides information manuals and videos to municipalities, and it has developed a data base that can be accessed through its regional centers. Under the municipal reform program of 1986, ESAP receives a regular grant from central government, equivalent to 0.1 percent of VAT proceeds and earmarked specifically for training, consultancy, and technical assistance to local government.

In 1991 a U.S.$24 million interministerial program, the Programa de Desarrollo Institucional (PDI) was established with funding from the World Bank and the United Nations Development Programme to support the institutional development of local government. The program aims to cover 70 percent of those municipalities with fewer than 100,000 inhabitants, and it envisages the establishment of mechanisms for intermunicipal coordination of service delivery activities. Under this program, ESAP is expected to play a major part in providing technical services to local government.

CITIZEN PARTICIPATION

Until recently the absence of citizen participation was a noticeable and hotly debated feature of Colombian local government. Repeated attempts to introduce legislation permitting the establishment of neighborhood councils at the submunicipal level were resisted by political elites fearful of local democracy. Community action committees (*juntas de acción comunal*) had invariably been co-opted by such elites and had served primarily as means of maintaining traditional systems of patronage. Following the upsurge of civic strikes in the 1970s, a national congress of civic movements and popular organizations, held in 1983, called for a range of measures to enable genuine citizen participation in local government.

This bore fruit in the 1986 municipal reform, which introduced three such measures. Municipal authorities were empowered to create submunicipal administrative units, known as *comunas* in urban areas and as *corregimientos* in rural areas, in order to improve service delivery. They were also empowered to establish local administrative boards (*juntas administradoras locales,* or JALs) in both comunas and corregimientos. The requirement that a comuna should have a minimum population of 10,000 before it may be officially recognized, however, effectively prohibited the formation of JALs in the urban areas of 75 percent of Colombian municipalities (Eljach:96). The JALs comprise between three and seven members. Although by law only a third must be elected, the most usual practice is that at least five members are elected, with the remainder appointed by the mayor. The JALs carry out administrative functions delegated by the council, as well as an advisory and monitoring role, although their attributions vary widely from one municipality to another (Eljach:102–104).

The Municipality of Cali has pioneered the introduction of JALs, each of which has been granted delegated powers to allocate funds for social investment purposes. At the first JAL elections held in April 1989, an average of nineteen separate lists of candidates were presented in each of the twenty comunas, and 25 percent of elected members were women. Most elected members were poorly informed about the purposes of the JALs, and a high proportion of them were affiliated with political parties, suggesting that the JALs may end up replicating traditional practices of clientelism at the local level (González and Duque:82). Despite the Cali experience, the program has advanced slowly. By 1990 only fifteen municipalities had decided to establish JALs (Pulido:93), and electoral turnout at JAL elections has been surprisingly low (Eljach:99).

Provision was also made for the representation of consumer groups on the boards of municipally controlled public utilities, such as those for electricity, water, telecommunications, and solid waste management. But the significance of this reform has been lessened by the fact that few municipalities retain provision for public utilities. Even fewer have legally constituted consumer groups, and social services such as health and education were specifically excluded from the provisions of the decree (Rojas et al.:10). Local referendums were allowed on matters over which the municipality had responsibility, but the council, not the mayor, retained the right to approve referendums; this led to the limited use of referendums in practice.

PROSPECTS FOR LOCAL GOVERNMENT

Beginning in the early 1980s, Colombia has been undergoing the most serious process of decentralization in the whole of Latin America. In sharp contrast to the decentralization process in Bolivia and Peru, the Colombian reform movement has given priority to the strengthening of municipal government rather than departmental government. By the year 2002, according to constitutional requirements, the combined transfer to municipalities from the situado fiscal and the transferencia is likely to surpass 30 percent of national fiscal revenue, the highest share in Latin America. However, the capacity of local government to respond adequately to the challenge of new responsibilities cannot be taken for granted. A study of two major intermediate cities, Cartagena and Santander, suggests that the major political reforms introduced in 1986 did not bring about any reform of municipal management style. Instead, the deep-rooted practice of clientelism maintained the inefficient use of municipal resources and blocked the development of citizen participation in local government (Velásquez:119). Furthermore, a study of ten municipalities between 1988 and 1990 revealed a great range among municipalities in the degree of satisfaction expressed by citizens over the impact of the local government reform (Dugas et al.:119). By 1994, 700 mayors and former mayors were under investigation by the attorney-general's office on charges of embezzlement, unlawful enrichment, or mismanagement of public funds.

Following the 1991 Constitution, there has been a noticeable shift in the decentralization debate toward strengthening the departmental tier of government. This has been stimulated by the introduction in October 1991 of direct elections for departmental governors. Departments have historically received a much smaller share of fiscal revenue than municipalities, with virtually no own revenue generation. Although they have not been granted any intermediary role in the coordination and planning of municipal development programs with national government, they have now been given responsibility for the administration of financial transfers to municipalities. Clientelist considerations are most likely to influence decisions by departmental councils concerning the allocation of transfers among municipalities (Santana, 1993:68), and conflicts have already emerged between departments and municipalities over the sharing of central government transfers earmarked for health and education expenditure. This has highlighted the lack of clarity with regard to the allocation of responsibilities between these two tiers of government. It has also raised the specter, as in Bolivia and Paraguay, that departmental governments may assert their newfound authority by stifling municipal financial autonomy.

15

COSTA RICA

Costa Rica is a unitary nation divided for administrative purposes into seven provinces. Below the province level, the country is covered by eighty-one cantons (*cantones*), each of which has municipal status. Municipalities are divided for administrative purposes into 435 districts. The Metropolitan Area of San José comprises eleven municipalities in and around the capital city of San José. In 1976 a national municipal congress proposed the creation of a metropolitan government for San José, but this idea was rejected by central government; today the Metropolitan Area of San José lacks any political or administrative significance (Lungo and Pérez:74).

The variation in population size among the eighty-one municipalities is much less pronounced than in the rest of Latin America. In 1993 six municipalities had populations between 100,000 and 500,000, nine had between 50,000 and 100,000, thirty-four had between 20,000 and 50,000, and a further twenty-three had between 10,000 and 20,000. Only six municipalities had populations between 5,000 and 10,000, and only three had fewer than 5,000.

HISTORICAL DEVELOPMENT

The establishment of the short-lived Central American Federation in the early postindependence period, of which Costa Rica formed a part, granted increased powers to local government. This encouraged the emergence of strong localist feeling and led to the eventual dissolution of the federation. During this period, local government became the major vehicle for early social provision. Following the collapse of the federation, the process of centralization that accompanied nation building led, as elsewhere in Central America, to a gradual decline in municipal autonomy, as formalized in the

1871 Constitution and the municipal code of 1909. Nevertheless, local government continued to occupy a significant role in service delivery until the 1940s, most notably in the area of primary and secondary education.

A new constitution in 1949 formally reasserted the autonomy of local government and granted specific functions to municipalities for the first time. During the 1940s and 1950s, however, new state corporations for water and electricity supply were also created; together with central government ministries such as the Ministry of Public Works, they spread their operations rapidly throughout the country, in the process stripping important functions from municipalities. This led to a further decline in the importance of local government.

In the late 1960s a municipal reform movement sought to strengthen local government. This bore fruit on 30 April 1970 with the promulgation of a new municipal code, Código Municipal No. 4574, and with the creation of a municipal training and advisory body, the Instituto de Fomento y Asesoría Municipal (IFAM). Municipal autonomy was enhanced by the removal of centrally appointed provincial governors as executive heads of the municipalities that were provincial headquarters, and by ending the appointment of central government nominees, known as *jefes políticos,* as executive heads and police chiefs in all other municipalities. However, these initiatives proved incapable of halting the secular decline of local government, which continued during the 1980s. This was in marked contrast to the trend in the rest of Latin America.

ORGANIZATIONAL STRUCTURE

The organization of the Costa Rican municipality breaks with Latin American tradition and has more in common with that found in parts of the United States. There is no elected mayor. Instead, the executive head, known as the *ejecutivo municipal* or *gerente,* is a city manager appointed by the legislature (concejo municipal). Seven geographically large municipalities have deconcentrated administrative units at the submunicipal level, known as *concejos municipales de distrito* (CMDs), whose deliberative authorities (concejales) and executive head (intendente) are all appointed by central government.

The number of councillors (regidores) is dependent upon the population size of the municipality and ranges from a minimum of five in those with a population of fewer than 25,000 inhabitants to a maximum of thirteen in those with more than 200,000 inhabitants. The councillors elect a council president from their midst on an annual basis, and this person is the most senior political authority at the municipal level. The executive head attends council meetings, has no voting rights, and may be removed from office by a two-thirds majority of councillors. Both the executive head and councillors serve a four-year term of office. The executive head may be reappointed, and councillors may stand for immediate reelection.

Local government elections are held at the same time as presidential and congressional elections, and local government councillors are elected for the same term as their national counterparts. This linkage means that local government elections are overshadowed in importance by the national elections held at the same time. There have been repeated attempts, dating from as far back as the first national municipal conference held in 1940, to change the timing of local government elections to the midpoint of the period of office of the national legislature. So far these efforts have not succeeded.

The selection of party candidates for local government elections is determined more often by the support those candidates can generate for their counterparts in congressional and presidential contests than by their own capabilities for municipal office. This results in the subordination of councillors to the wishes of national political parties and is to the grave detriment of municipal interests (Ortíz:285). Extreme political centralization is reinforced by the closed party list system (*papeleta colectiva*) for the presentation of candidates in municipal elections.

FUNCTIONAL RESPONSIBILITIES

Article 4 of the 1970 municipal code grants to Costa Rican municipalities probably the widest competencies anywhere in Latin America, covering virtually every conceivable area of local economic activity. In practice, however, this carte blanche is effectively nullified by the very next article within the code, which stipulates that these competencies do not override the attributions already granted to other tiers of government. For example, although local government is formally responsible for regulating local building activity, building permits and regulations over land use are still issued by the national housing institute.

Despite the initiatives to strengthen local government, as expressed in the 1970 municipal code and the creation of IFAM, local government continued to be relatively neglected and by the late 1980s had lost most of its important competencies except water supply. Municipalities were characterized by a very low level of activity and carried out only residual functions. A survey by IFAM in 1990 showed that the main functions carried out by local government were road maintenance (in 100 percent of the cases), solid waste management (94 percent), street cleaning (87 percent), cemeteries (74 percent), parks (63 percent), water supply (55 percent), markets (44 percent), and provision of scholarships for low-income students (44 percent).

Only 34 percent of all municipalities operated slaughterhouses, only 24 percent operated bus terminals, only 22 percent operated public libraries, and only 5 percent operated public lighting. The Municipality of Heredia was exceptional in supplying both water and electricity to most of the municipalities in the Province of Heredia. Nevertheless, the survey revealed that municipalities were keen to assume responsibility for road and bridge construction, local police, education, and water and sewerage (Chan and Vargas:20–24).

PERSONNEL SYSTEM

In 1987 there were 6,470 municipal employees, accounting for 4 percent of all public sector employment in the country (Murillo:47). The geographical distribution of municipal employees was a far more adequate reflection of the distribution of population than in most of Latin America. The 292 inhabitants per municipal employee in the Province of San José, where the capital city is located, was only half as many as in the least populated Province of Limón, where there were 649 inhabitants per employee (Murillo:47).

Local government employees are not covered by the 1953 civil service law. The 1970 municipal code gave special attention to the introduction of norms for personnel management (job descriptions, salary scales, and job stability), and since then IFAM has sought to establish a separate municipal employment code (Monge:6). Despite efforts to put these norms into practice, by the late 1980s the personnel system of Costa Rican municipalities was characterized by many of the features common throughout much of Latin America—low salary levels relative to central government, high rotation of staff, and clientelist patterns of recruitment.

The fact that the executive is not elected, a feature unique to Costa Rican municipal organization, caused additional problems. It was originally hoped that appointed executive heads would improve municipal management. But the overwhelming importance given to party political considerations rather than to technical competence in the selection of these city managers has led to widespread difficulties in municipal management.

FINANCIAL STRUCTURE

The financial significance of Costa Rican local government started to decline in the 1950s, reflecting the reduction in municipal functions. Total municipal expenditure as a proportion of central government expenditure fell from 12 percent in 1950 to 5 percent by 1987 (Murillo:45). During the 1980s, the share of municipal expenditure in total public sector expenditure varied between a minimum of 2.5 percent and a maximum of only 4.1 percent. Over the period 1970–1988 as a whole, local government expenditure rose by only 36 percent, whereas central government expenditure rose by 137 percent, and expenditure by state companies rose by 216 percent (Chan and Vargas:6–7).

Although municipal finances during the 1960s and 1970s were highly dependent upon transfers from central government, by the late 1980s locally generated revenues accounted for most municipal income, and transfers from central government had declined to insignificant levels. During the period 1983–1987, the share of local revenue in total municipal income rose from 66 percent to 71 percent, whereas the share from central government transfers fell from 16 percent to only 2 percent.

Property taxation is totally administered by the Ministry of Finance, although proceeds were transferred to municipal control starting in 1969. It is now the major source of local revenue. Other important local revenue sources are business licenses, a tax on building construction, a charge for road maintenance, and service charges for solid waste management, street cleaning, public lighting, and water supply. Central government transfers to local government are not only insignificant but are highly discretionary. Revenue sharing is limited to the proceeds of a national sales tax on domestic and imported liquor, divided equally between IFAM and all municipalities, which then divide the rest amongst themselves. Proceeds are insignificant, accounting for less than 1 percent of total municipal income. The municipal code imposes a number of restrictions on municipal flexibility with regard to expenditure. No more than 40 percent of recurrent income may be spent on personnel costs, at least 20 percent of municipal income must be spent on health, and 10 percent of proceeds from property taxation must be destined for the support of local education boards.

In 1991 IFAM made three major proposals for tax reform as part of its decentralization program. First, it proposed to strengthen central government transfers by modifying Article 170 of the Constitution to provide local government with a guaranteed share of public revenues, beginning at 2 percent and rising gradually to a maximum of 10 percent. Second, it proposed the reform of property taxation, including the transfer of its administration to local government, the introduction of legally binding declarations of property values by owners, and a new cadastral survey to bring property values up to date. Third, it proposed improved administration of two other major local taxes: the business and building construction taxes. By 1994 none of these proposals had been implemented.

INTERMUNICIPAL COOPERATION

The creation of IFAM in 1970 encouraged the growth of intermunicipal cooperation, and by 1991 every municipality belonged to a provincial municipal league. Under the 1970 municipal code municipalities may sign agreements with each other for joint service provision. The few cases in which this has happened to date are limited to management of solid waste disposal sites.

The first national congress of municipalities was held in 1940. A national local government association, the Unión Nacional de Gobiernos Locales (UNGL), was created in 1977 and comprises all municipalities and thirteen province-based municipal leagues in the country. The UNGL lacks financial and political strength and has been largely overshadowed by IFAM. Its weakness in negotiating with central government is a reflection of the prevailing electoral system under which municipal officeholders remain dependent upon the goodwill of national political parties for their election.

SUPPORT SERVICES

As discussed earlier in this chapter, IFAM, a public sector institute offering technical and financial assistance to local government, was created in 1970. It is the strongest municipal development institute in Central America, employing 245 staff in 1992, and it has a good loan repayment record. Its administrative operations and municipal credit program are financed by a 10 percent share of the proceeds from property tax, by a 50 percent share of the proceeds from a national liquor tax, and by soft loans from foreign aid donors. Over the period 1977–1984, its credit program focused on the purchase and reconditioning of road-building equipment and the extension of water supply systems. Its technical assistance has focused on tariff revision studies for municipal water supply and methods to improve tax collection (Jagger:55–57). Municipal subordination in relation to IFAM is exemplified by the fact that there is no municipal representation on the institute's board of directors.

CITIZEN PARTICIPATION

Community participation in development is strong in Costa Rica, although citizen participation in local government is weak by comparison with the rest of Latin America. In 1967 a national network of community groups, known as *asociaciones de desarrollo comunal* (ADCs), was set up as part of a central-government-backed community development program (DINADE-CO), and over 1,400 such groups now receive funding directly from central government for local projects, effectively bypassing local government. Although required to coordinate their activities with municipalities, the ADCs often function as parallel bodies at the submunicipal level in competition with local government. This has led to considerable duplication of activities and has seriously weakened efforts to strengthen citizen involvement in municipal affairs (IFAM:83).

District-level councils (*consejos de distrito*) exist at the subcanton level and serve as a channel of communication and cooperation between local communities and municipal authorities. Each district council has five members. It is headed by an elected leader, known as the síndico, although the remaining members are appointed by the city manager. The síndico serves as the representative of the district council in the municipality and attends council meetings, but he or she does not have the right to vote.

PROSPECTS FOR LOCAL GOVERNMENT

The small size of the country and the relative competence of service delivery activities by central government agencies in coordination with a strong national network of community groups have reduced the pressure for decentralization to local government. As a result, and in sharp contrast to most Latin American countries, recent years have seen a continuing decline in the fortunes of Costa Rican municipalities. Repeated attempts since 1968 to reform Article 170 of the Constitution in order to guarantee municipalities a share of the national budget have failed. The highly centralized political system has been reinforced by an electoral system that gives overwhelming importance to national political considerations in the choice of municipal candidates and campaign issues.

In 1991, as part of a wider program to reform the Costa Rican state, IFAM proposed a decentralization program aimed at reducing regional economic disparities through the strengthening of local government. The proposal envisaged the transfer back to local government of former competencies, a strengthening of its financial resources, and a reform of the electoral system. The proposed transfer of competencies was also designed to overcome a growing problem in the coordination of service delivery activities by national, regional, and local government bodies. The proposal failed to generate political support, suggesting that prospects for a significant strengthening of local government remain weak.

16

DOMINICAN REPUBLIC

The Dominican Republic is a unitary nation divided for administrative purposes into twenty-eight provinces, each of which is headed by a governor who is appointed by the president of the republic. Below the province level, the country is covered by 138 municipalities, including the National District of Santo Domingo (the capital city), which has municipal status.

HISTORICAL DEVELOPMENT

The dictatorship of Rafael Trujillo (1930–1961) severely restricted municipal autonomy. In 1936 Santo Domingo was declared a national district, and its elected municipal authorities were replaced by an administrative committee whose members were appointed by the president. This was followed in 1952 by the replacement of elected municipal councils in the rest of the country by appointed committees. On 21 December of the same year, municipal codes were introduced: Ley sobre Organización Municipal No. 3455 and Ley sobre Organización del Distrito Nacional No. 3456. The overthrow of Trujillo had little impact in reversing the assault on municipal autonomy, which has continued to the present day.

ORGANIZATIONAL STRUCTURE

Local government in the Dominican Republic comprises a unipersonal executive head, or mayor (síndico), and a legislature (consejo municipal). The minimum number of councillors (regidores) is five, and an additional member is elected for every 14,000 inhabitants, except in Santo Domingo (one per 25,000) and the Municipality of Santiago (one per 17,000). The mayor and councillors are elected for four-year terms of office and may stand for immediate reelection.

Municipal authorities are elected jointly and concurrently with national political authorities. This occurs through a voting system known as the *boleta tipo arrastre,* whereby a vote for a presidential candidate automatically includes a vote for a slate of candidates for congressional and municipal office. This undemocratic electoral system virtually destroys minority representation in local government because candidates cannot stand for municipal office unless they are included in the slate of a presidential candidate (Pérez:22–23). It also ensures that clientelist considerations largely determine the selection of councillors. The principal role of the councillors is to mobilize the local vote for presidential candidates, and for this service they are rewarded with their council seats.

FUNCTIONAL RESPONSIBILITIES

A strong process of centralization began during the Trujillo dictatorship in the 1950s. Responsibility for electricity supply, public works, and even cemeteries was transferred from municipal to central government control. The process of centralization continued during the 1960s despite the return to democratic rule. Responsibility for water supply and sewerage in the capital city was transferred to an autonomous agency, the Corporación de Acueducto y Alcantarillado de Santo Domingo (CAASD), and this body also collects the service charge for solid waste management on behalf of the municipality. Regulation and organization of public transportation also passed from municipal control to a state institution, the Oficina Nacional de Transporte Terrestre (ONATRATE).

In sharp contrast to the rest of Latin America, during the 1980s the Dominican Republic was still undergoing a process of demunicipalization, as central government continued to absorb a growing share of service delivery functions at the local level. These included such tasks as maintaining roads and storm drains. As late as 1987, a combined urban affairs commission and public works coordination unit that excluded municipal authorities, especially in the National District, from further involvement in urban planning decisions was set up. By 1990, most service provision at local level was carried out by central government, with municipal activity reduced to parks and gardens, solid waste management, and traffic planning (Jiménez and Peguero:302–303).

PERSONNEL SYSTEM

In 1994 there were 19,346 municipal employees, equivalent to 8 percent of total public sector employment. As far back as 1854 a constitutional amendment granted the president of the republic the authority to remove any civil servant from office, except in exceptional circumstances. This legalized the practice of appointing and dismissing staff on the basis of patronage, which has dominated the personnel system of the civil service right up to the present day. Repeated attempts, from as early as 1913, to introduce a civil service and administrative career law have all floundered as a result of the opposition of vested political interests.

FINANCIAL STRUCTURE

Municipal finance in the Dominican Republic is extremely weak by Latin American standards, with local government accounting for only 4 percent of total public spending in 1986 (Chaves:8). Urban property taxation does not exist in the Dominican Republic, though this is unique in Latin America. Furthermore, the vehicle road tax is a central government tax. The municipal tax legislation is extremely outdated. Hence, municipal own revenue sources are extremely limited, composed principally of taxes collected on public events and on hotels.

Given this limitation on its own tax sources, municipalities rely heavily upon financial transfers from central government. In 1962 municipalities were granted a 20 percent share of the national fiscal revenue. This law soon fell into abeyance, however, and was replaced in 1966 by a system that granted monthly transfers to municipalities in proportion to their internal revenue generation. In 1983 the 1962 initiative was partially resurrected by a law that assigned 20 percent of the fiscal proceeds from national domestic taxation to local government. By 1988 even the National District of Santo Domingo derived 59 percent of its income from central government transfers (Aybar de Sanabria:8).

INTERMUNICIPAL COOPERATION

Although the Liga Municipal Dominicana (LMD) was created in 1939 and was the first national municipal association in Latin America, it has not been successful in strengthening municipal autonomy. On the contrary, under the Trujillo dictatorship it functioned as a mechanism for political control over local government because discretionary financial transfers from central government were channeled through it. Following the overthrow of Trujillo, a 1961 law expressly restricted the functions of the LMD to the provision of technical assistance to municipalities in the areas of finance, urban planning, and public works. In practice, however, the LMD has carried out these functions only to a limited extent. Instead, it has retained a continuing control function through the financial resources placed at its disposal by successive central governments. In 1965 this control was formalized when the LMD was granted the legal authority to approve all municipal budgets, a task carried out in most Latin American countries by the Ministry of the Interior or by the comptroller-general's office. In 1983 the LMD was once again authorized to distribute financial transfers from central to local government.

The LMD hosts an annual congress of municipalities that elects a seventeen-member executive committee comprising representatives of municipalities and the Ministry of the Interior. The secretary-general of the LMD has always been appointed by the president of the republic, with the exception of a short break in 1962–1964 when the annual congress made the appointment.

SUPPORT SERVICES

There is no permanent training institution in the Dominican Republic for local government.

CITIZEN PARTICIPATION

Administrative units exist at the submunicipal level. In semiurban areas there are nineteen such units, known as *delegaciones municipales,* that are administered by a municipal junta, which is appointed and supervised by the mayor. In rural areas, they are known as *secciones rurales,* and are headed by an auxiliary mayor (*alcalde pedáneo*), who is proposed by the provincial governor, appointed by the municipality, and directly supervised by the mayor.

No legal framework yet exists to promote citizen participation in local government, but despite their lack of legal recognition, neighborhood groups (juntas de vecinos) have increasingly influenced the policies of municipal authorities in the National District of Santo Domingo by convening cabildos abiertos.

PROSPECTS FOR LOCAL GOVERNMENT

The Dominican Republic remains one of few countries in Latin America where the process of demunicipalization continues and where the regional trend toward decentralization has had little impact. Municipalities have continued to operate under legislation passed during the Trujillo dictatorship. Municipal officeholders bear primary allegiance to national government and therefore have little interest in reforming the current electoral system. The delinking of municipal elections from the national electoral process is an essential first step in order to "free up" the municipalities, to overcome public indifference to local government, and to redirect the purpose of the LMD toward striving for greater municipal autonomy.

17

ECUADOR

Ecuador is a unitary nation divided for administrative purposes into twenty-one provinces. Each province has an elected executive head (*prefecto*) and a provincial council. A governor appointed by central government shadows the elected representatives at the provincial level. Below the province level, the country is covered by 193 districts (cantones), all of which have municipal status. Administrative units exist at the submunicipal level in the form of about 1,000 rural and urban parishes. There is no metropolitan government in either Quito, the capital city, or Guayaquil, both of which have more than one million inhabitants.

HISTORICAL DEVELOPMENT

A modern system of local government dates from 31 January 1966, when the municipal code, Ley de Régimen Municipal, was passed. Although the law was substantially reformed in 1971, subsequent national legislation relating to municipal activity frequently contradicted and effectively overrode the municipal code. This often resulted in administrative paralysis by municipal authorities who feared legal sanctions by the comptroller-general's office.

The recent fortunes of local government have been closely linked to petroleum revenues. From 1972 to 1979 Ecuador experienced an oil boom, during which the share of municipalities in total public spending rose rapidly, reflecting a strong urban bias in the allocation of the oil revenues by the military government of that time. The heavy financial dependence on central government that took root during the oil boom strengthened clientelism and therefore decreased the pressure for greater municipal autonomy.

Although the municipal code stipulated a minimum population of 50,000 before a municipality could be created, an exception was granted in the case of municipalities in the eight frontier provinces. Here parish-based groups began to exert strong pressure to subdivide existing municipalities in order to obtain greater access to growing central government financial transfers during the oil boom. As a result, the number of municipalities rose rapidly from 105 in 1974, to 116 in 1980, and to 193 in 1993, by which time half of all municipalities had populations of fewer than 10,000.

ORGANIZATIONAL STRUCTURE

In the case of Ecuadorean municipalities that either have populations of more than 100,000 or are provincial headquarters, local government comprises a unipersonal executive head, or mayor (alcalde), and a legislature (consejo municipal). Elsewhere the executive role is filled by the council leader (*presidente del consejo*), who is elected from among councillors (consejales). The number of councillors ranges between five and fifteen according to the size of the municipal population. Municipal elections are held simultaneously with those for central and provincial government, and the four-year terms of most municipal officeholders run concurrently with those of central and provincial government authorities. This linkage means that local government elections are overshadowed in importance by the national elections held at the same time. This has strengthened the exercise of clientelism in the selection of councillors, whose principal role is to mobilize the local vote for presidential candidates. Clientelism has also been encouraged by the practice of the quota system, whereby congressional deputies are granted decisionmaking powers over the disbursement of annual sums of money for carrying out development expenditure in their own constituencies.

Depending upon their position in the voting list, councillors are elected either for a four-year term or for a two-year term with the possibility of immediate reelection. For example, in the case of a fifteen-member council, the seven members receiving the least votes must stand for reelection after two years, although the eight who received the most votes continue until the end of the four-year term. At the end of the four-year term of office, mayors are not permitted to stand for reelection. The council leader and councillors may stand for reelection after a break of one term.

FUNCTIONAL RESPONSIBILITIES

Legal imprecision in their respective attributions often leads to conflicts between municipal and provincial authorities, especially when leadership is exercised by different political parties. In practice there is a tendency to divide responsibilities on a geographical basis, with local government taking responsibility for urban areas and provincial government for rural areas. Unlike municipalities, provincial councils have no revenue-generating capacity and depend exclusively on central government transfers linked to oil income.

The 1966 municipal code assigned local government the responsibility of pursuing "local welfare" in the form of eleven functions: water supply and sewerage; construction and maintenance of roads, parks, and public places; solid waste management; city lighting; food hygiene; moral welfare; authorization of new buildings; licensing of industrial, commercial, and professional activity; cemeteries; promotion of tourism; and slaughterhouses and provision of markets. There is no comparable definition of the responsibilities of provincial councils. They are charged with providing similar services as municipalities, with a stronger emphasis in practice on feeder roads and rural school building.

From the early 1970s municipal autonomy was severely circumscribed by the rapid expansion of central government programs at the municipal level, which were financed by the oil boom. Municipalities were henceforth obliged to coordinate their activities with a wide range of central government agencies, most notably the Ministry of Public Works, the state water corporation (IEOS), and the state electricity corporation (INECEL). In the process they were subjected to financial supervision by a plethora of central government institutions, such as the Ministry of Finance, the comptroller-general's office, the state bank (BDE), and the national preinvestment fund (FONAPRE). All municipal budgets had to be approved by the national planning body, CONADE. The government of President Febres Cordero (1984–1988) went so far as to set up special central government units, known as *unidades ejecutoras,* in order to implement public works programs at the local level, although these were later abandoned because of widespread municipal protest. As a result of this growing domination by the institutions of central government, local government was relegated to the role of "shock absorber" for regional and local social conflicts (Carrión and Velarde:52), a role that strengthened the deep-rooted clientelism that already pervaded local government, especially among smaller municipalities. By the early 1990s, local government activities were limited to solid waste management, markets, road maintenance, parks, and cemeteries. Involvement in education and primary health care was marginal, although many municipalities still operated their own water supply and sewerage systems.

PERSONNEL SYSTEM

In 1994 there were 15,000 municipal employees, accounting for 5 percent of total public sector employment in the country. White-collar municipal employees are covered by the 1964 public sector civil service law, which prohibits trade unions, and blue-collar workers are covered by the general labor code, which allows such unions. Provision in the 1964 law for a merit-based career system governing the recruitment, training, promotion, and job stability of white-collar employees could not be implemented because of a deeply entrenched system of political patronage. As a result, the greater job stability and negotiating strength of blue-collar workers has virtually eliminated effective salary differentials between the two groups. This has contributed to very low motivation among white-collar municipal employees, leading to widespread corruption and moonlighting. A 1982 reform of the municipal code allowed municipalities to opt out of the public sector employment code altogether and to establish their own merit-based personnel systems. To date, however, no municipality has actually implemented such a scheme.

FINANCIAL STRUCTURE

Local government accounted for around 10 percent of total public expenditure during the 1980s, and municipal finances have been closely linked with petroleum exports in recent years. A national fund, Fondo Nacional de Participaciones (FONAPAR), was established in 1971 within the Ministry of Finance in order to distribute to municipalities and provincial councils the revenue-sharing proceeds from stamp duty, a cigarette sales tax, and a 10 percent share of the income tax. Starting in 1972, the oil boom led to contributions from a national petroleum tax becoming by far the major source of FONAPAR's revenue, with the bulk of its funds destined for municipalities. As a result, municipal income grew rapidly during the 1970s.

There were no objective criteria for allocating FONAPAR transfers, known as participaciones, among municipalities; two-thirds of the funds were distributed for earmarked investment projects, and one-third went to cover recurrent expenditure. Access to future allocations depended primarily on the level of current expenditure rather than on any assessment of its efficiency, and this encouraged a rapid growth in municipal expenditure. The complex administration of FONAPAR led to long delays in the disbursement of central government transfers, and the imprecise allocation criteria greatly increased the discretion given to the Ministry of Finance. Provision existed for consideration of the "economic and financial situation" of individual municipalities, and the discretionary nature of such "special case" considerations encouraged rampant clientelism in the allocation procedure (Fawcett:58).

The combination of rapidly rising disbursements by FONAPAR and the shortcomings of its allocation mechanism gave little incentive to local tax effort and produced a rapid increase in the financial dependence of local government on central government transfers. The share of own revenue in total municipal income fell from 40 percent in 1975 to 25 percent by 1985. In 1989 the major sources of locally generated municipal revenue were property taxation (55 percent), a business tax levied on asset values of property (16 percent), a vehicle road tax (7 percent), a betterment levy (7 percent), and a business registration license (6 percent).

The inadequacy of urban cadastres contributed to the weak municipal tax effort. Responsibility for cadastral surveying was transferred from municipal control to a central government agency, DINAC, as part of a 1964/65 tax reform. Thereafter municipalities were prohibited from carrying out their own cadastral surveys despite the fact that the 1966 municipal code attributed responsibility for cadastral surveying to local government. By the mid-1980s only 10 percent of urban properties in the country had been surveyed, representing an enormous loss of potential municipal tax revenue. Meanwhile, rural property valuation was carried out by a separate central government body, the Oficina Nacional de Avalúos.

In marked contrast to much of Latin America, local government finances weakened considerably during the 1980s. A sharp decline in state revenue from petroleum exports led to a severe fiscal crisis and the imposition of a structural adjustment program by the International Monetary Fund. The amounts transferred by central government through FONAPAR fell sharply, bringing about a growing financial crisis for municipalities and highlighting the urgent need to raise local tax effort. The municipal share in total public expenditure fell from 14 percent in 1981 to 9 percent by 1987 (Fuhr:169).

This municipal fiscal crisis was felt especially in the Municipality of Quito. Although municipal income per head there had risen in real terms by 20 percent from 1970 to 1978, this was due almost exclusively to rapidly rising external resources (18 percent a year), rather than to locally generated resources (1.5 percent a year). Over the period 1970–1978, 50 percent of total municipal income derived from external resources, of which 60 percent came from foreign loans and 40 percent from central government transfers. Foreign loans, almost exclusively from the Inter-American Development Bank, were destined for basic infrastructure investment by the municipal water supply company, EMAP, but they did not contribute toward improving locally generated revenue. As a result, the municipality faced a growing debt crisis during the 1980s because of its weak capacity to meet debt service obligations on these foreign loans (Carrión:151–154).

By the late 1980s dissatisfaction with the discretionary nature of central government transfers to local government was running high. The absence of any transparent allocation formula meant that municipalities could not program their activities because they had no clear estimate of the amount of funds to be transferred from one year to the next. In April 1990 FONAPAR was replaced by the Fondo de Desarrollo Seccional (FODESEC), which had two aims. One was to make local government less dependent upon central government transfers, and the other was to make the allocation procedure itself more equitable and less discretionary. Between 1991 and 1993, 3.2 percent of public sector expenditure was distributed to local government via FODESEC. The formula allocating transfers among municipalities gave weight to population size (60 percent), area (30 percent), and tax effort (10 percent). Transfers carried out in a discretionary and arbitrary manner via congressional deputies (the so-called quota system), the president of the republic, and various ministries, however, continued to greatly exceed those effected through the transparent FODESEC system.

The discretionary criteria in the allocation of transfers exacerbated the marked disparities that had developed in municipal expenditure per head, both by region and by municipal population size. In part this reflected much higher central government transfers to smaller municipalities, especially to those in the strategically important and underpopulated eastern (*oriente*) region, where petroleum is produced. Generally speaking, the level of municipal income per head in the medium-sized municipalities of the highlands (sierra) was much higher than in those of the coast (*costa*) because of the former's greater capacity for locally generated fiscal revenue and their greater willingness to charge on a cost-recovery basis for municipal services (Rosales, 1990:112). These perceived inequalities in the allocation mechanism, as well as the inability of municipal authorities to compensate for the decline in transfers by raising the local tax effort, led to a noticeable deterioration in basic service provision, especially for water supply, starting in the mid-1980s. This contributed to the eruption of widespread municipal protest in 1991, which took the form of civic strikes against central government.

INTERMUNICIPAL COOPERATION

Although the first national municipal congress took place in 1941, a national association, the Asociación de Municipalidades Ecuatorianas (AME), was not founded until 1968, following successful municipal lobbying to ensure legal provision for such a body in the 1966 municipal code. Although membership of AME was made compulsory for all municipalities, its slow consolidation reflected opposition to its aims from patronage-based politicians. Nevertheless, its Quito headquarters provided much-needed logistical support for municipal authorities during their negotiations with central government. In the late 1980s the establishment of a training arm and involvement in the PDM (discussed later in this chapter) provided a new impetus to the work of AME.

SUPPORT SERVICES

Ecuador's national municipal association, AME, has also been the major source of support services to local government—an unusual circumstance in Latin America. AME provided training programs starting in the mid-1970s, and in 1982 it began to assist municipalities in the elaboration of project proposals for funding and in cadastral surveying. In 1987 the Instituto Nacional de Fomento y Desarrollo Municipal (INFODEM) was formally established as the training arm of AME. Financing came from a municipal code reform that raised the contribution of municipalities to the funding of AME to 0.4 percent of their annual income. By 1989 INFODEM was sufficiently consolidated to be chosen as the training body for the PDM (discussed later in this chapter). In the mid-1980s the Municipality of Quito established its own training arm, the Instituto de Capacitación Municipal (ICAM), which also provides room in its classes for staff from other municipalities.

CITIZEN PARTICIPATION

Formal mechanisms to promote citizen participation in local government have proved largely ineffective and have operated instead as subtle means of social control (Unda:232). An advisory body known as the *cabildo ampliado* exists ostensibly as a mechanism for consultation with citizens. It may be convened at times of crisis, but only with the agreement of two-thirds of the councillors, and its role in promoting local participation is minimized by the fact that its members are not directly elected. Instead the body's membership includes, in addition to councillors, the five previous mayors or council presidents, provincial deputies to the national legislature, a representative of the provincial prefect, a central government representative, a representative of state corporations, three local journalists, and a representative of AME. Three-member parish councils (*juntas parroquiales*), which exist at the submunicipal level in both urban and rural areas, were directly elected until 1982, after which time their members were appointed by the municipal council for terms of two and a half years.

A case study of Santo Domingo de los Colorados, the fastest-growing medium-size city in the country, showed that high levels of citizen participation in local government were stifled starting in the mid-1970s as the municipality became an instrument of central government. As a result of growing alienation, the demands of civil society became increasingly articulated through housing cooperatives, which were seen to be more responsive to citizens' problems. As the municipality lost credibility, community organizations preferred to bypass it and to express their needs directly to central government (Allou and Velarde:173).

PROSPECTS FOR LOCAL GOVERNMENT

An ambitious U.S.$300 million interinstitutional program for municipal development was launched in 1990 that sought to introduce cost recovery in municipal service provision through its lending program, thereby enabling municipalities to offset the decline in central government transfers through greater own revenue generation. The Programa de Desarrollo Municipal (PDM) was jointly funded by the World Bank, the Inter-American Development Bank, and Gesellschaft für Technische Zusammenarbeit (GTZ), and it involved a number of state agencies, including AME. Although the bulk of the funds (91 percent) were to be spent on urban infra-structure investment, an estimated 6.5 percent was earmarked for institu-tional development and 2.5 percent for training. By 1993, 145 out of the 193 municipalities were participating in the PDM.

By 1994 the program was already beginning to encounter problems in carrying out reform initiatives in the clientelist-ridden environment of Ecuadorean public administration. It was experiencing difficulties in coor-dinating project activities among competing central government agencies, each keen to maximize its own input into the program. BDE officials tend-ed to approve loan disbursements in such haste that they undermined PDM conditionality, and numerous municipalities avoided the institutional reform obligations that had been agreed upon with the PDM (Fuhr:179).

18

EL SALVADOR

El Salvador is a unitary nation divided for administrative purposes into fourteen departments. Below the department level, the country is covered by 262 municipalities. The Metropolitan Area of San Salvador (Area Metropolitana de San Salvador, or AMSS) comprises the Municipality of San Salvador, which is the capital city, and twelve neighboring municipalities. In 1992 the AMSS had a population of 1.1 million (22 percent of the national total), of whom 45 percent lived in the Municipality of San Salvador. There is no metropolitan government in the AMSS. In 1987 mayors of municipalities within the AMSS formed a consultative committee known as COAMSS. In 1994 a new urban development law established a metropolitan development council (CODEMET) for the AMSS, consisting of central government ministries and COAMSS. Its powers of control over land use zoning, building regulations, and environmental protection were exercised through a metropolitan planning office (OPAMSS), which was firmly under central government control, although the COAMSS had consultative status through CODEMET.

Most municipalities are small. In 1991 only eleven had more than 80,000 inhabitants, twenty-one had between 40,000 and 80,000 inhabitants, forty-eight had between 20,000 and 40,000 inhabitants, and 182 had fewer than 20,000 inhabitants.

HISTORICAL DEVELOPMENT

Until very recently, El Salvador was one of the most highly centralized countries in Latin America. An uninterrupted succession of harsh military regimes ruled the country from 1931 to 1984. During this period, political parties of all persuasions were practically nonexistent, and local government played an insignificant role in the life of the country.

Departmental governors, appointed by the president of the republic, exercised extensive supervision over municipalities under their jurisdiction and even had the power to sack municipal employees. This departmental control over local government was carried out through an intermediary administrative tier of thirty-nine districts throughout the country. The chief executive officer at the district level functioned as a sort of assistant governor and was appointed as mayor of the municipality in the district headquarters. This official was also empowered to impose fines on other mayors in the same district.

The civil war that engulfed the country between 1981 and 1992 served as the catalyst that placed decentralization on the political agenda. The Christian Democratic government elected in 1984 rejected the previous harsh counterinsurgency strategy against the revolutionary forces of the Frente Farabundo Martí de Liberación Nacional (FMLN), a left-wing guerrilla movement. Instead it sought to win the "hearts and minds" of the rural population by demonstrating the benefits of a democratic system of local government in contrast to the allegedly authoritarian approach the FMLN took to the local administration of areas under their control. The 1983 Constitution formally recognized municipal autonomy. It also abolished the districts and ended the supervisory powers of departmental governors over local government. As part of this reform process, a new municipal code in 1986, Código Municipal No. 274, replaced legislation that had been in existence since 1908.

ORGANIZATIONAL STRUCTURE

Local government in El Salvador comprises a unipersonal executive head, or mayor (alcalde), a legal officer (síndico), and a legislature (concejo municipal). The number of councillors (regidores or concejales), ranges between five and thirteen according to municipal population size. All local government officers serve a three-year term of office and may stand for immediate reelection. The electoral system is not based on proportional or majority representation, a unique situation in Latin America. Instead, voting is by closed party lists, and the party that wins the largest number of votes automatically takes possession of all council seats. Hence there is no minority representation whatsoever in municipal councils.

FUNCTIONAL RESPONSIBILITIES

El Salvador has inherited a highly centralized administrative system under which central government ministries and state corporations have provided basic services at the local level. Under this arrangement, functional departments of municipalities operate principally as the administrative liaison for the activities of line ministries, and local government itself provides only supplementary services.

Although the 1986 municipal code empowers municipalities to carry out no fewer than twenty-eight functions, almost all of these tasks conform to a traditional and highly restricted perception of local government activity. The only exception is the power granted to finance housing and urban renewal programs. The continuing subservience of local government to central government is reinforced by a provision in the municipal code itself, which states that any of the responsibilities granted to municipalities may be overridden by attributions conferred upon agencies of central government. In practice, local government functions are still restricted to solid waste management, street cleaning, public lighting, bus terminals, public markets, slaughterhouses, and cemeteries, as well as civil registration. Although seventy-two municipalities were responsible for their own water and sewerage systems in 1993 (Murphy et al.:11), virtually all health, welfare, and education services continue to be provided by central government.

A much-vaunted decentralization program for primary education, urban road construction and maintenance, environmental health, and public hygiene was launched in the late 1980s. The thrust of this program was administrative deconcentration rather than devolution to local government (Molina:110). Following the end of the civil war, the government has pursued a social welfare program that seeks to target assistance to those households believed to be living in absolute poverty. By 1991 four ministries and central government agencies, each funded by different foreign aid donors, were operating nine separate initiatives in the poorest municipalities. Local government was denied any significant coordinating role in these programs, and this led to widespread duplication of activities, as well as increasing congestion as programs amassed at the community level (Sollis:455–456).

PERSONNEL SYSTEM

In 1994, the total number of municipal employees was 10,924, equivalent to 9 percent of total public sector employment. The Municipality of San Salvador accounted for 31 percent of total municipal employment. Only twelve municipalities employed more than 100 staff, and 127 employed less than ten staff. A 1990 survey of the staff of 100 municipalities revealed that 41 percent had completed only primary education, 44 percent had secondary education, 9 percent had professional training, and 6 percent had received university education (INCAE:63–64). Although local government employees are theoretically covered by the national civil service law of 1979, there is no municipal career system.

FINANCIAL STRUCTURE

Local government finances remain weak and subject to strong control by the municipal division of the Ministry of the Interior. In 1993 municipal expenditure still accounted for only 6 percent of total public expenditure, and half of this came from foreign aid (Murphy et al.:35). Municipalities have extremely limited sources of income. Neither property tax nor vehicle road tax are municipal taxes, an uncommon feature in Latin America. A municipal credit bank was set up in the 1970s but proved unsuccessful. As a result, municipalities are extremely dependent upon transfers from central government and foreign aid donors, the distribution of which, until recently, was subject to very arbitrary political criteria.

Two fiscal reforms in the late 1980s, which also increased dependence on central government transfers, nevertheless increased municipal income. In 1988 a central government municipal fund (Fondo Municipal) was established. Its proceeds are distributed on the basis of an annual sum (x) per head of population, according to a formula that discriminates in favor of smaller municipalities. Municipalities with fewer than 10,000 inhabitants receive $2.5x$ per head, and municipalities with more than 100,000 inhabitants receive only $1.5x$. The transfer is primarily designed to boost municipal investment, and only 20 percent of the funds may be used for current expenditure.

In 1989 the central government tax on coffee exports was reformed, with 3 percent of the proceeds henceforth distributed to municipalities on the following revenue-sharing basis: 25 percent to the twenty-five largest coffee-exporting municipalities on an origin basis, and the remaining 75 percent divided equally among the remaining municipalities.

The impact of these two reforms upon municipal income was limited, and the Fondo Municipal remained equivalent to less than 1 percent of recurrent government revenue in 1994. Consequently, the reforms were unable to offset the enormous disparities in own revenue generation among different municipalities. In 1987 the income per head of the Municipality of San Salvador was already 5.5 times higher than the national average, and 20 times greater than for municipalities in the impoverished Department of Morazán. By 1990 the Municipality of San Salvador alone still accounted for 42 percent of the total income of all municipalities in the country, with the Municipality of Santa Ana accounting for a further 6.4 percent.

During the civil war, municipalities received capital aid from a USAID-financed public works program, known as CONARA, which was designed as a counterinsurgency effort. Following the ending of the war, municipalities have also received sizeable grants from foreign aid donors for reconstruction. This produced a marked disincentive for local tax effort and reduced the pressure from municipalities for an increase in the size of the

Fondo Municipal. The easy availability of grant aid has also made unworkable the development of a revolving credit program for municipalities.

INTERMUNICIPAL COOPERATION

An early attempt to form a national municipal association was made in 1941 with the establishment of the Corporación de Municipalidades de la República de El Salvador (COMURES), but this organization soon became inactive. At the end of the civil war, COMURES was resurrected, and its revised statutes were officially recognized by the central government in 1992. Despite the extremely polarized political situation that then prevailed, COMURES soon gained a high degree of acceptability thanks largely to the political pluralism of its governing body. At the eighth national municipal congress hosted by COMURES in 1993, all presidential candidates for the period 1994–1999 signed a joint declaration committing their parties to greater autonomy for local government.

SUPPORT SERVICES

Two institutions provide support services to local government. The Instituto Salvadoreño de Administración Municipal (ISAM) is a private body established in 1979 that receives support from the Konrad Adenauer Foundation of Germany. It provides legal and technical assistance to municipalities and carries out training programs in financial administration, management development, and municipal legislation. The Instituto Salvadoreño de Desarrollo Municipal (ISDEM) is a public sector body established in March 1987 that has responsibility for administering the revenue-sharing agreement for the coffee export tax and the financial transfer to municipalities from the Fondo Municipal. In 1994 it established a municipal training school.

CITIZEN PARTICIPATION

The 1986 municipal code sought to promote citizen participation in local government through a number of means. First, municipal authorities were obliged to convene cabildos abiertos every three months in order to report on the implementation of municipal programs and to discuss matters raised by community groups, and the council could not act against the wishes of a majority expressed at such meetings. Second, popular consultations (*consultas populares*) were encouraged, whereby municipal initiatives were to be subjected to public scrutiny before their approval. Third, official recognition was granted to community groups (*asociaciones comunales*), which had to have a minimum of twenty-five members. Representatives from such groups could be invited to serve as advisors to the council. Although 718 community groups had been officially recognized by 1994, the legacy of mistrust engendered by the civil war meant that citizen participation in local government was still extremely limited by comparison with the rest of Latin America. Three out of four municipalities studied in depth in 1993 as part of a USAID-funded municipal development program did not have council meetings open to the public or even the press (Murphy et al.:13).

PROSPECTS FOR LOCAL GOVERNMENT

In 1993 COMURES was the driving force behind the establishment of an official interinstitutional commission on decentralization and local government under the Ministry of Planning, on which COMURES itself and ISDEM were both represented. In the wake of the inconclusive outcome of the civil war, prospects for local government strengthening remain limited in the medium term.

19

GUATEMALA

Guatemala is a unitary nation divided for administrative purposes into eight regions and then again into twenty-two departments. Each department is headed by a presidentially appointed governor, whose primary function is to oversee law and order. Below the department level, the country is covered by 330 municipalities. The Municipality of Guatemala City and the other sixteen municipalities in the Department of Guatemala constitute a metropolitan region, although there is no metropolitan government.

There is considerable variation in municipal population size, and municipalities are classified into four categories. There are twenty-two municipalities that either have a population of over 100,000 or are departmental headquarters. There are 114 municipalities that have populations of between 20,000 and 100,000 or are ports, ninety-seven municipalities with populations of between 10,000 and 20,000, and a further ninety-seven municipalities with populations of fewer than 10,000.

HISTORICAL DEVELOPMENT

For most of its history, local government in Guatemala has been tightly controlled by central government. This situation reflects the long-standing domination of the country by authoritarian military regimes. The campaign for greater local government autonomy has also been limited by the repeated exclusion from the electoral system, through assassination and disappearance, of those political forces advocating decentralization and municipal freedoms.

Starting in 1931, municipalities served as a branch of central government, with their executives appointed directly by the president. Following the democratic revolution of 1944, municipalities were granted a degree of political autonomy by the 1945 Constitution. In 1957 the first significant municipal code was enacted, and a national municipal development institute, the Instituto de Fomento Municipal (INFOM), was established to provide technical assistance, training, and soft loan finance to local government.

Municipal autonomy was reaffirmed in the 1965 Constitution precisely at a time when central government institutions were stripping municipalities of many of their functions. To this end, in 1966 the Panajachel conference brought together central and local government officials and sought to promote the myth of municipal autonomy by formulating the motto "partners in development" (McIntosh, 1980:18).

In 1982 political autonomy was once again contradicted by the appointment of municipal executives. The 1985 Constitution reasserted a degree of political autonomy to local government by means of provisions for the direct election of municipal officeholders and an 8 percent share in national fiscal revenue. The national legislature nevertheless retained the exclusive power to approve all municipal taxes.

In 1987 a comprehensive system of urban and rural development councils was announced, with councils operating at the national, regional, departmental, municipal, and submunicipal levels. This system was designed in order to coordinate government development efforts more effectively throughout the country. Although projected as a decentralization strategy, in reality it represented merely a deconcentration of central government administration. Each local group of elected municipal officeholders was incorporated into this new system by being renamed a municipal urban and rural development council (*consejo municipal de desarrollo urbano y rural*). A new municipal code, Código Municipal No. 58, of 12 October 1988, and a large increase in central government funding for local government were to form key components of this corporativist strategy. INFOM was to play a key role in ensuring that local government investment decisions conformed with nationally defined priorities. The imposition of these new structures faced considerable resistance from municipal authorities, and by 1990 the structures had fallen into disuse as effective planning mechanisms (Mencos:13).

ORGANIZATIONAL STRUCTURE

Guatemalan local government, known as the *corporación municipal,* comprises a unipersonal executive head, or mayor (alcalde), a legal officer (síndico), and a legislature consisting of between eight and twenty councillors (consejales) according to the population size of the municipality. Councillors are elected according to the D'Hondt system of proportional representation. Guatemala has a system of strong mayors and weak councils, and the mayors chair council sessions. Officeholders in the Municipality of Guatemala City have a four-year term that is concurrent with that of politicians elected to national office. All other municipalities have two-year terms of office, with elections held at the same time as national elections and then again midway through the term for national political office. All municipal officeholders may stand for immediate reelection.

The Guatemalan municipality has an unusual internal organizational structure that reflects its extreme dependence on central government. Every municipality is required to establish ten committees—one each for finance, public health, education, culture, tourism and sport, agriculture, cattle ranching, urban planning, urban and rural development, and financial probity. The primary function of these committees is to coordinate local government activity with the respective central government ministry or state corporation operating at the local level.

FUNCTIONAL RESPONSIBILITIES

Central government remains wedded to a strategy of decentralization that involves administrative deconcentration rather than the devolution of responsibilities to local government. In contrast to the 1957 municipal code, which defined the mandatory and discretionary responsibilities of local government, the 1988 municipal code granted only a vaguely defined coordinating role to local government without specifying its functional responsibilities at all. In practice, municipal functions normally include markets, solid waste management, slaughterhouses, and community sports centers. In addition, Guatemala remains unique in Latin America in that virtually all municipalities operate their own water supply system, and eleven also provide electricity.

A 1991 study carried out in fifty-seven municipalities of local government investment projects gave an indication of municipal service delivery priorities. The most common projects, listed in order of frequency, involved water supply, street paving, sewerage, school building, community sports halls, bridges, markets, electrification, pavements, road construction, cemeteries, slaughterhouses, and solid waste management (Echegaray, 1991:58).

PERSONNEL SYSTEM

In 1989 there were 14,133 municipal employees (excluding the employees of eleven municipally owned electricity companies), accounting for 8 percent of total public sector employment. Of the total, 29 percent worked for the Municipality of Guatemala City. Only six municipalities employed more than 100 staff each, and 262 municipalities each employed fewer than twenty staff (Sánchez:132). All municipal requests for new staff posts must be approved by the national civil service office following prior agreement by INFOM that funds are available to pay for the post. Although a separate municipal labor code exists, there is no local government career system.

A 1982 study carried out by INFOM showed that the educational level of mayors was very low—72 percent of them had received only primary education. The post of mayor was generally considered unattractive because of the extremely poor salary level, which was even below that of municipal secretaries and treasurers. Skill levels remain very low, and municipalities have been technically and administratively ill equipped to undertake the dramatic increase in investment activities since 1986.

FINANCIAL STRUCTURE

Local government finance in Guatemala, which had been weak for many decades, has been significantly strengthened in recent years. During the period 1971–1976 municipalities accounted for only 8.1 percent of total public expenditure. The Municipality of Guatemala City accounted for half of the national total, although the vast majority of small and rural municipalities did not generate sufficient resources to provide even the most basic services (McIntosh, 1980:60). For these municipalities, locally raised revenue was barely sufficient to cover recurrent expenditure, and as a result the municipalities carried out hardly any capital expenditure.

INFOM played a significant role in local government finances, serving as a conduit for small-scale revenue shares assigned to municipalities from export taxes on coffee (since 1965), as well as from domestic taxes on gasoline (since 1956), beer (since 1964), and liquor (since 1965). It used the proceeds from these taxes, as well as soft loan finance from USAID and the Inter-American Development Bank, to provide the only source of credit available to local government. Its loan portfolio concentrated on water supply and sewerage, with most projects geared toward repair or expansion, rather than the construction of new installations (McIntosh, 1978:65–66).

This situation changed dramatically as a result of a provision in the 1985 Constitution requiring that 8 percent of the national budget, known as the *aporte constitucional,* be transferred henceforth to municipalities and earmarked exclusively for investment purposes. The aporte constitucional had a major impact on local government finances, as a result of which municipalities acquired a new dynamism, to the point where they now form the bulk of public investment in the country. Total municipal income rose rapidly starting in 1985, reaching 13.8 percent of national fiscal revenue in

1986–1987, probably the highest such share in Central America (Sánchez:131, 136).

Although local government finances improved dramatically, they became highly dependent upon the aporte constitucional and other transfers from central government. These other transfers included a wage subsidy for municipal employees and the proceeds from property taxation collected by the Ministry of Finance. The latter remained low because of widespread undervaluation, numerous exemptions, and outright evasion. By 1987, 73 percent of total municipal income derived from central government transfers (Sánchez:130), compared with only 40 percent in 1974 (McIntosh, 1980:20).

The capacity of most Guatemalan municipalities to raise own revenue is severely constrained by their economic base. In 1988 the twenty richest municipalities together accounted for 72 percent of all locally raised municipal revenue in the country (Linares:5). Own revenue generation is also constrained by central government legislation. Annual requests to raise fees and tax rates, known as the plan de arbitrios, must first be reviewed by INFOM and then approved by the Ministry of Finance. Service charges for water consumption and slaughterhouses, however, may be fixed by municipalities without central government approval. In 1986 municipal own revenue derived from forty-eight different sources, of which the most important were a head tax (*boleto de ornato*), business licenses, and a charge for public lighting (CEDAL:45).

The aporte constitucional is distributed among municipalities according to a mildly redistributive formula as follows: 25 percent in equal parts among all municipalities; 25 percent in proportion to the total population of each municipality; 25 percent in proportion to the own revenue per head of each municipality; 15 percent in proportion to the number of villages and hamlets in each municipality; and 10 percent in inverse proportion to the own revenue per head of each municipality. The impact of this formula is to reduce somewhat the inequalities in income per head between large, urban municipalities and small municipalities with dispersed populations. There is little evidence that the transfer system has encouraged greater local tax effort, despite the inclusion of an element in the distribution formula that seeks to reward it.

INTERMUNICIPAL COOPERATION

A national municipal association, the Asociación Nacional de Municipalidades (ANAM), was founded in 1969. Membership in ANAM is obligatory for all municipalities, and the mayor of the Municipality of Guatemala City heads the association's board of directors. For two decades ANAM remained firmly under the control of central government. Amongst its principal aims was support for government programs under the "partnership in development" slogan. Many municipalities fell into arrears with their annual quotas to ANAM, and the association became heavily dependent upon a subsidy from central government to cover its operating costs. During the 1970s and 1980s a major concern expressed at the annual conferences of ANAM was life insurance coverage for mayors, many of whom have been killed in the civil war that has plagued the country for many years.

In the late 1980s, ANAM became more independent and began to campaign against central government interference in the way municipalities spent resources obtained under the aporte constitucional. It also demanded representation on the governing boards of a number of central government agencies, such as the national telecommunications company, the social security institute, and the land reform institute, all of which had refused to coordinate their activities with local government. Despite the twenty-five-year existence of ANAM, intermunicipal cooperation remains minimal, and there is no example to date of joint funding of projects under the aporte constitucional.

SUPPORT SERVICES

INFOM has been in existence since 1957. In addition to its role as a supplier of cheap credit and a channel for distribution of shared taxes to municipalities, INFOM also carries out limited training for municipalities. Throughout the institute's life, central government has exercised strict control over INFOM through majority representation on the governing board and through the requirement that the president of INFOM be appointed by the president of the republic. The sudden increase in municipal investment activity after 1986 as a result of the aporte constitucional revealed the urgent need for municipal training in project selection, implementation, and evaluation. By 1990 municipalities were campaigning through ANAM for a change in the statutes in order to reduce central government control over INFOM.

CITIZEN PARTICIPATION

Successive authoritarian military regimes in Guatemala have severely restricted citizen participation in local government because they viewed such behavior as subversive. There is provision in the municipal code for citizen consultation through a cabildo abierto, but this is not mandatory and must have the approval of two-thirds of the councillors. The corporativist national system for urban and rural development introduced in 1987 included community development councils (*consejos de desarrollo local*) at the submunicipal level. These local committees were designed to generate "controlled" participation by citizens in the selection and implementation of investment projects to be financed by the aporte constitucional, although they soon fell into disuse. A 1991 study of fifty-seven municipalities revealed a general recognition by municipal staff that the views of citizens were rarely considered during the selection of municipal investment projects, and that citizen participation in project implementation was minimal (Echegaray, 1991:40, 45).

PROSPECTS FOR LOCAL GOVERNMENT

The introduction of the aporte constitucional radically strengthened municipal finances and enabled local government to play a major role in the development of Guatemala for the first time (Mencos:11). Municipal authorities have gained a new self-confidence that has enabled them to reject their previously subordinate role vis-à-vis departmental governors. Two problems will need to be resolved in order to maximize the long-term benefits of this major reform. First, the maintenance of public infrastructure by municipalities has been poor, most noticeably in the case of water supply systems. This problem is caused by a severe shortage of qualified technical and administrative staff. These shortages have become even more severe as a result of the rapid expansion of municipal investment since 1986. For this reason, a comprehensive training program is needed to ensure that the new investment projects operate efficiently. A second problem (related to the first) is the need to meet the rapid increase in operating and maintenance costs of the new municipal investment program, which has granted priority to road construction and water and sewerage systems (Echegaray, 1991:12). Although some of these costs may be recovered by charging fees, others will have to be met out of general municipal revenue. It will therefore be necessary to strengthen municipal financial management and so improve the collection of a wide range of locally raised municipal taxes in order to sustain the dramatic increase in municipal investment.

20

HONDURAS

Honduras is a unitary nation divided for administrative purposes into eighteen departments. Each department is headed by a governor appointed by the president of the republic and is administered by a departmental council, comprising the governor and two municipal councillors. The latter are elected by an electoral college consisting of representatives from each municipality in the department. Below the department level, the country is covered by 291 municipalities, which are subdivided for administrative purposes into 3,072 units known as *aldeas* in suburban areas and 19,756 units known as *caseríos* in rural areas. The capital city of Tegucigalpa and the adjacent city of Comayaguela together form the Central District (Distrito Central). This district was previously governed by a metropolitan council, with an executive head appointed by the president of the republic. It now has municipal status with its own directly elected mayor.

There is enormous disparity in population size among municipalities. In 1988 six municipalities, each with more than 80,000 inhabitants, accounted for 34 percent of the national population, most industrial production and exports, a sizeable share of agricultural production, and most social infrastructure. On the other hand, 193 small rural municipalities, each with fewer than 10,000 inhabitants, together accounted for only 12 percent of the national population. In between was a band of ninety medium-size municipalities that together accounted for over half of the national population (Guzmán:149).

HISTORICAL DEVELOPMENT

In contrast to the rest of Central America, the Honduran state remained very weak during the nineteenth century. Competing elites, none of them strong enough to impose total control, fought a series of battles for power. The inaccessibility of many areas, the frequent civil wars, and the power of regional landowners over the peasantry preserved a high degree of local autonomy. National politics became dominated by the competing interests of foreign banana companies. An end to this rivalry in the late 1920s opened up the possibility of greater political stability, and the first municipal code was passed in 1927.

Under the dictatorship of President Tiburcio Carias Andino (1932– 1948) a highly centralized system of government gradually evolved. In 1939 local government autonomy was suppressed following the division of the country into thirty-one districts, administered by councils whose members were appointed by the president and supervised by the Ministry of the Interior. The emergence of a powerful elite of coffee growers in the 1940s encouraged the growth of state involvement in the economy.

In 1957 the district system was abolished, and municipal elections were held until 1972, after which time all municipal officeholders were appointed by military rulers until 1981. Various articles in the 1982 Constitution once again reaffirmed municipal autonomy, and in October 1990 a new law, Ley de Municipalidades No. 13,490, finally replaced the antiquated municipal code of 1927.

ORGANIZATIONAL STRUCTURE

Honduran local government, which is known as the corporación municipal, comprises a unipersonal executive head, or mayor (alcalde), and a legislature consisting of between four and ten councillors (regidores) according to the population size of the municipality. In 1987 the term of local government officeholders was increased from two to four years. As a result, it is now concurrent with that of national political office. The mayor is not elected separately. Instead municipal officeholders are elected according to a closed party list headed by the candidate for mayor. In the 1993 elections, local political accountability was increased when, for the first time, voters elected local and national officeholders on separate ballot papers. Municipal officeholders may stand for reelection.

The mayor chairs council meetings and heads the local government administration, although it is the council that appoints municipal employees on the basis of recommendation by the mayor. The role of the mayor as the local representative of the president of the republic is particularly strong in Honduras. As such, the mayor is responsible for ensuring local compliance with all laws and decrees emanating from central government. Given that most authority and resources at the disposal of local government are ultimately controlled by central government, mayors have been forced to give priority to their role as the representatives of central government, and this has contributed to a diminution of municipal autonomy. A striking manifestation of the political centralization of the country is the fact that basic decisions on the creation of new municipalities are still taken by presidential decree, not by laws passed through Congress; this is a very uncommon situation in Latin America.

FUNCTIONAL RESPONSIBILITIES

The 1927 municipal code, which was passed when the urban population of the country was a fraction of what it is today, granted a wide range of functions to local government. From 1965 to 1975, local government operations were rapidly circumscribed by the growth of state companies with operations at the local level. These companies included the state water corporation (SANAA) and the state electricity corporation (ENEE), which gradually acquired existing municipal and private electricity companies. By the mid-1980s, of the municipalities with between 10,000 and 80,000 inhabitants that had electricity supply systems (three-quarters of the total in this category), 61 percent were the responsibility of ENEE, 31 percent were still operated by municipalities, and 9 percent were privately owned.

By the mid-1980s, SANAA operated 95 urban and rural water supply systems in the five largest municipalities, and it cooperated with local administrative boards in the operation of 285 rural water supplies in municipalities with fewer than 10,000 inhabitants. Of the municipalities having between 10,000 and 80,000 inhabitants, almost all of which had some form of water supply, 63 percent of the supply systems were directly operated by the municipalities themselves, SANAA was responsible for 19 percent, and the remaining 18 percent were contracted out to private firms.

The creation of a national agrarian institute removed the ownership of communal land from local government, and the creation of a Honduran corporation for forest development (known as COHDEFOR) removed forest resources from municipal control. The state telecommunications, public works, and transport secretariat (SECOPT) assumed responsibility for local road construction and maintenance. Coordination between all of these state companies and local government has been weak.

As a result of this process of demunicipalization, the provision of basic municipal services is meager. A 1986 study of the eighty-six middle-range municipalities, each with between 10,000 and 80,000 inhabitants, was carried out for the Inter-American Development Bank; it showed that only fifty-five had slaughterhouses, forty had public markets, seventeen had surfaced roads, seven had street cleaning, and only one had a bus terminal. Furthermore, even in the case of those services for which the level of munic-

ipal provision was apparently high—such as water supply and electricity—
the coverage of the system was confined to limited areas of the urban center, and supply was restricted to only a few hours per day. The new 1990
municipal code, like its 1927 predecessor, continued to give local government the responsibility for an unrealistically wide range of services, many
of which are currently undertaken by state enterprises and for which local
government lacks the financial and administrative capacity to undertake
(Moncada:14).

PERSONNEL SYSTEM

In 1994 there were approximately 5,900 municipal employees in Honduras,
equivalent to 6.9 percent of total public sector employment. There is no
municipal career service. Instead, staff are proposed by the mayor and
appointed by the corporación. Most employees are replaced every four years
along with the change of political leadership. The only exceptions to this
general rule are the posts of municipal secretary and treasurer, as well as
staff belonging to the municipal cadastral service, where a degree of job stability and professionalization has taken root. As a result of the serious defi-
ciency in human resources, municipal planning and program budgeting are
restricted to the Central District and the larger Municipalities of San Pedro
Sula and La Ceiba.

Remuneration for elected officeholders and salaries for municipal
employees are both extremely low. This is a major factor explaining why the
general educational level of local government officeholders and personnel
remains extremely low, even by Latin American standards. A 1986 study of
169 (mainly small) municipalities revealed that 46 percent of elected officeholders had not even completed primary education and that only 7 percent
had received secondary education. Among municipal employees, 32 percent
had not completed primary education, and only 20 percent had received secondary education (Guzmán:158).

FINANCIAL STRUCTURE

The share of local government in total government income (central and
local) averaged 7.9 percent between 1983 and 1985 (Guzmán:160, 163).
This low share was mainly attributed to the fact that, until recently, central
government transfers were not a significant source of local government
income and represented only 8 percent of the total in 1986. Revenue sharing
between central and local government did not begin until 1987, when eight

port municipalities began to receive 4 percent of customs receipts accruing to the national ports authority.

In the absence of significant transfers from central government, municipalities have traditionally relied on locally raised sources of revenue. In 1986 middle-range municipalities (10,000–80,000 inhabitants) were heavily dependent on own sources of income: tax, 58 percent; nontax, 17 percent; and service charges, 16 percent. The major local revenue sources are a property tax; a head tax; and a tax on commercial, industrial, mining, and agricultural business, which is levied on the volume of production or sales. Other sources include a tax on the exploitation and extraction of natural resources (mining, forestry, fishing, and hunting), a property sales tax, a betterment tax, and user charges for municipal services such as water, street cleaning, and public lighting.

Until very recently, municipal financial management was hindered by the outdated features of the 1927 municipal law. The ad specie (i.e., fixed-fee) nature of taxes severely constrained financial buoyancy. All municipal budgets and loan operations, all contracts with private companies, and all changes in the rates charged for municipal services had to be approved by departmental councils. In addition, central government exercised de facto financial control over the Central District through the Ministry of the Interior. Furthermore, the absence of cadastres in 60 percent of municipalities made it virtually impossible to identify potential taxpayers (Moncada:27). By 1986 municipal income averaged only U.S.$8.68 per head, although even this figure masked an extreme concentration of financial resources in the largest municipalities. In the same year 40 percent of all municipalities received an income that was insufficient to cover minimum operating costs. The incomplete, confusing, and delayed system of recording municipal income and expenditure, as well as the absence of any municipal finance law, made analysis of local government finances virtually impossible.

The 1990 municipal code introduced several fiscal reforms. First, it made provision for municipalities to receive a gradually increasing percentage of the national budget, rising from 2 percent in 1992 to a maximum of 5 percent by 1994. This is allocated among municipalities according to the following formula: 20 percent in equal parts and 80 percent in proportion to the population of each municipality. Second, ad valorem (i.e., percentage) rates replaced ad specie rates on all major municipal taxes. Municipalities were also granted freedom to vary the rates of property and local business taxation, in the range of 0.15 percent to 0.5 percent, although this decision was criticized on the grounds that the discretion it allowed would exacerbate administrative corruption (Moncada:26). Third, the new code also gave municipalities full responsibility for drawing up, approving, and administering their own budgets. They were no longer required to sign contracts exclusively with state corporations for the delivery of basic services and were henceforth allowed to contract out to the private sector.

INTERMUNICIPAL COOPERATION

A national municipal association, the Asociación de Municipios de Honduras (AMHON), was founded in 1960. After two decades of relative inactivity, it began to exert influence on central government policy toward local government, and this gave rise to the 1990 municipal code. From 1991 to 1993, AMHON was reorganized and strengthened with technical assistance from the International City Management Association of the United States. By 1994 AMHON was represented on the presidential commission for the reform of the state and had succeeded in establishing a congressional committee for local government.

SUPPORT SERVICES

The Banco Municipal Autónomo (BANMA), founded in 1961, is the principal state institution that grants credit and technical assistance to local government. It is the largest source of loan finance for municipal investment and serves as its principal financial intermediary. BANMA finances its activities primarily from foreign loans (USAID and the Inter-American Development Bank), although municipalities are supposed to allocate 5 percent of their income to the purchase of its shares. BANMA has suffered from the poor loan repayment record of municipalities, as well as from their defaults on the commercial bank loans it has guaranteed. By the end of 1988, outstanding debts were equivalent to 130 percent of the paid-up capital of BANMA. Debts by the Central District alone made up 77 percent of the total. As a result of this growing debt problem, by the mid-1990s BANMA had severely curtailed both its lending program and its technical assistance services to local government.

CITIZEN PARTICIPATION

Citizen participation in Honduran local government has historically been very weak, and the traditional form of community organization, known as the *patronato,* has received little encouragement from municipalities. The 1990 municipal law required municipal authorities to hold five cabildos abiertos a year and to publish the municipal budget. It also made provision for plebiscites to be held for the first time. Nevertheless, its impact on the promotion of citizen participation has been slight.

PROSPECTS FOR LOCAL GOVERNMENT

Honduras remains one the few countries in Latin America where there has been little sign of a resurgence of local government during the 1980s. The highly centralized system of government continues to restrict severely the financial and administrative autonomy of municipalities. The promulgation of the new 1990 municipal code, which was preceded by minimal public debate, is unlikely to alter this panorama significantly.

21

MEXICO

Mexico is a federal nation composed of thirty-one states and the Federal District of Mexico City, the capital. Below the state level, the country is covered by 2,397 municipalities. The system of government is highly centralized. The power of the national legislature to amend the Constitution with the approval of a majority of state legislatures considerably dilutes the country's federal character. Although local government's right to exist is enshrined in the Constitution, municipalities remain the creatures of state legislation.

Few major cities in the world have less local democracy than Mexico City. Its executive head (*regente*) is appointed by the president of the republic, as are the local executive heads (*delegados*) of the sixteen zones (*delegaciones*) into which the city is divided for administrative purposes. Legislative functions for the Federal District are carried out by the national legislature. In 1988 a separately elected assembly of representatives was introduced but it has only consultative status. The Mexico City Metropolitan Area (MCMA) embraces the Federal District and seventeen municipalities in the State of Mexico. One-quarter of the national population and approximately half of national production is located there. The MCMA is a geographical rather than administrative entity, and there is no metropolitan structure of government. The urgent need to tackle environmental pollution in Mexico City has focused attention on the undue administrative complexity of the MCMA.

There is enormous heterogeneity among Mexican municipalities. In 1980, 83 percent of the 2,378 municipalities at that time had fewer than 30,000 inhabitants, 10 percent had between 30,000 and 60,000 inhabitants, a further 6 percent had between 60,000 and 300,000 inhabitants, and only twenty-four municipalities, equivalent to only 1 percent of the total, had more than 300,000 inhabitants (Martínez and Ziccardi, 1989:298). In 1990,

23 percent of the national population lived in just 294 municipalities, which together covered 53 percent of the national territory (G. Martínez:148–149). The number and average population size of municipalities varies enormously among states. In 1992 the State of Baja California had only four municipalities, each with an average population of 306,359, and the State of Oaxaca had 570 municipalities, each with an average population of only 4,418.

HISTORICAL DEVELOPMENT

Mexico has a particularly centralist system of government, even by Latin American standards. Political power is highly concentrated in the hands of the presidency. The leaders of the Mexican Revolution of 1910 had raised the call for "the free municipality" (*municipio libre*), which demanded freedom for the overwhelmingly rural municipalities from the controls imposed by the Napoleonic prefectoral system. However, this aspiration was opposed by congressional deputies to the constitutional assembly (Olmedo:186–192). They engineered a compromise to ensure that Article 115 of the 1917 Constitution purposely granted municipalities an ill-defined status.

Local government was subsequently subsumed within the corporativist system led by the Partido Revolucionario Institucional (PRI), the party that came to monopolize the political life of the country. The PRI pursued a rapid, state-led industrialization strategy that was implemented by a highly centralized administrative system granting minimal importance to municipal development.

This industrialization strategy generated massive rural-to-urban migration and extreme urban-rural inequalities. During the 1960s and 1970s policies to promote regional development and the deconcentration of federal bodies were pursued. As a result of the 1980 debt crisis, the federal government was no longer able to cope financially with the spiraling demand for urban services. This prompted a major policy shift in favor of a "controlled" decentralization.

In 1983, an amendment to Article 115 of the Constitution was heralded as a major step in this direction because it aimed at granting municipalities greater autonomy from federal and state control. The amendment granted municipalities responsibility for basic urban services, provided them with greater financial resources, and for the first time made proportional representation obligatory in order to introduce a semblance of multiparty democracy in local government.

The impact of the constitutional reform was disappointing. Federal and state government continued to determine local investment priorities for basic urban services. Financial independence for local government did not materialize. Instead, control over municipalities shifted from the federal government to the state government, although the degree of municipal subordination remained the same (Rodríguez, 1992:136). Although opposition political parties began to contest municipal elections following the introduction of proportional representation, local democracy continued to be denied through the widespread use of vote rigging by the PRI.

In 1989 the Programa Nacional de Solidaridad (PRONASOL), a massive social investment program, was established as part of the federal government's antipoverty strategy designed to fill the social deficit caused by the introduction of neoliberal reforms. Solidarity, as the program became known, introduced a new thrust to the overall decentralization program, especially through its municipal subprogram, Fondos Municipales de Solidaridad, which provided grants for social welfare and agricultural and basic infrastructure projects. By 1992 Solidarity's expenditure represented 1.1 percent of Mexico's gross domestic product.

ORGANIZATIONAL STRUCTURE

Mexican local government, known as the *ayuntamiento,* comprises a unipersonal executive head, or mayor (presidente municipal), a legal officer (síndico), and a legislature consisting of between five and twenty councillors (regidores) depending on the population size of the municipality. All municipal officeholders are elected for three-year nonrenewable terms. There is no separate election of the mayor. Instead, officeholders are elected collectively according to a closed party list through systems of proportional representation that vary from state to state. The candidate who heads the list of the party that gains the most votes becomes the mayor. The runner-up becomes the síndico, who acts as a watchdog on the executive, countersigning all expenditure vouchers and having the right to inspect all executive reports. Councillors have a supervisory function, each being allocated a responsibility to oversee a specific area of the administration. The fact that the mayor and councillors are elected on a common party list acts as an integrating force, and the separation between executive and deliberative power is not as clear-cut as in most Latin American countries. Integration among tiers of government is also tight—in practice the vast majority of mayors owe their election to the support of either the president of the republic or the state governor (Batley:21).

FUNCTIONAL RESPONSIBILITIES

In contrast to most Latin American countries, in Mexico there is a high degree of coordination among different tiers of government in the provision of services. The duplication, competition, and lack of vertical coordination found elsewhere is virtually nonexistent. This situation reflects the extreme subordination of municipalities within the Mexican political system. State governments have no functions exclusively reserved for them in the Constitution, but within their own constitutions they can define the distribution of functions between themselves and their municipalities. For decades considerable legal ambiguity regarding the specific services for which local government had exclusive responsibility enabled the gradual encroachment by federal and state-level institutions into service provision at the local level.

The 1983 amendment of Article 115 of the Constitution for the first time specified those public services for which municipalities had prime responsibility. These included water supply and sewerage, cleaning, roads, parks, urban transportation, slaughterhouses, markets, cemeteries, public lighting, police, and traffic police. The amendment also empowered municipalities to carry out land use planning, development control, and environmental protection. In practice, however, municipal dependence on state government often leads to the de facto performance of many of these functions by state governments. This is especially so in the case of water supply, land use planning, local road construction, and the collection of local taxes (Batley:29). Local government involvement in basic education and primary health care remains slight. Until the 1980s these were primarily federal functions. By 1987 responsibility for primary and teacher education had been fully transferred to the state level, and by 1994 responsibility for health services had been transferred to fourteen states.

Municipal subordination to state government is reinforced by the present legal framework (Massolo, 1993:208–209). Municipal administration is the outcome of state laws that define their municipal statutes in accordance with state-level municipal codes. State congresses can suspend a municipal administration for failure to discharge its duties. Municipalities may legislate only in a manner backed up by a state or federal law. For example, municipalities cannot vary the rates of their own taxes or user charges, and municipal borrowing requires the approval of the state government.

Municipalities discharge their functions either by direct provision, through a decentralized federal government agency, or, as in the case of water supply, by agreement with a state government agency. With the general exception of investment projects, the use of private contractors is less common than elsewhere in Latin America, although passenger road transportation is largely operated by private companies.

Within Mexico's corporativist political system, local government is an integral part of the national planning system. Local-level plans are formulated by municipal planning committees (*comités de planeación del desarrollo municipal*) within guidelines established by the national development plan and according to priorities established by the respective state planning bodies. Despite the rhetoric of coordination, cooperation, and participation, in practice this operational system greatly restricts municipal autonomy. Three federal bodies—the Ministry of Finance, the comptroller-general's office, and the Ministry of Social Development—closely monitor municipal activities to ensure that they conform with centrally determined priorities. The existence of municipal development plans gives a false view of the extent of municipal autonomy. The financial and administrative capacity to implement activities established by such plans depends crucially upon "development agreements" (*convenios de desarrollo social,* or CDSs) between federal and state authorities. A 1992 survey of planning officers in sixteen municipalities in the State of Mexico revealed that such municipal plans were rarely used as a basis for decisionmaking (Hernández and Mejía:21). Instead, key decisions are made through the complex and concealed process of bargaining known as *concertación,* which continues to be a dominating feature of central-local relations in Mexico.

PERSONNEL SYSTEM

In 1991 there were an estimated 113,000 municipal employees, accounting for 2.6 percent of total public sector employment (including state corporations and the social security system) in the country. Because of the modest functions of Mexican local government, municipal staffing levels are low by Latin American standards—in 1991 the Municipality of Campeche had 121 inhabitants per employee, and the Municipality of Hermosillo had 192 inhabitants per employee (Batley:46–47).

There are three basic categories of municipal employees. Virtually all senior management and policymakers occupy confidence posts at the discretion of the mayor, and they lack security of tenure. Skilled technical officers are recruited on short-term contracts to fulfill specific tasks within the three-year municipal cycle. Routine administrative and unskilled workers are recruited to so-called basic posts in which they have a high degree of job security. Their system of recruitment is not systematic, they have no guaranteed salary or career progression, and there is no performance assessment or reward for merit.

The share of confidence posts in total staff numbers varies enormously among municipalities, ranging between 5 and 57 percent (Batley:44). Generally, smaller municipalities have higher proportions of confidence posts. Staff occupying confidence posts circulate among state and municipal administrations, decentralized public sector agencies, and regional offices of the federal government, and their career progression is dictated by attachment to political leaders with whom they are linked by a network of personal contacts. Leaders take their followers in a zigzag career among organizations (Batley:45).

There is great variation in municipal salary levels. Larger municipalities pay salaries comparable with those in state government. At the other end of the scale, small municipalities are sometimes obliged to employ senior citizens because they cannot afford to pay the statutory minimum wage. In the State of Yucatán all municipalities pay the same scales laid down by the state government. By contrast, in the State of Mexico, each municipality decides its own salary levels.

FINANCIAL STRUCTURE

The highly centralized system of government in Mexico is reflected in the distribution of taxing powers among tiers of government. In 1984, 93 percent of all public sector revenue was collected by the federal government. Spending powers have been redistributed somewhat in recent years as part of the decentralization program. As a result, the share of local government in total public sector expenditure rose from 2.3 percent in 1980 to 4.0 percent in 1990. Local government obtains its income from a combination of federal government transfers (known as participaciones), discretionary grants, and locally generated revenue. The transfers derive from revenue-sharing agreements with central government and state government that were consolidated in a major tax reform in 1980. The share of central government transfers in total municipal income rose sharply thereafter, from an average of 17 percent in 1976–1980 to 58 percent in 1984–1986 (INEGI:65), falling again slightly to around 52 percent by 1990.

The 1980 tax law distributes federal revenues among states and municipalities through three mechanisms. First, there is a general fund, the Fondo General de Participaciones (FGP), which comprises a share of general federal tax revenue that has risen from 13 percent in 1980 to 21 percent by 1994. The FGP is distributed to states on the following criteria: 45.17 percent on the basis of state population, 45.17 percent on the basis of state contribution to federal tax receipts, and 9.66 percent in inverse proportion to the receipt per head of each state resulting from the first two criteria. The redistributive coefficient (i.e., the third percentage value) is designed to provide a minor corrective to the disparities of the origin basis coefficient (the second percentage value). Second, there is a tax on vehicle ownership that is collected by the federal government, but all of the proceeds from it are received by state governments. Third, there is a municipal development fund, the Fondo de Fomento Municipal (FFM), comprising 1 percent of general federal tax revenue; it is exclusively destined for municipalities. In order to provide an incentive for local tax effort, FFM funds are distributed preferentially to municipalities in those states where the collection of municipal property tax and water charges has risen fastest. Under the 1980 tax law, states must in turn distribute among their municipalities at least 20 percent of their allocations from both the FGP and the tax on vehicle ownership, as well as 100 percent of the allocations from the FFM. There is also special provision for the direct sharing with sixty frontier municipalities of revenue from foreign trade taxes.

By comparison with previous arrangements under which municipalities were totally dependent on the funds that state legislatures decided to allocate to them, the greater transparency built into the 1980 tax reform has strengthened municipal finances. Disbursements are made according to a preestablished calendar, and state governments must reallocate federal funds assigned to municipalities within five days of receipt, without deductions for administrative expenses. In theory, the allocations received by municipalities as transfers are not earmarked and may be used according to locally determined (rather than state government) priorities.

Nevertheless, although the federal law stipulates that municipalities must receive a minimum of 20 percent of the FGP transfer received by each state, the criteria for allocating this share among municipalities is a matter exclusively for state legislation. In practice, the criteria differ considerably from state to state, with population size, relative poverty, and tax effort being among the most common factors used. In the States of Puebla and Coahuila, the transfer is almost exclusively based on population size. In the States of Nayarit and Colima, the municipalities of the state capitals automatically receive 39 percent and 34 percent, respectively. And in the States of Chihuahua, Campeche, and Durango, there is no stated formula at all (INDETEC:41–53).

This absence of any common nationwide criteria for the allocation of resources from states to municipalities increases the potential for political favoritism (Gershberg:15). In practice, many state legislatures do use arbitrary and subjective political judgments in deciding on the allocation of transfers among municipalities. This practice has been heavily criticized. State governments are accused of not distributing the transfers in cash and instead retaining part for state-selected and -executed projects at the municipal level. Similarly, the importance given to tax origin in a number of state formulas has been criticized for the distortions it produces at the municipal level. The tendency for people to commute to work across municipal boundaries means that revenues, especially for value-added tax, accrue in the municipalities where those people work and not in those where they live.

In addition to these revenue-sharing transfers, local government also receives investment grants from the federal and state government. The regional development budget of the federal government finances local projects through the CDSs, with matching contributions from state budgets. Municipalities may be parties to these agreements, contributing a share of the cost of the project in the form of communal labor, local materials, and technical supervision. Some states have parallel programs financed entirely from their own and municipal budgets.

Since 1989 the Solidarity program has provided municipalities with another source of federal transfers, for both investment and recurrent costs of local projects. Because Solidarity transfers are distributed directly to municipalities, they offer greater freedom from the kind of arbitrary interference by state governments associated with the participaciones. The fact that municipalities are not required to provide matching funds is an added advantage of the Solidarity program. By 1992 Solidarity represented the major source of investment funding for most municipalities.

As a result of the increasing dependence on fast-growing transfers from federal revenue sharing and grants, municipal tax effort declined sharply during the 1980s, and municipal own income remained static in real terms. Property taxation remains by far the major source of locally generated revenue. Other less significant sources include a mixed bag of fees, charges, and fines, referred to variously as *derechos, productos,* and *aprovechamientos.*

Property tax was previously collected by state governments, and the extent to which proceeds were distributed to local government was left entirely to the discretion of each state. The 1983 amendment to Article 115 of the Constitution transferred the collection and retention of property tax receipts to municipalities. Two major problems have arisen as a result. First, rates of municipal taxation, fees, and charges are still determined by state governments, which are usually very keen to hold down tax rates for political reasons. Findings from a study of four states (Querétaro, Tlaxcala, Campeche, and Nuevo León) show that municipal property tax yields had declined sharply in real terms since 1983, that the proportion of tax bills paid was less than 40 percent, and that there had been no general revaluation since the 1970s (IHS:15). Given the inability of municipalities to adjust property tax rates, to reassess property values, or to index property values against inflation (all of which require state approval), it is not surprising that the real value of property tax receipts fell sharply during the 1980s. Second, the lack of municipal infrastructure for tax collection, in particular the widespread absence of up-to-date property cadastres, has obliged most smaller municipalities to make collaborative agreements with their state government for the assessment and collection of property taxation. The charge for this service can be exorbitant, often amounting to as much as 30 percent of the gross value of tax receipts.

Borrowing by large municipalities is more common than in the rest of Latin America. The federal public works bank, BANOBRAS, has had a long-standing credit program for municipal development, although with a history of cumbersome procedures and a loan portfolio based on political rather than financial criteria (Gershberg:31, 34). In the past its heavily subsidized lending program focused on low-cost housing, water supply systems, and the construction of markets and slaughterhouses. The introduction of near-market interest rates since 1988 has seen a switch toward providing credit for improvement of municipal property cadastres. Municipal borrowing has been severely limited by the unwritten but almost universally applied rule that incoming administrations should not be faced with debt repayments on borrowing incurred by their predecessors. In practice, this restricts borrowing to a maximum three-year repayment period (IHS:26–27).

States exercise strict financial control over municipalities under their jurisdiction. They control the right to levy local taxes and the extent of external subsidy, and they must approve all increases in municipal tariffs and user charges. A state auditor's office can annul municipal expenditure that it considers illegal or contrary to the public good. Federal and state treasury departments retain a joint office at the municipal level that operates a supervisory control over local government expenditure. A 1991 study of municipal financial officers in fifteen municipalities in the State of Mexico shows that this municipal audit function was basically corrective rather than preventive, and was geared toward legal vigilance rather than providing support and guidance to local government in better management practices (Medina and Mejía:29).

INTERMUNICIPAL COOPERATION

Because of the highly centralized political system, there is little tradition of intermunicipal cooperation in Mexico, and no national municipal association exists. Although the 1983 constitutional reform specifically empowered municipalities to form associations to discharge functions jointly, in practice this rarely happens (World Bank:23). State governments usually discourage intermunicipal cooperation, which they see as a threat to their own continued intervention in municipal affairs.

SUPPORT SERVICES

Systematic training provision for Mexican local government staff did not begin until the 1970s, when the State of Mexico began to offer the first such courses and the State of Guerrero undertook a program of municipal strengthening. By the 1990s, a variety of federal institutions were providing technical assistance to municipalities. Foremost among these are two institutions. The Instituto para el Desarrollo Técnico de las Haciendas Públicas (INDETEC), a public finance institution sponsored jointly by the federal and state secretariats of finance, provides state-level courses on fiscal and financial administration for the public sector as a whole. The Centro Nacional de Desarrollo Municipal (CNDM), a branch of the federal Ministry of the Interior, was set up in 1984 and publishes manuals and guidelines for state legislation and municipal regulations. The CNDM is connected with state-level branches by a sophisticated nationwide municipal geographic information system. Other institutions providing training support for municipalities include the Instituto Nacional de Administración Pública (INAP) and the municipal department of BANOBRAS. At the state level, training is often available in specific areas of municipal administration from professional associations, universities, and colleges. The availability varies from state to state and depends largely on the interest of the respective state government.

CITIZEN PARTICIPATION

Since the Mexican Revolution of 1910, the country's corporativist political system has strongly influenced the nature of citizen participation in local government. Provision has long existed for the establishment of submunicipal local area offices, known variously as *comisarías* and delegaciones. These offices are headed by officials appointed by the mayor, and they operate as conduits for local demands and the disbursement of patronage. Citizen participation in local government, which is channeled through these structures, takes the form of neighborhood groups (juntas de vecinos), which are sometimes grouped in municipal-wide consultative committees. All these semiofficial community organizations operate under the strict supervision and guidance of the municipal authorities.

The Solidarity program introduced in 1989 highlighted the role of participation by the urban and rural poor in the selection and implementation of projects for whom they are designed. The Fondos Municipales de Solidaridad, a municipally controlled fund using voluntary labor, is a significant subprogram within Solidarity, which was operating in 87 percent of all municipalities in the country by 1992. Under this program, citizen participation is mobilized for small-scale physical infrastructure, social welfare, and productive investment projects. It is administered by local committees, *consejos municipales de Solidaridad,* which are made up of municipal authorities. These committees liaise with the citizen groups (*comités locales de Solidaridad*) that generate projects for consideration. Although these citizen groups are nominally independent, projects are to a large extent still generated and selected through official processes and the PRI.

PROSPECTS FOR LOCAL GOVERNMENT

There is no tradition in Mexico of independent local government as found, to varying degrees, elsewhere in Latin America. Municipal administration still operates as an integral part of a centralized system of government dominated by the PRI. Local autonomy is extremely limited, and municipalities are highly dependent financially on the federal government and, in the exercise of powers, on state government. The impressive degree of functional integration among tiers of government is a product of the one-party model. Multiparty democracy is gradually being introduced into local government, and a growing number of municipalities are now controlled by opposition parties. This has led to a noticeable demand by mayors for greater political autonomy. If this process continues, local government is indeed likely to assume a new vitality.

In recent years, controlled decentralization has been introduced by the federal government in order to bolster the faltering legitimacy of its centralist political system. Although federal and state governments remain very much involved at the local level, under the Solidarity program, municipalities are for the first time receiving investment funds directly from the federal government, thereby potentially loosening their ties to state government. It remains to be seen whether this will lead to the empowerment of local government, or whether it forms part of an overall project of sustained political control from the center (Rodríguez, 1993:136).

22

NICARAGUA

Nicaragua is a unitary nation divided for administrative purposes into nine regions and fifteen departments. Below the department level, the country is divided into 143 municipalities. The capital city of Managua had a population of 974,000 in 1992, equivalent to 33 percent of the national total, but it lacks any metropolitan government. In 1929 it was declared a national district. Thereafter, it was directly administered by a central government ministry specially created for that purpose until 1989, when its municipal status was reinstated. Larger municipalities may be subdivided for administrative purpose into districts, of which the Municipality of Managua has seven.

As with the rest of Latin America, there is an enormous disparity in population size among municipalities. In 1992 only twelve municipalities had more than 50,000 inhabitants, another forty-six had between 20,000 and 50,000 inhabitants, thirty-four had between 10,000 and 20,000 inhabitants, and the remaining fifty-one municipalities, equivalent to 36 percent of the total, had fewer than 10,000 inhabitants.

HISTORICAL DEVELOPMENT

Although local government legislation in 1901 granted formal autonomy to municipalities, their role was reduced to a minimum by the extremely weak development of the Nicaraguan state until the 1950s. From 1937 to 1979, local government suffered the additional misfortune of the Somoza regime. This autocratic political system was highly centralized and enforced its control by military repression. Under the 1939 Constitution, municipal elections were abolished, and elected officeholders were replaced by presidential appointees. In 1963 municipal autonomy was officially recognized once again, although local government remained under the strict supervision of central government.

Although elections were reintroduced, municipal officeholders were invariably wealthy landowners or businessmen who received power and illicit income in exchange for mobilizing political support for the Somoza regime at the local level. The National District of Managua remained under the direct control of a presidentially appointed chief executive and had no legislative body.

Strict supervision of local government was carried out through a national audit office and the municipal services department of the Ministry of the Interior, which had to approve municipal budgets and which exercised control over the planning and implementation of all projects at the local level. Local government had no right of appeal against decisions made by central government.

In 1979 a popular insurrection led by the Frente Sandinista de Liberación Nacional (FSLN, or the Sandinistas) overthrew the Somoza regime. The FSLN quickly recognized the municipal reconstruction juntas (juntas municipales de reconstrucción, or JMRs) that had sprung up throughout the country to replace the corrupt municipal officials, who invariably fled in the wake of Somoza's defeat. The JMRs were made up of three to five members, usually prominent local citizens who had participated in the struggle against Somoza. JMR members were ratified by popular assemblies for an unspecified term of office. Each JMR was headed by a salaried coordinator (coordinador) chosen from among its membership. A secretariat for municipal affairs (Secretaría de Asuntos Municipales, or SAMU), with ministerial rank, was created in October 1979 in order to coordinate the activities of the JMRs.

The precise role of local government became the subject of intense debate during the Sandinista government. A traditional view, reinforced by orthodox Marxists within the FSLN, was that local government should be limited to a minor role in the delivery of basic services. According to this view, a major role should be assigned to central government agencies, which had already begun to expand their activities throughout the country in order to further the social objectives of the revolution.

Alternatively, grassroots organizations argued that the role of local government should be expanded to plan, coordinate, and evaluate all activities by state agencies within its area of jurisdiction. This perception of local government had been strongly influenced by the de facto powers exercised by the newly established JMRs during the final phase of the popular insurrection against Somoza. Such a view was strengthened by growing reports from SAMU that the highly centralized decisionmaking and lack of intersectoral coordination among central government agencies in the field was leading to poor delivery of basic services.

The regionalization program initiated in 1982, which was motivated by military considerations because of the growing external threat from U.S.-government-sponsored counterrevolutionaries (Rodríguez, 1991:53), involved a process of administrative deconcentration. It appeared at first to have settled the argument over the role of local government. Nine administrative regions were created: six regions (each composed of two to four departments) and three special zones (all on the Atlantic Coast). Presidentially appointed governors (delegados) with ministerial rank coordinated the activities of state agencies in each region, and key ministries were required to deconcentrate their activities through the appointment of regional heads. By 1985 each governor was also the head of the regional committee of the ruling party, the FSLN.

Far from strengthening municipal autonomy, the regionalization program removed the de facto power that JMRs had exercised over the activities of state agencies in the larger municipalities. A major consequence of the program was the abolition of SAMU, whose advocacy role had been so crucial for generating support of local government. SAMU was replaced by a new secretariat for regional coordination (known as the SCR), which served as a liaison between the presidential office and the governors. The SCR had no responsibility for local government affairs and delegated that function entirely to regional governments. As a result, local government was left without any powerful national institution to speak on its behalf. Instead municipalities were subject to the regional secretariats that oversaw their activities.

The new regional administrations were accountable neither to the JMRs at the municipal level nor to grassroots organizations. Their degree of concern for local government varied greatly. Some regions supported a municipal role in government, but others treated local government as largely irrelevant. In all cases, municipal governments had less authority than during the 1979–1982 period because their broader functions were absorbed by the new regional structure. The nadir in local government autonomy was reached in 1983–1984 with the creation of subregional administrative zones. Zonal chiefs simply regarded municipalities as the lowest administrative tier of government. Coupled with the virtual extinction of the JMRs, this led to the obliteration of local government autonomy.

A reaction soon set in, prompted by the growing alienation of the population from central government. From 1985 the gradual demise of the top-down development strategy pursued hitherto by the FSLN led to the abandonment of the regional planning structures. A highly critical survey of municipalities carried out in 1986 led to a growing recognition within the Sandinista government of the importance of local government. These policy shifts were reflected in the abolition of the SCR and its replacement by a directorate for municipal and regional affairs (Dirección General de Asuntos

Municipales y Regionales, or DAMUR). Over the next five years (1986–1990) DAMUR spearheaded a major program for municipal strengthening in Nicaragua, which represented a complete reversal of the highly centralized development strategy pursued from 1979 to 1985. In 1988 this process culminated in the promulgation of a new municipal code, Ley de Municipalidades No. 40.

ORGANIZATIONAL STRUCTURE

Nicaraguan local government comprises a unipersonal executive head, or mayor (alcalde), and a legislature (concejo municipal). These replaced the former coordinators and JMRs following the municipal elections of 1990, the first to be held under the new municipal code. The number of councillors (*consejales proprietarios*) varies from five in municipalities with populations of fewer than 20,000, to ten in municipalities that are departmental headquarters or have a population of more than 20,000, and to twenty in the Municipality of Managua.

Nicaraguan local government is characterized by a system having a weak mayor and a strong council; this system derives from a number of features that are unusual within Latin America. Although each feature dates from the 1963 reforms carried out during the Somoza regime, they were all nevertheless incorporated within the new 1988 municipal code. First, there is no separate election of the executive head. Instead, the mayor is elected indirectly by a simple majority vote from among councillors. Second, councillors are elected for a six-year term of office, the longest in Latin America. Municipal elections are also held at the same time as national elections, thereby diverting voter attention away from local issues and toward national electoral considerations. Third, the mayor is elected for only a two-year term of office and may be removed by a majority vote of councillors. This has led to considerable administrative instability. Between February 1990 (when the first municipal elections were held under the new law) and June 1992, seventy-three attempts were made by councillors to remove mayors, with nineteen cases proving successful (Ortega:51). Fourth, unlike in most of Latin America, the electoral system is not based on proportional representation. In the case of Managua, departmental capitals, and other municipalities with more than 20,000 inhabitants, the party that wins the largest number of votes automatically receives half plus one of the council seats, with the remaining seats divided among the other parties according to their share of the vote. In the case of municipalities with fewer than 20,000 inhabitants, the party that obtains the largest number of votes automatically receives three council seats, and the two remaining seats go to the party that receives the second-highest vote.

FUNCTIONAL RESPONSIBILITIES

The 1980 law that recognized the JMRs assigned a wide range of functions to municipalities in pursuit of the general objective of promoting local economic development. These functions included health care, education, sanitation and civil registration, tax collection, bus terminals, markets, road construction and maintenance, cemeteries, and recreational facilities, as well as the provision of basic infrastructure such as water, sewerage, and electricity. The rapid expansion of central government activities throughout the country, however, almost immediately negated the thrust of the 1980 law, as newly created ministries and state corporations assumed growing responsibility for many of the above-mentioned services. This process was facilitated by the low technical and financial capacity of the JMRs themselves. An early attempt to resolve this problem by the formation of regional program-coordinating committees, bringing together state agencies and delegates from JMRs and popular organizations, proved abortive because powerful ministries virtually ignored them.

The 1988 municipal code gave only a vague definition of municipal functions. It distinguished between competencies that were solely the responsibility of municipalities themselves and those that were to be shared with other, undefined tiers of government. It did not state which municipal competencies were obligatory. The fifteen functions granted to municipalities were limited in scope and excluded any responsibility for basic services such as public transportation, water and sewerage, health care, or education. In practice many municipalities undertake functions not specified in the 1988 code, such as the construction of schools and primary health care centers, water supply systems, libraries, restoration of historical monuments, and the promotion of cooperatives and handicrafts.

Ambiguity in the definition of the respective responsibilities of central and local government has contributed to a double neglect of basic service provision, both by municipalities, which are not legally required to fulfill certain basic functions, and by central government, which is not obliged to provide sufficient funding for such functions. By 1989 only forty-two municipalities were providing six basic services (solid waste management, street cleaning, parks, cemeteries, slaughterhouses, and markets), and ninety-four provided two, three, or four of these services. Seven municipalities provided no services at all. Only half of all municipalities carried out solid waste management, and only one-fourth operated markets (Rodríguez, 1993:58). Water supply and sewerage remain the responsibility of a state corporation, INAA. In response to intense dissatisfaction with INAA, in 1991 an experiment in municipal water provision began in the Municipality of Matagalpa and surrounding municipalities.

PERSONNEL SYSTEM

In 1994 there were an estimated 6,754 municipal employees, accounting for 9 percent of total public sector employment. The Municipality of Managua accounted for 32 percent of total municipal employment. The 1979 Sandinista revolution had led to an almost total turnover of municipal staff. Almost without exception, the JMRs were composed of citizens with no previous experience in local government, and only 5 percent of the administrative employees whom they oversaw had worked under the Somoza regime (Downs, 1987:365). Yet the JMRs were assigned the daunting tasks of recovery and rehabilitation of the local economy after the damage caused by the war. At the same time, they had to redirect local government priorities to meet the new social and political demands of the population. Foremost among these was the demand for popular involvement in local government policymaking. The lack of administrative experience, combined with pressing demands from the local population, who viewed the JMRs as responsible for all that occurred in their municipalities, led to a rapid turnover of JMR membership. Many left to occupy administrative posts within the municipality itself, leaving the coordinator as the executive head. As a result, replacements were chosen from among leading activists of the many popular organizations that had arisen during the revolution. This led to a complete transformation in the social composition of local government. In stark contrast to the Somoza period, municipal government was now controlled by those who represented the aspirations of the broad majority of the poor. By 1981 the lack of trained personnel and the enormous demands placed upon local government led to a situation in which 90 percent of JMR members held full-time administrative posts and represented 40 percent of administrative staff (Downs, 1987:368).

FINANCIAL STRUCTURE

Local government finances remained very weak during the Somoza regime. Limited income came from some locally generated taxes and fees, an origin-based revenue-sharing agreement for gasoline and tobacco taxes, and irregular and discretionary central government grants. The Municipality of Managua absorbed the lion's share of municipal income, accounting for 74 percent of the total in 1975. Over half of its income came from a 1 percent sales tax levied within its jurisdiction.

Municipal finances were greatly strengthened during the Sandinista government. During the early years, direct transfers from central government became an important source of municipal income as significant amounts of foreign aid were channeled through SAMU for reconstruction of the war-damaged economy. SAMU set up a revolving fund for municipal development, FODEMU, to provide soft loans to municipalities for investment projects. These transfers remained ad hoc, and the JMRs were unable to prepare municipal budgets on the assumption of a regular flow of funds from central government. In 1981, 40 percent of all municipalities had total projected incomes of under U.S.$4,000, and 67 percent had projected incomes of less than U.S.$10,000. Roughly half of all projected income came from local taxes, one-quarter from local user fees (especially markets and slaughterhouses) and the remainder from a variety of sources, including central government transfers (Downs, 1987:372).

In the second half of the decade, central government transfers were severely curtailed because of a growing economic crisis. Between 1986 and 1990, only 14 percent of municipal income derived from central government transfers (Rodríguez, 1993:16). The only exception was Managua, which as late as 1989 still received 62 percent of its income from a central government transfer that was ten times the size of the combined transfer received by all other municipalities in the country. This situation was in marked contrast to most other Latin American countries, where capital cities invariably displayed a much greater reliance on own sources of revenue than other municipalities. Nevertheless, the income of other municipalities grew more rapidly than that of Managua, so that the latter's share of total municipal income had fallen to 35 percent by 1989. In 1990 two revenue-sharing agreements with central government—for 2.5 percent of the proceeds from fuel tax and for 2 percent of receipts from electricity charges—were abolished. As a result, by 1992 transfers to local government had fallen to only 1 percent of municipal income.

A major municipal tax reform was introduced from 1986 onward. The anachronistic system whereby municipalities had to draw up a detailed annual schedule of local taxes and service charges for approval by central government, known as the plan de arbitrios, was finally abolished. Instead, the tax schedule was simplified and universalized, first at a regional level and subsequently throughout the whole country by 1988, with the sole exception of Managua. Most municipal taxes were replaced by a single sales tax levied at a standard rate of 2 percent (and at 1 percent on unprocessed agricultural goods). Municipal tax registers were established to improve collection rates.

As a result of the reforms, larger municipalities experienced a rapid growth in own revenue, and this more than offset the decline in central government transfers. It also enabled these municipalities to maintain tax buoyancy during a period of hyperinflation from 1987 to 1990. Overall, the share of municipal income in total public sector income rose to an average of 13 percent during 1986–1990, one of the highest shares in Central America (Rodríguez, 1993:15). And in 1991 municipal finances were strengthened even further by the transfer from central government of responsibility for three major sources of fiscal revenue: the vehicle road tax and business licenses (both of which had once been under municipal control) and the property tax (which had hitherto always been a central government tax). By 1992 Nicaraguan local government derived a higher share of its income from own sources of revenue (94 percent) than almost any country in Latin America.

Although the municipal tax reform significantly increased the financial strength of larger municipalities, it weakened the finances of the vast majority of poorer municipalities, where about 25 percent of the population still lived. These municipalities were unable to counter the virtual disappearance of central government transfers, a key feature of the reforms, with own revenue sources because they lacked the economic base to generate significant revenues from a vehicle road tax, sales tax, or property taxation. This led to growing disparities in municipal expenditure per head between richer and poorer municipalities. In 1992 mayors proposed that 6 percent of central government revenue should be transferred to local government, to be allocated preferentially to poorer municipalities, but this was rebuffed by central government.

INTERMUNICIPAL COOPERATION

There is no national association of municipalities in Nicaragua. During the Sandinista government, SAMU encouraged the formation of intermunicipal associations in each department. Departmental councils were also established, made up of JMR coordinators and field representatives of central government ministries. Central government officials, however, proved hostile to this initiative.

SUPPORT SERVICES

The lack of experience of local government employees appointed following the Sandinista revolution soon meant that even the most basic administrative procedures were not followed. A key role of SAMU was to provide technical assistance to municipalities. The training of municipal staff in project identification and formulation became a major priority. In 1985 DAMUR replaced SAMU as the major institution offering technical assistance to local government. In February 1990, DAMUR was replaced by the newly created Instituto Nicaragüense de Fomento Municipal (INIFOM). Unlike its predecessors, INIFOM comes under the firm control of municipalities, which appoint thirty-four of the forty members on the institute's board of directors.

CITIZEN PARTICIPATION

In the early years of the Sandinista government, popular municipal development councils were established to provide a formal channel of communication between the JMRs and local citizens. In some municipalities public assemblies were also held, modeled on the style of the cabildo abierto. Many JMRs regarded these assemblies as counterproductive so long as municipalities still lacked the legal autonomy and financial resources to meet the pressing demands that were expressed.

Given the limited local financial resources and the growing unreliability of central government transfers, the capacity of municipalities to bring about material improvement in living standards was largely determined by the extent to which they were able to mobilize poorer communities to undertake voluntary labor input in capital investment projects. In this way, local government often played a crucial intermediary role between state agencies and the grassroots organizations that supported the FSLN.

Citizen participation in local government was eventually institutionalized in the 1988 municipal code. This required mayors to convene at least two cabildos a year—one to consider the municipal budget and another to review its implementation. In addition, the mayor was empowered to establish consultative bodies, known as popular municipal councils (*consejos populares municipales*), as a means of ensuring citizen participation in local government. In 1991 a survey of fifty-one municipalities revealed that over half had not yet held a cabildo despite the legal requirement to do so, and that only 40 percent had set up popular municipal councils (Ortega:53).

PROSPECTS FOR LOCAL GOVERNMENT

The turbulent experience of the Sandinista government from 1979 to 1990 had a galvanizing effect on local government in Nicaragua. For a short time, the degree of citizen participation in local government was unsurpassed in the rest of Latin America. Local government was strengthened as a consequence of a major fiscal reform program. Despite its electoral defeat in 1990, the Sandinista government left an important legacy in the form of the widespread political consensus that recognized the importance of local government in the development process. Combined with strengthened municipal finances and a tradition of citizen participation, this legacy bodes well for the future development of local government.

A 1991 municipal survey revealed a high degree of arbitrary behavior by mayors who failed to consult with, and were unaccountable to, both councillors and local citizens. This behavior was all the more surprising given that mayors may be dismissed at any moment by councillors (Ortega:53). The findings of this chapter suggest that clientelist practices may continue to hamper the development of local government for some years to come despite the significant improvements that have been made.

23

PANAMA

Panama is a unitary nation divided for administrative purposes into nine provinces. Below the province level, the country is covered by sixty-seven districts, each of which has municipal status, including one (San Blas) that has special status as an Indian reservation. Provincial governors are appointed by the president of the republic and have a limited brief to supervise the municipalities under their area of jurisdiction through a provincial coordinating council made up of municipal representatives. At the submunicipal level there are 510 electoral wards (corregimientos), as well as neighborhood-based administrative units that are variously referred to as *regidurías,* barrios, and *comisarías.* There is no metropolitan government in the capital, Panama City.

There is considerable variation in population size among municipalities. In 1985 only three municipalities had more than 100,000 inhabitants, nine had between 20,000 and 100,000 inhabitants, and the remaining fifty-five municipalities each had fewer than 20,000 inhabitants.

HISTORICAL DEVELOPMENT

Panama has historically had a highly centralized system of government. Both the 1941 and 1972 Constitutions severely restricted municipal autonomy, defining the functions of local government as essentially administrative. This restricted constitutional role for local government has overridden the political autonomy granted to it by the 8 October 1973 municipal code, Ley sobre Régimen Municipal No. 106. The 1972 Constitution empowered the national legislature to decide whether the municipal executive head should be either a central government appointee or an elected mayor. From 1972 to 1994, the executive head was selected by councillors from a slate of three

candidates presented to them by central government. Under this arrangement, executive heads were effectively appointed by the president of the
republic, thereby highlighting their primary role as the local representatives
of central government in the area of public security. Nevertheless, during the
1970s Panamanian local government was described as having a "weak
mayor" system in which the council held considerable power (Alder-
fer:273). For example, it was not the executive head, but the council president, elected from among councillors, who chaired council sessions. In
1994, though, this system of appointment was replaced by the direct election
of mayors.

ORGANIZATIONAL STRUCTURE

Local government in Panama, known as the corporación, comprises a
unipersonal executive head, or mayor (alcalde), and a legislature (consejo
municipal). The mayor fulfills a dual role as head of the municipal administration and also as the local representative of the national government. This
latter role has often associated the mayor with acts of political repression
through his or her status as titular head of the local police force. The number of councillors (representantes) ranges between a minimum of five and a
maximum of nineteen (in the case of Panama City). Municipal elections are
held at the same time as presidential and congressional elections, and the
five-year municipal term of office is the same as that of the national legislature. All officeholders may stand for immediate reelection.

The system of election for councillors is unique in Latin America.
Instead of the system of proportional representation found elsewhere, the
municipality is divided for electoral purposes into wards in accordance with
population size. A councillor is elected to represent each ward on a "first
past the post" basis, as in the Anglo-Saxon tradition.

FUNCTIONAL RESPONSIBILITIES

The 1972 Constitution did not mandate municipal autonomy; this is unusual for Latin America. Instead it assigned municipalities a purely administrative role in the development process, which was to be carried out in association with central government. This subordinate relationship was reflected
in the 1973 municipal code. This authorized municipalities to carry out a
wide range of functions including public works, public utility services,
health and welfare services, planning and urban development, education,
markets, street cleaning, sports facilities, and libraries, as well as the formulation of local development policies. But these activities could be carried

out only in collaboration with and with the advice of the Ministry of Planning.

A lack of funds and trained personnel prevents local government from carrying out most of these assigned functions, and central government provides almost all basic local services. The Ministry of Public Works has almost complete responsibility for highways and roads within municipal boundaries. It also regulates the services and tariffs for gas, electricity, and telephone utilities, and it even carries out solid waste management in the two largest municipalities (Panama City and Colón). Health and education are administered entirely by central government ministries. A housing and urbanization institute plans and implements low-income housing projects. An institute for water and sewage provides water supply and sewerage facilities in all urban and metropolitan areas. And an institute for hydraulics and electrification produces electricity for municipalities and is responsible for all public lighting.

PERSONNEL SYSTEM

In 1989 there were 5,061 municipal employees, accounting for 7.9 percent of total public sector employment in the country. There is no municipal career system, and clientelism strongly influences the recruitment of personnel. A survey of municipal employees carried out in 1987 by the Ministry of Planning and Economy revealed that 55 percent had changed jobs during the previous twelve months.

FINANCIAL STRUCTURE

Local government finances in Panama are very weak by comparison with the rest of Latin America, and contrary to the regional trend, they became even weaker during the period 1970–1990. By 1991 combined municipal income was equivalent to only 4.7 percent of central government income (González:31). Property taxation is not under municipal control, and locally raised revenue derives principally from construction permits, a vehicle road tax, and a range of eighty licenses, including slaughterhouse and market fees. In 1991 financial transfers from central to local government accounted for less than 1.3 percent of total municipal income and a minuscule 0.05 percent of central government income. These transfers were not allocated according to any clearly defined criteria, and twenty-five municipalities did not receive any transfer at all (González:35). Municipalities do receive indirect funding from central government in the form of an annual investment grant that is uniformly allocated to all 510 submunicipal community boards. In 1991 the combined value of these transfers was twenty-six times greater than the transfer to municipalities (González:37).

INTERMUNICIPAL COOPERATION

Although the municipal code provides for intermunicipal associations, they are extremely rare. A national municipal association, Asociación Panameña de Cooperación Intermunicipal (APCI), was founded in 1954 but functioned for only five years. It was reactivated in 1985 but had ceased functioning by 1994.

SUPPORT SERVICES

There is no government body that provides training, technical assistance, or research in support of local government. In 1992 the Instituto Panameño de Desarrollo Municipal (IPADEM), a nongovernmental organization, was established for these purposes with funding from the Konrad Adenauer Foundation of Germany.

CITIZEN PARTICIPATION

Panama has a nationwide system of citizen participation at the submunicipal level. This system is unique in Latin America, but it is also controversial and has been accused by its critics of being little more than a means of political control. In each of the 510 municipal wards, in addition to the elected councillor, there is a local representative (corregidor) appointed by the mayor, whose duties are primarily those of law and order. Five local citizens appointed by the councillor, together with the corregidor, constitute a community board (junta comunal). This board, which is presided over by the councillor, functions as a miniature unit of local government at the submunicipal level and receives grant funding directly from central government.

At the neighborhood level, there are over 6,000 elected bodies (juntas locales), which liaise with the community board through nominated spokespersons. In coordination with both municipal and central government agencies that provide limited funding, the juntas locales are responsible for mobilizing citizen participation in a wide range of local development activities.

PROSPECTS FOR LOCAL GOVERNMENT

The parallel structures of elected and appointed officers at the provincial, municipal, and ward levels continue to hinder development prospects. This dual system is the outcome of ideological conflict within the armed forces who have ruled Panama for the past two decades. As a result, layer after layer of new laws and procedures have been applied, creating widespread confusion and confrontation at the local level. The creation of IPADEM in 1992 and the introduction of direct election for mayors in 1994 suggest that local government reform is beginning to take place in Panama, and that this process has been strongly influenced by the experience of neighboring countries in Central America. Nevertheless, Panamanian municipalities remain extremely weak, as exemplified by the very limited range of functions they carry out and by the correspondingly low level of finance that is available to them. The overthrow of General Noriega by a U.S. invasion of the country in 1989 did not lead to any major rethinking of central-local relations, and decentralization was not an issue in the 1994 presidential election. Prospects for strengthening local government in the medium term are not bright.

24

PARAGUAY

Paraguay is a unitary nation divided into seventeen departments, each of which has a regional government comprising a directly elected governor and a departmental council. Below the department level, the country is covered by 212 districts, each of which has municipal status. The Municipality of Asunción, the capital city (population 502,426 in 1992) does not belong to a department. The Metropolitan Area of Asunción (Area Metropolitana de Asunción, or AMA) comprises the Municipality of Asunción and ten surrounding municipalities and has a population of 1.3 million. It has no metropolitan government.

There is considerable variation in population size among the 213 municipalities. Only one municipality (Asunción) has a population of more than 500,000, three have between 100,000 and 500,000, nine have between 50,000 and 100,000, thirty-seven have between 20,000 and 50,000, and a further fifty-seven have between 10,000 and 20,000. In addition, 107 municipalities (50 percent of the total) have populations of fewer than 10,000, and fifty municipalities (23 percent of the total) have fewer than 5,000.

HISTORICAL DEVELOPMENT

Until very recently Paraguay was probably the most highly centralized country in Latin America. There are several reasons for this: the perceived threat to national sovereignty resulting from its involvement in two of the three wars fought between Latin American nations in the postindependence period; a generally low density of population that, until the 1970s, was heavily concentrated around the capital city, which retains a virtual monopoly of all major economic and political decisionmaking; and the absence of any strong regional identities based on cultural differences.

The centralist tradition was reflected in early municipal legislation passed in 1882, 1909, and 1927; it was markedly reinforced during the regime of President Stroessner (1954–1989). New central government corporations stripped local government of basic functions, and the ruling Colorado Party was converted into a hierarchical political machine extending down to the submunicipal level. This administrative and political centralization had its legislative counterpart in an electoral code according to which all congressional deputies and senators were elected on the basis of closed party lists to a single national constituency. Under the "majority plus" electoral system, the party obtaining the most votes automatically received two-thirds of seats in the national legislature and municipal councils, and the remaining seats were distributed among the other contesting parties in proportion to their respective shares of the vote. Through a mixture of repression and electoral fraud, the official share of the Colorado Party in the total votes cast in the local government elections held during the Stroessner period actually rose from 72 percent in 1965 to 88 percent in 1985, when, as in the previous four elections, the Colorado Party won control of every municipality. In 51 of the 190 municipalities, no votes at all were recorded for opposition parties.

Modern legislation began with a 1954 municipal code under which the executive head of larger municipalities was appointed by central government. In the smaller municipalities, a council president, elected from among councillors, exercised the executive role. In 1971 a government municipal support agency, the Instituto de Desarrollo Municipal (IDM), was established with the support of foreign aid donors in order to provide credit, training, and technical assistance to local government. In 1987 a new municipal code, Ley Orgánica Municipal No. 1294, was introduced. It divided municipalities (except Asunción) into four categories according to the size of their municipal budgets. The executive head was henceforth appointed by central government in all municipalities, and his or her powers were strengthened vis-à-vis the council.

Local government was granted very low priority during the Stroessner period. Although the number of municipalities doubled from 104 in 1954 to 199 by 1989, this primarily reflected the overriding concern of the regime to maintain political control at the local level during a period of rapid internal population migration to areas of new colonization in the eastern border region of the country.

Local branches of the Colorado Party exercised absolute control over the formal structure of local government. The merging of party and government institutions was such that it became common practice for the same person to hold the post of municipal executive head and head of the Colorado Party branch, either concurrently or consecutively. This arrangement was reinforced by the close identification of the local police force with the

Colorado Party. As a result, the municipality as an institution became widely confused in people's minds with that of the ruling party (Marín, Silvero,
and Sosa:1).

Mismanagement and corruption were rife under this undemocratic system of local government. Municipal office was generally viewed as a mechanism for personal enrichment rather than for displaying civic responsibility. Municipal budgets were rarely published; the granting of municipal
licenses for the operation of slaughterhouses became a lucrative business for
municipal executives; and municipally owned public land was regularly sold
off in flagrant contravention of municipal bylaws. Avenues for citizen participation in municipal affairs were extremely limited. The popular image of
local government was extremely negative, as manifested by high rates of
electoral abstention, widespread evasion of municipal taxes, and generalized
fear of local government authorities.

The overthrow of the Stroessner regime in 1989 led to the introduction
of democracy at the local government level. In May 1991, municipal elections were held under a new electoral code that introduced the direct election of mayors for the first time in Paraguayan history. This reform put an
end to over a century (1882–1991) during which municipal executive heads
were appointed by central government, despite guarantees of municipal
autonomy in successive constitutions. The electoral code also replaced the
undemocratic majority plus system for electing councillors with one involving proportional representation. The elections led to the establishment of a
multiparty system at the local government level after decades in which all
municipalities had been controlled by the Colorado Party. Opposition parties
won control in forty-three municipalities, including Asunción.

ORGANIZATIONAL STRUCTURE

Paraguayan local government comprises a unipersonal executive head, or
mayor (intendente), and a legislature (junta municipal). Municipalities are
divided into four categories depending upon the relative size of their annual budgets, and the number of councillors (concejales) ranges accordingly
between nine and twelve, except for the Municipality of Asunción, which
has twenty-four councillors. All municipal officeholders are elected for a
five-year term of office, but mayors may not stand for immediate reelection.

FUNCTIONAL RESPONSIBILITIES

The 1987 municipal code granted responsibility to local government for
twenty different functions, including urban planning, road construction, reg-

ulation of public transportation, public housing, and employment generation. Water supply and sewerage were also defined as municipal responsibilities in locations where this service is not provided by other government
agencies. The respective competencies of local and central government are
not defined in the code. Instead, the code states that there should be coordination between municipalities and other government agencies in the public
interest.

This lack of definition of municipal authority reflects the highly centralized political system during the Stroessner period, which gave rise to the
proliferation of service delivery activities at the local level by a range of
central government ministries and state enterprises, each one operating independently. Although successive municipal laws referred to local government
involvement in the coordination of service delivery at the local level, in
practice such involvement hardly ever took place. The extreme centralization of service delivery is exemplified by the situation over water supply, for
which two separate state institutions exist. CORPOSANA supplies water for
urban centers with more than 4,000 inhabitants, and SENASA supplies
water for smaller urban centers. SENASA operates through local water
boards set up to represent water users; each municipality has a single representative on its respective local board. A public housing corporation,
CONAVI, was established in 1989 and built over 20,000 low-cost housing
units throughout the country by December 1994. However, it had undertak-
en minimal coordination with municipalities, which were subsequently
obliged to provide road access and installation of basic services.

As a result of centralization, by 1994 local government activities were
limited to a largely ceremonial role, comprising only minimal functions
(essential street cleaning, road repair, cemeteries, and slaughterhouses) and
without any exercise of regulatory functions. In the absence of land use zoning for any municipality, including Asunción, municipal regulation of property development was minimal. The weakness of local government was
highlighted in 1991 when the Supreme Court ruled that the Ministry of
Public Works, not the Municipality of Asunción, was responsible for public
transportation in the AMA.

PERSONNEL SYSTEM

In 1989 there were 5,245 municipal employees, accounting for 4.4 percent
of total public sector employment in the country. This number was barely
double that of the number of executive heads and councillors (2,084). The
Municipality of Asunción alone employed 2,408 staff, 46 percent of the
national total, and thirteen larger municipalities employed a further 1,078
staff. The vast majority of smaller municipalities, totaling 185 in number,

employed a total of only 1,759 staff, equivalent to an average of only nine staff per municipality, the same as their number of local government office-holders (Nickson, 1993:8).

Although the municipal code states that local government should have its own personnel system, at present none exists. In the absence of specific municipal labor legislation, local government employees are covered by a 1971 law that provides for a public administration service, but this law has likewise never been implemented. As a result, issues such as staff rights and duties, recruitment, promotion, discipline, salary scales, and social benefits have no legal structure and are in practice dealt with in an arbitrary fashion by municipal authorities. In theory unfair dismissal can be challenged in the court of appeal. However, reinstatement, even if authorized by the tribunal, can still be refused on the grounds that a vacancy no longer exists, in which case the maximum compensation is four months' salary. In common with the rest of public sector employees, municipal employees suffer from the complete absence of a career system, and a pension scheme for municipal employees exists only in embryonic form. The lack of job stability, the low salaries, and the rapid turnover of staff represent a serious obstacle to efforts to professionalize the municipal service.

The administrative capacity of local government remains very weak, and there is a serious shortage of trained personnel of all kinds. More recently, the institutional memory and administrative continuity of local government have been severely dented by five major changes in municipal leadership, leading to widespread disruption from 1987 to 1992. Although the educational level of the newly elected municipal authorities increased considerably after the 1991 elections, mayors and councillors are often surprisingly ill informed about the role of local government in the overall development process, as well as about the respective roles and responsibilities of elected officers and administrative staff.

FINANCIAL STRUCTURE

Paraguayan local government operates on an extremely weak financial basis by Latin American standards. Contrary to the regional trend during the 1980s, the share of local government in total public sector expenditure actually fell from 3.3 percent in 1980 to only 1.9 percent in 1988, by which date it was probably the lowest in the whole of Latin America (Nickson, 1993:7). In 1992 the combined budgeted expenditure of all municipalities was equivalent to that of the national university in the same year.

Local government receives no financial transfers from central government, neither in the form of revenue sharing, earmarked funds, nor conditional grants; this is a unique situation in Latin America. With the exception

of small-scale soft loan finance on-lent from international agencies, municipalities are almost totally dependent upon their own locally generated
sources of revenue in order to finance recurrent and capital expenditure. In
1992 the major sources of revenue were an industry and business tax; the
rental of municipal land; a vehicle road tax; a passenger transportation tax;
and a composite charge for solid waste management, public lighting, and
cemeteries.

The buoyancy of municipal own tax revenue has been adversely affected by the prevailing 1976 municipal fiscal law, under which most of the
fifty-one municipal taxes and fees are levied on the basis of fixed amounts
rather than percentage rates. But even those municipal taxes that are ad valorem (property tax, industrial and commercial licenses, and vehicle road
tax) have not been protected from the effects of inflation because of widespread underdeclaration of real asset values, as well as company turnover.
As a result, the share of taxes and fees in total municipal revenue declined
during the 1980s, and the share from services and sales (rental of municipal
land, market stall income, slaughterhouse fees, administrative charges) rose.
Constrained by this inadequate revenue base, the level of local government
expenditure has been extremely weak, even by Latin American standards.
Municipal expenditure fell considerably in real terms during the 1980s, with
a rising share accounted for by administrative personnel costs, which
reached 60 percent of recurrent expenditure by 1989 (Furst:116–120).

There are marked disparities in expenditure among municipalities. In
1992 the Municipality of Asunción accounted for 44 percent of total budgeted municipal expenditure, and twelve larger municipalities accounted for
a further 33 percent. Meanwhile 150 smaller municipalities together
accounted for only 11 percent of the total municipal expenditure. Average
municipal expenditure per head was U.S.$10.52, but this masked consider-
able variation among municipalities, ranging from U.S.$37.77 in the
Municipality of Asunción to only U.S.$0.37 in the Municipality of Tacuaras
(Nickson, 1993:13). Furthermore, these figures may be overestimates; a
detailed study of municipal finances for 1986 revealed that budgeted municipal expenditure was typically 20 percent higher than actual expenditure
(Furst:122).

The 1992 Constitution provided a major potential boost to local government finances by transferring control over the assessment and collection
of urban and rural property taxation from the Ministry of Finance to municipalities. Local governments are allowed to retain 70 percent of the proceeds
from property taxation, with 15 percent going to finance departmental governments and a further 15 percent destined for a municipal compensation
fund to assist poorer municipalities. The transfer of property taxation to
local government control enormously increases the potential for raising
municipal revenue, through increasing taxpayer registration, increasing the
rate of collection, and increasing the valuation base for the tax itself. But this

potential can be realized only when municipalities have both accurate cadastral surveys (in order to increase registration) and improved administration (in order to increase the collection rate). Incomplete national cadastral surveys were carried out in rural areas (in the 1960s) and in urban areas (in the 1970s). They were not maintained, and widespread evasion led to property tax receipts remaining low. As late as 1988, the Municipality of Asunción alone accounted for 49 percent of property tax receipts for the whole country. Although the share originating from the urban areas of other municipalities grew during the 1980s, by 1988 it still accounted for only 17 percent of the national total. In 1992 twenty-six municipalities alone accounted for 89 percent of total property tax receipts. This reflects the fact that only thirty municipalities currently have accurate urban cadastres (Goldenberg:1–2).

INTERMUNICIPAL COOPERATION

Intermunicipal cooperation is weak in Paraguay. Although a national municipal association, the Organización Paraguaya de Cooperación Intermunicipal (OPACI), was founded in 1954, it remained firmly under central government control throughout the Stroessner period. It was financed through a compulsory contribution of 1.5 percent of current municipal income, and its main function was to control the issuing of driving licenses. OPACI was ineffective as a lobby group for local government at the national level. In particular, it failed to address a major grievance of local government—namely, the refusal of the Ministry of Finance to implement the provision in the 1976 municipal fiscal law that 30 percent of the proceeds from property tax should be earmarked for municipalities. Instead the municipalities received only 4.4 percent (Nickson, 1989:3–4).

OPACI organized five national municipal congresses during the Stroessner period, although the first was not held until 1977. On each occasion the demand for greater municipal autonomy was stifled. A loose coalition of municipalities in the Metropolitan Area of Asunción, the Asociación de Municipalidades del Area Metropolitana (AMUAM), was formed in 1979 but failed to develop into a policymaking body for metropolitan planning. By 1990, 123 of the 200 municipalities in the country belonged to regional associations, but none of these had evolved into effective decisionmaking bodies (Marín, Silvero, and Sosa:1).

SUPPORT SERVICES

The IDM provides soft loan project finance, training, and technical assistance to local government. By 1992 it had provided over 900 individual loans worth a total of U.S.$15 million, mainly for the construction of municipal headquarters, multiuse centers, slaughterhouses, markets, and bus terminals. During the Stroessner period, it was financed by a deduction of 10 percent of property tax receipts owed to municipalities, a deduction of 2 percent of current municipal income, and a 2 percent surcharge on the import tax for alcoholic beverages.

Political considerations usually outweighed economic viability in IDM project selection. The institute's financial supervision was limited to design and construction, and monitoring of project implementation was virtually nonexistent. Audits carried out since 1989 have revealed widespread corruption by municipal authorities and heavy arrears in loan repayments to IDM, problems that by 1993 had led to serious difficulties in the IDM meeting its debt service obligations to foreign borrowers.

From 1974 to 1989 nearly 10,000 participants attended over 500 IDM training courses, but these were usually mere one-day events at which municipal staff were instructed in how to comply with financial and administrative regulations imposed by the Ministry of the Interior. The neglect of serious municipal training has left local government poorly equipped to undertake the growth in functions now demanded of it by civil society. The initial hostile attitude toward the IDM among municipal leaders elected after the overthrow of Stroessner reflected this bitter legacy. However, a subsequent reorganization of IDM management and a frank recognition by municipal authorities of their extreme shortage of trained personnel have combined to bring about a resurgence in support for IDM.

CITIZEN PARTICIPATION

Although the 1954 and 1987 municipal codes both made legal provision for citizen participation in local government, the exclusionary nature of the Stroessner regime severely restricted such participation in practice. All forms of citizen involvement in local government were actively discouraged, especially by the IDM, and the involvement of nongovernmental organizations in local government was banned altogether. As a result, despite growing recognition since 1991 of development commissions (*comisiones de fomento urbano*) in urban areas and community neighborhood committees (*juntas comunales de vecinos*) in rural areas, most municipal authorities remain wary of promoting citizen participation. Similarly, although the number of nongovernmental organizations has grown rapidly since 1989, their relationship with municipalities remains tenuous. Nevertheless, in 1993 the Municipality of Asunción began a program of administrative deconcentration involving the establishment of twelve neighborhood offices (*centros municipales*), with the declared aim that they would liaise with community groups in each suburb of the city.

PROSPECTS FOR LOCAL GOVERNMENT

There is a growing political consensus in Paraguay for a strengthening of local government. But its strength should not be overestimated, nor should the reasons for specific decentralization measures necessarily be attributed to a desire for greater municipal autonomy. Although the moves toward decentralization undertaken after 1991 did not reflect pressure from a wide-spread civic movement such as in Colombia and Venezuela, attitudes among the general population toward local government have begun to change. Increasingly, community groups are calling upon municipalities to solve their economic and social problems, whereas in the past they would have ignored local government. Prospects will be hampered in the medium term by the negative legacy of the Stroessner period, during which municipal development was regarded as a very low priority.

More specifically, the financial capacity of local government to respond to these demands is constrained by the continuing absence of any fiscal transfers from central government. Surprisingly, during the debate that led up to the 1992 Constitution, there was no call for a constitutionally guaranteed share of national revenue to be earmarked for local government, a practice that has become an increasingly common feature of constitutional reform in Latin America in recent years (e.g., in Brazil and Guatemala). Although the transfer of property taxation to local government does represent a major strengthening of local government finances, in the short term it is unlikely to produce any significant increase in fiscal revenue because the vast majority of smaller municipalities still lack the cadastres and administrative capacity for its collection. For these municipalities, the absence of any financial transfers from central government will continue to constitute the major constraint on the improvement in their level of service provision over the medium term. Ironically, the central government refusal to countenance the introduction of such fiscal transfers to local government in Paraguay is currently justified on the pretext that local government has been granted a major new source of fiscal revenue (property taxation) that obviates the need for further central government support.

The vague definition in the 1992 Constitution of attributions and sources of finance for the departmental tier of government, as well as that tier's future relations with municipalities under its area of jurisdiction, are further sources of concern for the future of local government in Paraguay. Although the Constitution states that 15 percent of property tax receipts collected by local government should be earmarked for the departmental government, there is no similar constitutional provision for central government funding of departmental government. This could encourage greater reliance on funding from municipalities. The Constitution also states that a further 15 percent of proceeds from property taxation should be used as a compensation fund for poorer municipalities, but it is not specified whether this financial redistribution will be made on an intradepartmental basis (in which case it would effectively be controlled by the new departmental governments) or on an interdepartmental basis (in which case the redistribution would be controlled by central government). In light of the marked interdepartmental disparities in municipal expenditure per head, an intermunicipal redistribution would be preferable on grounds of interjurisdictional equity, although the existence of widespread intradepartmental disparities, especially between departmental capitals and the rest, suggests that this redistribution should be combined with a preferential allocation in favor of smaller municipalities (Nickson, 1993:19). In a country where the decentralization process is still embryonic, there exists the danger, as in Bolivia, that the departmental tier of government may sap municipalities of the new lease on life that they have been granted since 1989.

25
PERU

Peru is a unitary nation divided into twelve regions, including the special region of Lima-Callao. Recent attempts to establish a regional structure of government have been fraught with political controversy. At the subregional level, the country is divided for administrative purposes into twenty-five departments. The country is unique within Latin America in having a two-tier local government system. At the subdepartmental level there are 189 provinces, which in turn are subdivided into 1,798 districts. Both provinces and districts have municipal status. At the subdistrict level, there is provision for the establishment of administrative units, known as *municipalidades de centro poblado menor* and *agencias municipales* in rural and urban areas respectively.

Economic activity is centralized in the capital city of Lima, which in 1993 had a population of 6.5 million, equivalent to 29 percent of the national total, and where no less than 50 percent of national production is concentrated. The Metropolitan Area of Lima comprises two provinces: Lima and Callao. The Province of Lima is governed by a provincial council and forty-two district councils; it is the nearest thing to a metropolitan government in Latin America. The central area of Lima, known as Cercado, is directly administered by the provincial council. The Province of Callao, the port of which is an integral part of the city, comprises six district municipalities and has the unique status of an honorary department. This fragmentation in the government of Lima has resulted in widespread administrative disorder (Olivera:62). The need to establish a metropolitan government for Lima has been left unresolved by the regionalization process.

The vast majority of municipalities are extremely small, even by Latin American standards. In 1983, 83 percent of the 1,676 district municipalities at that time each had populations of fewer than 3,000. Yet there is no categorization of municipalities, and all have the same rights and responsibilities.

HISTORICAL DEVELOPMENT

For over a century after independence, the presence of state institutions remained extremely limited in many parts of the national territory. This phenomenon was a reflection of deep ethnic divisions within Peruvian society and of an "enclave" economy dominated by both an agricultural oligarchy and foreign-owned mining companies. The first municipal code was passed in 1892 and remained in force for over ninety years. Although it assigned a wide range of urban functions to local government, it made virtually no provision for rural services.

The role of the state within the economy grew rapidly starting in the 1950s. In the process, most of the responsibilities formally assigned to local government were gradually assumed by ministries or state corporations, converting the municipality into a historical anachronism. The scale of demunicipalization was extreme even by Latin American standards. Responsibility for electricity supply was transferred from municipal control to a state corporation, ElectroPerú, although a separate state corporation, ElectroLima, was set up specifically to provide electricity for Lima. The state transportation corporation, ENATRUPERU, was created out of a company owned by the Municipality of Lima. Responsibility for issuing building permits was even transferred to the Ministry of Housing, and responsibility for public parks was passed to a state corporation, SERPAR. By the 1960s, the only functions retained by local government were solid waste management, civil registration, weights and measures, licensing of public events, and road maintenance. As a result of the growing centralization of service provision, as well as the financial dependence on central government, local government gradually assumed a residual function as an appendage of central government.

Despite a provision for direct elections in the 1892 municipal code, the appointment of local government officeholders by central government became the norm after 1909. Elections took place in 1963 and 1968, but were abolished once again by the military regime in power from 1968 to 1980. Despite its rhetoric of "full participation" (*participación plena*), the military granted no importance to local government, and the long-term process of centralization and demunicipalization was actually accelerated. A plethora of state companies were created that either directly assumed functions formerly carried out by local government or created problems of coordination and duplication of service provision with existing local government structures. For example, municipalities needed to obtain prior approval from the Ministry of Industry and Commerce before they could issue municipal business licenses. The authorization of fares for intraurban passenger transportation was handled by the Ministry of Transport. And public events such as fairs and film shows in cinemas had to be authorized by the national cultural institute (Murgia:18).

In reaction to the centralizing experience under military rule, the return to civilian government in 1980 was accompanied by pressure for decentralization and reform of municipal legislation. This movement represented a tacit alliance of two distinct groupings. One grouping included those, mainly on the political left, who saw the strengthening of municipal autonomy as a mechanism both for promoting citizen participation and for obtaining better service provision. The other grouping comprised technocrats within the public sector who hoped for a more efficient, cost-effective, and coordinated provision of basic services through stronger municipal structures.

In response to this pressure, in March 1981 a presidential decree finally replaced the 1892 municipal code. This decree was passed without public consultation, however, and was rejected by the National Congress on the grounds that it did not make adequate provision for increased revenue to meet the range of functions it restored to local government. In its place, a new municipal code, Ley Orgánica de Municipalidades No. 23853, was passed on 28 May 1984. This consolidated a host of amendments to the original 1892 legislation but did not represent a radical departure from the past. The code widened even further the theoretical ambit of local government, in keeping with the needs of a much more urbanized society. But it did not create any new sources of municipal finance. Nor did it counter the disincentive for local tax effort that was inherent in the centralizing bias of the prevailing two-tier system of revenue collection.

As in Bolivia, the problems of local government were somewhat neglected during the 1980s as the thrust of the decentralization initiative focused on the creation of a new regional tier of government. This process proved extremely conflictive. The territorial configuration of the new regions gave rise to widespread opposition, especially in the Lima region; the refusal of central government to transfer responsibilities and to relinquish fiscal control to the new regional governments highlighted the regions' total dependence upon central government funding; and the participation of all provincial mayors as automatic members of regional assemblies gave rise to fears that they would neglect their municipal duties. Twelve regional governments were eventually created by a 1989 regionalization law, but the process came to an abrupt halt in April 1992 when President Fujimori dissolved the National Congress together with the recently elected regional governments. Since then the regional tier of government has been emasculated to the point of virtual extinction.

ORGANIZATIONAL STRUCTURE

Peruvian local government comprises a unipersonal executive head, or mayor (alcalde), and a legislature (consejo municipal). The election of the mayor is not separate from that of the councillors (regidores). Instead, elections are held according to a closed list system under which the party that wins the most votes automatically obtains 51 percent of the council seats. The candidate heading the winning list is chosen as mayor, and the second person named in the list becomes deputy-mayor (*teniente-alcalde*). The remaining council seats are then distributed among other parties on the basis of proportional representation. The number of councillors in provincial councils ranges between a minimum of nine and a maximum of thirty-nine (in the case of the Province of Lima). In 1983 only 42 out of 1,676 district municipalities had more than five councillors. These included district municipalities within the Province of Lima that had up to fourteen councillors. All municipal officeholders are elected for a three-year term of office, with the possibility of immediate reelection.

Although the mayor presides over council meetings, councillors have considerable executive powers in comparison to local government systems elsewhere in Latin America. Under the system of inspection (inspectoría), each councillor is assigned to supervise a branch of the municipal administration. In practice, the distinction between supervision and actual decision-making has been blurred, and councillors have considerable power to recruit, dismiss, promote, and regrade staff.

The abortive presidential decree of 1981 had attempted a clearer demarcation of executive and deliberative roles by creating a new administrative post of municipal director (*director municipal*), appointed by the mayor as a confidence post but answerable to a subcommittee of the council. But this reform was widely opposed by councillors, who, as *inspectores,* feared the curtailment of their traditional powers of patronage. Consequently, the 1984 municipal code reinstated the inspectoría system and required the municipal director to act henceforth in accordance with guidelines established by the mayor and the inspectores.

FUNCTIONAL RESPONSIBILITIES

The division of responsibilities between provincial and district municipalities is only vaguely defined in the 1984 municipal code. District municipalities have prime responsibility for street cleaning, public hygiene, licensing of commercial premises, markets, slaughterhouses, road maintenance, public lighting, primary health care, public libraries, cemeteries, and civil registration. Provincial municipalities may also undertake these functions, but they are granted the additional responsibilities of land use planning, primary education, and public transportation. Meanwhile, responsibility for public health, secondary education, weights and measures, and urban transportation is shared jointly by both district and provincial municipalities.

A 1984 survey of half of all provincial municipalities revealed that, in practice, municipal functions were limited to traditional activities such as markets and solid waste management, whereas primary education, public transportation, and primary health care were all neglected functions (INFOM:119–194). Nevertheless, a high proportion of smaller municipalities provided water supply and electricity services, primarily because the central government agencies neglect these services (Althaus:38).

Imprecision in the municipal code has led to considerable disorder in the allocation of functional responsibilities between provincial and district municipalities. Even in the Metropolitan Area of Lima, the division of responsibilities between the Municipality of the Province of Lima and district councils remained unclear for decades (Olivera:63). Historically, most investment by the Municipality of the Province of Lima has been spent on arterial highways, which has greatly benefited the more affluent districts. Meanwhile, major road improvements linking the poorer districts with the city center have been carried out by the Ministry of Transport.

Despite the provisions of the Constitution and the municipal code that grant municipalities majority representation on the board of directors of state corporations providing basic urban services, central government has retained firm control over those services. The allocation of responsibilities for primary health care and basic education has also been hotly disputed. During the left-wing administration of the Municipality of the Province of Lima (1984–1986), this dispute led to conflict with central government, which refused to relinquish control of water supply, electricity, and urban planning. A comprehensive study in 1989 revealed that, in flagrant violation of the municipal code, almost all basic services in Lima were still delivered by state companies that were not operating under the authority of local government (Figari and Ricou:45).

PERSONNEL SYSTEM

In 1987 there were 38,745 municipal employees, equivalent to only 4.7 percent of total public sector employment. Of these, 55 percent were employed by provincial municipalities and 45 percent by district municipalities. The Municipality of the Province of Lima and the district municipalities within the Province of Lima together accounted for 37 percent of all municipal employees in the country (Polanco:214). The vast majority of municipalities employ very few staff by comparison with the rest of Latin America. In 1984, 51 percent of all provincial municipalities employed fewer than twenty staff, and 30 percent employed fewer than ten staff. District municipalities employed an average of only six staff members, and a very high proportion were believed to employ only one or two permanent staff (Althaus:23).

According to the 1984 municipal code, local government employees are covered by the same labor code as central government employees. Although nominally integrated into the general administrative service, in practice local government employees were generally accorded the lowest pay and conditions within the public administration. Local government rarely attracted university graduates, and the general educational level remained well below the norm for the public sector as a whole. This situation changed radically in the late 1980s as municipalities were allowed for the first time to enter into individual pay negotiations with their workforce, and as pay and conditions in central government deteriorated sharply because of the introduction of a harsh program of structural adjustment. As a result, by the mid-1990s salary levels in the larger municipalities exceeded those in central government by a significant margin.

Imprecision in the division of responsibilities between elected representatives and local government officers under the inspectoría system has contributed greatly to the continuing absence of job stability and a proper career structure. Political interference by councillors in the recruitment, posting, and promotion of municipal staff is common. As a result, the popular image of the local government officer is highly negative, characterized by a mixture of incompetence, ignorance, and corruption. This poor image has in turn contributed to the prevailing minimal importance that large sectors of society attach to local government as an institution for carrying out social reform.

FINANCIAL STRUCTURE

Local government finance in Peru has historically been very weak by comparison with the rest of Latin America. It was weakened even further during the period of military rule from 1968 to 1980, when the share of local government in total public sector recurrent and capital expenditure averaged 4 percent and less than 1 percent, respectively. At the same time, local government became even more dependent upon transfers from central government to finance its own expenditure (Greytak:17, 21). Municipal expenditure as a share of total public expenditure continued to fall during the early 1980s, to only 2.2 percent in 1983, when it was one of the lowest shares in Latin America (Althaus:18). As a result of municipal tax reforms carried out in 1983 and 1985, however, this share rose rapidly to reach 8.3 percent by 1987 (Arnao and Meza:48).

Since the 1950s, both the capacity of local government to generate own revenue and the level of central government transfers failed to keep pace with the explosion in urban population growth. Municipal finances were limited by the increasing control imposed by central government, which included the power of the Ministry of Economy and Finance to approve municipal budgets. By the 1970s the only significant sources of locally generated revenue that remained under municipal control were the residential property tax, professional and industrial licenses, a tax on vacant lots, and a user charge for public lighting and road sweeping. National legislation restricted the power of local government to create new taxes and even to alter rates on existing ones. Although provisions existed for municipal borrowing and for a betterment levy, neither was common.

The procedure for establishing the overall level of transfers, both from central government to provincial municipalities and from provincial municipalities to district municipalities, was surrounded in legal obscurity. Transfers were viewed more as a gesture of goodwill by central government than as a legal right to which local government was entitled. The system for allocating transfers among municipalities was based on political patronage rather than relative need. This led to a highly inequitable geographical distribution, whereby the Province of Lima alone typically absorbed over half of the total transfer to local government. This inequity was replicated within each province; the district municipality where the provincial headquarters was located usually absorbed the bulk of the transfer.

The vast majority of district municipalities barely raised enough revenue to pay for their own staff, let alone to finance other current expenditure. Capital expenditure was virtually nonexistent. As the collection of fiscal revenue became concentrated in the hands of central government, district municipalities typically became dependent upon meager transfers from central government for over half of their total income (Greytak:33).

During the 1980s a series of municipal tax reforms sought to meet the challenge posed by this fiscal stagnation. In 1980 provincial municipalities were empowered to establish municipal investment funds, such as the Fondo de Inversiones Metropolitanas (INVERMET) of the Municipality of the Province of Lima. The resources of these funds derived from several new tax sources: a vehicle tax levied on the sale of car fuel, which was collected by the state petroleum company and distributed in proportion to the number of vehicles registered in each municipality; a municipal royalty payment, in the form of a share in the national tax on the extraction of petroleum, gas, and gold, which benefited only selected municipalities; and a 10 percent share of the CERTEX, a rebate to producers of nontraditional exports, which was distributed on an origin basis. In 1983 responsibility for property tax was devolved from provincial to district municipalities, and its base was widened to include business properties.

Following a nationwide mobilization by municipal authorities of all political persuasions, the highly discretionary system of central government transfers was replaced in 1985 by a series of revenue-sharing agreements with local government. The most important of these was a municipal development tax (Fondo de Promoción Municipal, or FPM), which comprised a 1 percent surcharge (later increased to 3 percent) on the national sales tax. The Province of Lima received 30 percent of the FPM proceeds, and the remaining 70 percent was distributed among the other provincial municipalities on the following basis: half on an equal-shares basis and half according to their relative population sizes.

Other taxes for which the proceeds were now transferred to local government on an origin basis included a vehicle road tax, highway tolls, a tax on the sale of property, and a tax on vehicle purchases. Some of these transfers were earmarked exclusively for capital expenditure through the province-based municipal investment funds. Over the period 1985–1988, the contributions of different taxes to the combined municipal receipts from the new revenue-sharing agreements were as follows: FPM, 58 percent; petroleum canon, 18 percent; CERTEX, 13 percent; and vehicle road tax, 9 percent (Granda:9, 34). Together, these proceeds greatly exceeded the income that municipalities received under the previous haphazard system of transfers.

Although the recent fiscal reforms greatly strengthened municipal finances as a whole, they did little to correct the enormous disparity in municipal expenditure between the capital city and the rest of the country. In 1983, 54 percent of consolidated municipal expenditure took place in the Province of Lima (Althaus:21); and in 1987 municipal expenditure per head in the Department of Lima was U.S.$8.70, compared with only U.S.$1.10 in the poor mountainous Department of Apurímac (Arnao and Meza:58).

This disparity between the Province of Lima and the rest of the country was compounded by the bias inherent in the complex two-tier system of local revenue collection. Some taxes were collected directly by district municipalities (property tax, property sales tax, and the tax on vacant lots), and others (such as a tax on vehicle purchases and the business licenses) were collected by provincial municipalities. In all cases there was an extreme lack of clarity with regard to both the delegation of responsibility for collection and the redistribution of proceeds to the district level. These problems were exacerbated by the unequal relationship between provincial and district municipalities in the Peruvian two-tier local government system. Although an annual assembly of district mayors formulated overall plans for provincial development, these had to be approved by the provincial council. The budgets of district municipalities had also to be approved by their respective provincial councils, which could also reject fiscal proposals made by the districts.

Outside of the Province of Lima, this imprecision in fiscal powers gave rise to a notable "centralizing" bias in favor of the district municipality in which the provincial headquarters was situated. In turn, this resulted in a disincentive to other district authorities to improve the collection of those taxes for which the proceeds had to be passed first to the provincial government. In order to compensate for the basic inequity of this situation, central government came under continuous pressure to provide extra transfers to district municipalities on an ad hoc basis, a practice that failed to address the underlying inequity of the system.

As a result, disparities in municipal expenditure per head, both among provinces and within provinces, remained enormous, reflecting the extraordinary centralization of development resources in the Province of Lima and the associated neglect of the vast majority of the country's municipalities. Despite the existence of a quasi-metropolitan form of government in the Province of Lima, the absence of any municipal equalization fund meant that, even there, the extreme differences in the level of service provision between richer and poorer district municipalities, which derived principally from extreme differentials in property tax receipts, were not reduced. In 1985 expenditure per head by the Municipality of La Molina (U.S.$36.80) was twenty-two times greater than that by the Municipality of Villa María del Triunfo (U.S.$1.63) (Allou:160). During the period 1981–1986, the transfer of financial resources from the Municipality of the Province of Lima to district municipalities was negotiated by means of regular formal meetings between the provincial mayor and all of his district counterparts. This procedure, however, was subsequently dismantled by the incoming provincial mayor; instead, each district mayor had to negotiate the transfer to his or her municipality separately, giving rise to rampant clientelism and political favoritism.

In 1994, without prior consultation, President Fujimori assumed direct control of the FPM, the main source of central government transfers to local government. Henceforth 20 percent of FPM proceeds would be transferred to provincial municipalities and 80 percent to district municipalities, but the allocation among municipalities was left to the discretion of the presidential office. A minimum of 80 percent of the proceeds received by each municipality was earmarked for investment purposes. A new development program, FONCODES, was established in order to carry out local investment projects. It came under direct presidential control, with little involvement by local government.

INTERMUNICIPAL COOPERATION

Widespread municipal outrage at the 1981 attempt to force through a new municipal code by presidential decree was the catalyst for the foundation of a national municipal association, Asociación de Municipalidades del Peru (AMPE). This body was established following the first national municipal congress in January 1982. It receives considerable technical support from a number of nongovernmental organizations and hosts an annual congress of municipalities. In 1994 AMPE represented a major democratic challenge to the autocratic government of President Fujimori, opposing the plans to abolish the regionalization program and insisting that investment funds be channeled through municipalities instead of through FONCODES.

SUPPORT SERVICES

Local government training has been weak in Peru. Public administration training is carried out by a national institute for public administration (INAP), but this institution has assigned a low priority to local government training within its overall program of activities. A national municipal training body, the Instituto Nacional de Fomento Municipal (INFOM), was created in 1982 with financial assistance from USAID. By 1987 its 177 employees were providing technical assistance, training, and loan finance to municipalities. Under the populist government of President Alan García, however, a large part of INFOM's financial and human resources were wasted on an ill-conceived project to supply road-building equipment to municipalities. In 1992 INFOM was dissolved as part of the austerity program of the Fujimori government. Municipal training is also provided by two foreign-funded nongovernmental organizations, the Instituto de Investigación y Capacitación Municipal (INICAM), founded in 1984, and the Instituto para la Democracia Local (IPADEL), founded in 1987 (Dawson, 1992:95).

CITIZEN PARTICIPATION

Peru is noted within Latin America for its strong tradition of community organization. In highland peasant communities, it has long been common practice for the submunicipal official posts to be filled by traditional leaders who coordinate voluntary labor in agricultural and public works activities; these officials are appointed by the mayor and are known as *agentes municipales*. Starting in the 1950s there was a dramatic increase in migration to urban areas. Andean migrants brought with them a deep-rooted tradition of agricultural support networks, which was soon put into practice for the provision of urban shelter. Powerful community organizations that sought to put pressure on ministries and state corporations to provide basic services grew up in the shantytowns.

The military regime that ruled the country from 1968 to 1980 adopted a corporativist program of community mobilization, known as SINAMOS, but by the late 1970s the organizations that belonged to it had broken free of military control and had coalesced into a powerful, city-wide federation,

FEDPJUP. In response to the abject failure of central government agencies to provide basic services in squatter settlements, popular participation (*participación popular*) in local government became one of the organizations' major demands. They pressed for strong and independent municipalities backed by substantial financial transfers from central government in order to meet the ever-increasing demand for urban basic services in squatter settlements.

Left-wing political movements were a strong influence upon these community organizations. They placed great emphasis on the "capture" of municipal government and its transformation into a model of participatory socialism that could later be applied at the national level. They unfavorably contrasted representative democracy, in which citizen organizations held a consultative status, with direct democracy, in which citizen organizations would participate actively and independently in municipal decisionmaking (Távara:254–255).

In an understandable reaction to the tight control over community involvement in local development exercised by the military regime, the 1979 Constitution stated explicitly that municipalities should promote and support citizen participation. Despite the upsurge in community organization, however, the 1984 municipal code was surprisingly vague concerning the actual form that citizen participation in municipal affairs would take (Pease and Jibaja:358). In municipalities with populations of fewer than 3,000, a cabildo abierto could be held, but only with the agreement of two-thirds of the councillors. Furthermore, the mayor was required to hold quarterly meetings with recognized neighborhood associations. Official recognition of such associations, however, remained the exclusive prerogative of the mayor. When recognition was refused, as happened in the Municipality of San Juan de Miraflores in 1990, the impact of community organizations on municipal affairs was reduced to zero overnight (Dawson, 1993:408). Despite the limitations imposed by the 1984 municipal code, citizen participation in local government continued to grow, particularly in the district municipalities of the poor northern, southern, and eastern fringes of Lima, where over half of the city's inhabitants lived. For example, by 1991 the Municipality of San Juan de Miraflores (population 303,000) alone had over 1,000 community organizations (Zaaijer and Miranda:135).

Villa El Salvador provided a striking example of community self-management that attracted considerable international attention. This squatter settlement was created in 1971 following a large-scale land invasion on the desert outskirts of Lima (Peattie:21–24). It was granted the status of a district municipality in 1983. By 1989 its population had grown to over 300,000. Community participation was organized on the basis of blocks of twenty-four households each. Sixteen blocks constituted a residential group, each of which had a nursery school, recreation area, community center, and health post—all built by community residents themselves. These groups were represented by over 150 neighborhood committees, which elected members to a municipal-wide community council, the Comunidad Urbana Autogestionaria Villa El Salvador (CUAVES), which at times convened the whole community for important decisionmaking through cabildos abiertos. CUAVES functioned as a parallel body in coordination with the elected council and was responsible for appointing a network of voluntary "popular inspectors" who controlled public hygiene and juvenile delinquency.

The Glass of Milk program, started in 1984 as a community initiative with support from the Municipality of the Province of Lima, was another highly successful example of citizen participation in local government. By 1992 it reached 750,000 children under the age of seven in thirty-three district municipalities, who were supplied daily with a glass of milk by a network of 7,500 voluntary women's committees, though only twenty-nine municipal employees were assigned to the program. As a result of a march by 30,000 women to the National Congress in late 1984, the program was extended to cover the whole country (Pease, 1989:56, 86). Municipalities also supported mothers' clubs and soup kitchens organized by voluntary women's committees in response to the severe economic crisis of the 1980s. From 1984 to 1986, 40,000 families at Huaycán in the Municipality of Ate-Vitarte and at Pampas de San Juan in the Municipality of San Juan de Miraflores benefited from self-help housing projects supported by the Municipality of the Province of Lima (Chirinos, 1991:118).

Less successful was an emergency preventive health care program started in 1984 in eleven poor district municipalities within the Province of Lima, which involved citizen organizations and health workers seconded from the provincial municipality. When the district municipalities failed to assume responsibility for the continuation of the program, it simply collapsed (Dawson, 1993:409). Similarly, evidence from the city of Cusco, in the far south of Peru, between 1980 and 1987 drew attention to the manipulation of neighborhood associations by municipal authorities of all political persuasions, who used the rhetoric of popular participation in order to conceal political clientelism (Villafuerte:222–223).

During the 1980s, local government entered the everyday political vocabulary of Peru to an extent unparalleled in Latin America. The return to civilian rule produced an upsurge of citizen participation and a strong lobby in favor of decentralization, both of which focused attention on local government. Starting in the late 1980s, however, a severe economic crisis and the inability of local government to counter the decline in living standards contributed to a growing disillusionment with citizen participation in local government. The assassination by the counterrevolutionary organization Sendero Luminoso of mayors and councillors in rural municipalities of the sierra and of community activists in the poorer district municipalities of Lima exacerbated this decline in citizen organization.

The election of independent, nonparty candidates to municipal office reflected a growing belief that municipal authorities should demonstrate managerial efficiency rather than the ability to generate and support citizen participation. So strong was this new tide of thinking that, in the January 1993 municipal elections, candidates of left-wing parties also emphasized efficiency over participation in their campaigns. The capacity of municipalities to demonstrate this greater efficiency still depended upon access to adequate financial resources, yet this was increasingly called into question by a resurgence of political centralization.

PROSPECTS FOR LOCAL GOVERNMENT

Within Latin America, Peru is surpassed only by Bolivia in the extent to which the colonial structure of government has survived to the present day. The deep ethnic discrimination that underlies urban-rural inequalities in Peruvian society has been legitimized in the country's unique two-tier system of local government. The vast majority of the rural poor still live in district municipalities that fulfill a purely ceremonial role, receiving little income, employing very few staff, and carrying out hardly any service delivery activities whatsoever.

The advocates of decentralization and reform of the state have given priority to the need for an elected regional government and have largely disregarded the need to strengthen local government. The decentralization movement is still led by provincial urban groups outside the capital city of Lima, and peasant interests are virtually unrepresented (Wilson and Garzón:332). There is ample evidence that this is already creating a new centralization at the level of each regional headquarters. As in Bolivia, there is an urgent need for the decentralization process to proceed beyond the regional level and to strengthen the role of local government. An important first step is to reform the inequitable two-tier system of local government. One measure would involve the introduction of a transparent and equitable revenue-sharing formula between central and local government to put an end to the capture of transfers by provincial councils. Other measures would involve the legal recognition of traditional systems of local government among peasant communities at the district municipality, as well as the abolition of the supervisory-subordinate relationship between provincial and district municipalities.

26

URUGUAY

Uruguay is a unitary nation with a highly centralized system of public administration. There is one major tier of government at the subnational level, consisting of nineteen departments; this is unusual in Latin America. Strictly speaking, there is no local government in Uruguay, although the departments are often referred to as municipalities. The departmental tier of government is more akin to that of a provincial government, although it includes municipal responsibilities for the departmental headquarters (Arocena:79). At the subdepartmental level, five-member local boards (juntas locales) may be created, except within the urban area of the departmental capital. These boards have no constitutional status, their members are nominated by the mayor, and they have minimal responsibilities. The absence of a genuinely municipal tier of government means that, outside the headquarters of many departments, there are sizable urban communities that are devoid of any semblance of local government. All nineteen departmental governments have a uniform character. The Department of Montevideo, the capital city, despite having 45 percent of the national population and 65 percent of industrial employment, has no metropolitan form of government, and for administrative purposes it is treated exactly the same as any other department.

HISTORICAL DEVELOPMENT

In a manner unique within Latin America, the formation of the Uruguayan nation and the subsequent process of economic growth have greatly hindered the development of local government. Among the special factors in Uruguay are the practice of extensive cattle ranching and the associated small proportion of the population who live in rural areas; the weak development of urban centers capable of countering the overwhelming political and economic predominance of Montevideo; and the uniform low-lying terrain, which has stifled the development of a strong sense of local identity.

The extreme centralization that immediately followed independence was the product of the peculiar geopolitical instability of the country. Uruguay is wedged between Argentina and Brazil, and the latter country occupied Uruguay from 1819 to 1825. The cabildos that had led the independence movement were suppressed by the 1830 Constitution. The nine departments existing at the time were headed by a central government appointee in collaboration with a council that had five to seven members and was elected for a three-year period; these councils initially exercised only an honorary role. Starting in 1868, the councils began to assume new powers at the expense of the appointed executive, reflecting their growing role in the legal administration of land titling, a crucial factor in the development of the rural economy (Martins:135). This new division of power was recognized by a 1903 municipal code that established nine-member councils, which were elected for a three-year term and had the power to name auxiliary commissions with five to seven members in all urban settlements within each department. A 1908 law, Ley de Intendencias, reaffirmed central government control through the appointment of departmental executives (intendentes). By contrast, the 1917 Constitution granted the highest degree of political and financial autonomy to local government in the history of Uruguay. This was expressed in a 1918 law, Ley Orgánica de Gobiernos Locales, which created departmental legislative assemblies as well as collegiate administrative councils that assumed the executive functions previously carried out by intendentes.

The world recession of 1929 led to a new wave of centralization, as the severe fiscal crisis of the state was now blamed on the financial profligacy of departmental governments. This led to a military coup in 1933, followed by a constitutional reform in 1934 and a new October 1935 municipal law, Ley Orgánica Municipal No. 9515, which was still in effect as of 1994. Under this new arrangement, executive functions were henceforth concentrated in the figure of the intendente, and legislative functions were carried out by councils (*juntas departamentales*). At the submunicipal level, five-member local boards (juntas locales) were appointed by the intendente with the approval of the council. From 1938 onward, all of these officers were elected for a four-year term of office. In 1942 the number of departmental councillors was raised from nine to fifteen, and from eleven to thirty-one in the case of Montevideo.

In 1952 a constitutional reform reintroduced the collegiate system of government, which involved the sharing of power between the two major political parties on a rotational basis. This was replicated at the departmental level, where executive powers were henceforth shared among members of a directly elected executive team, known as the *consejo departamental,* consisting of seven members in Montevideo and five members in the other departments. The departmental council size was also further increased to thirty-one. This collegiate system was abandoned in 1966, with the return to the intendente as the unipersonal executive head.

Local democracy was abolished by the military rulers who seized power in 1973. The intendentes, who were henceforth directly appointed, also assumed the responsibilities of the juntas locales. The elected departmental councils were replaced by corporativist bodies, known as juntas de vecinos, whose members were appointed by the military. The return to democratic rule in 1984 led once again to the direct election of both mayors and councils, but the outdated electoral system remained unchanged.

ORGANIZATIONAL STRUCTURE

Uruguayan local government comprises a unipersonal executive head, or mayor (intendente), and a thirty-one-member legislature (junta departamental). The mayor and departmental councillors (consejales) are elected simultaneously for five-year terms of office. The electoral system subordinates local government to national political considerations. All local government officeholders are elected on the same date as the national political leadership (the president and members of Congress), and their terms of office are coterminous. Voting takes place according to a single closed party list, containing candidates for national and departmental office. Hence there is no opportunity on the ballot paper for voters to select one party for national office and another for departmental office. The electoral system is not based on proportional representation; this is unusual in Latin America. Instead, the party that gains the most votes automatically receives a majority of the seats in the legislature.

FUNCTIONAL RESPONSIBILITIES

The Uruguayan system of "local" government is unusual in so far as the departmental government combines functions that in most countries would be carried out by either regional or municipal government. Prior to the military intervention of 1973, departmental functions were limited to the delivery of basic services such as public lighting, solid waste management, and parks, as well as basic regulation of private sector activities with regard to public transportation, building regulations, and food hygiene. Water supply was handled by a single state corporation for the whole country. Sewerage was handled in the Department of Montevideo by the department itself, but a state corporation handled the remaining eighteen departments. Public health, education, and housing remained under the control of central government. Central government ministries and state corporations carried out a wide range of activities at the departmental level, although their own departmental branches were granted minimal decisionmaking authority. Furthermore, they rarely consulted with department governments. This poor level of interinstitutional coordination had negative consequences for the efficiency of service delivery activities.

With the return to democracy in 1984, and in response to the crisis of the Uruguayan welfare state, departmental governments came under increasing pressure to fulfill a new role both as agents for the promotion of industrial and agricultural development and as the provider of basic social services. The pioneering example of the Department of Tacuarembó, which had established an organization for agricultural and industrial development as far back as 1972, was replicated by most departments by the late 1980s (Arocena:81–83). This new role was assumed in an unplanned manner, without the necessary financial transfers from central government. In order for this new role to be met adequately, there were new demands for the institutional strengthening of departmental government and for decentralization.

In 1988 the government introduced a decentralization program aimed at devolving functions from line ministries to the departments, deconcentrating line ministry decisionmaking from headquarters to departmental offices, and enabling the departmental authorities to coordinate the activities of line ministries within their areas of jurisdiction. The central personnel office, Oficina Nacional del Servicio Civil (ONSC), was given the task of implementing this program. Although progress was slow, in April 1993 the government announced plans to transfer responsibility for state hospitals to departments as part of a restructuring program for the national health service.

PERSONNEL SYSTEM

In 1993 there were 34,956 municipal employees, accounting for 12.7 percent of all public sector employment in the country. Of these, 31 percent were employed by the Department of Montevideo. Each departmental government is empowered to establish a labor code for its own employees, although some common principles are set down in the Constitution. In the past, gross overstaffing of departmental governments had operated as a form of social safety net, as in many Argentine provinces. This practice was greatly curtailed during the late 1980s under the impact of a structural adjustment program imposed because of a severe fiscal crisis.

FINANCIAL STRUCTURE

The 1935 municipal code ensured that departmental finances were tightly controlled by central government, and the consolidated recurrent expenditure of departmental government accounted for only 4.1 percent of total public expenditure in 1986. Financial transfers from central to departmental government accounted for 10–20 percent of departmental expenditure in 1990, although only 4 percent in the case of Montevideo. They take several forms: 5 percent of the proceeds from the fuel tax; 5 percent from the proceeds of the cigarette sales tax; and earmarked transfers for investment purposes, notably highway construction and public housing. Since 1985 departmental governments have also made increasing use of World Bank and Inter-American Development Bank credits channeled through central government.

In 1990 municipal own revenue generation totaled U.S.$214 million, equivalent to 7.5 percent of national fiscal revenue. The Department of Montevideo alone accounted for 45 percent of this total, the Departments of Canelones and Maldonado accounted for a further 17 percent, and the remaining sixteen departments together accounted for 38 percent. Municipal own revenue per head varied from U.S.$217 in Maldonado to U.S.$47 in Canelones (Bervejillo:13–14). Own revenue generation is barely sufficient to cover recurrent expenditure. Taxes and fees make up around 75 percent of the total. There are four principal taxes: urban and rural property taxes, a vehicle road tax, and a tax on the sale of cattle. Although rural property tax rates are determined by central government (an unusual situation in Latin America), departmental governments have discretion to fix tariff rates for urban property taxation. The yield from urban property taxation is typically only one-eighth of that from rural property taxation, except in the highly urbanized Departments of Montevideo and Canelones, as well as in the tourism-based Department of Maldonado. Central government reserves the exclusive right to levy new taxes. In practice, most fees (e.g., on public lighting, public hygiene) are levied as a consolidated surcharge on the urban property tax. Given that these charges are unrelated to the cost of service provision, such fees function in effect as another tax.

INTERMUNICIPAL COOPERATION

A national movement to represent the interests of local government has emerged only recently in Uruguay and is largely the product of the growing role of departments in the promotion of agricultural development. By 1990 nine national meetings had taken place to exchange experience in this field, and they were followed in 1991 by a national meeting of mayors, the Congreso Nacional de Intendentes. The latter group still lacks any legal status and is unlikely to exert powerful pressure on the national government until the prevailing electoral system is reformed.

SUPPORT SERVICES

A striking manifestation of the political centralization and historically weak role of local government in Uruguay is the fact that no national municipal training and research body exists in the country. The Department of Montevideo runs the Instituto de Estudios Municipales for the training of its own employees as well as those from other departments. In 1985 a central public administration department, the ONSC, was established, and in 1993 its training unit began offering courses to departmental governments.

CITIZEN PARTICIPATION

Under the municipal code there is provision for the mayor to appoint members to local boards (juntas locales), five-person consultative bodies that may be established outside the departmental headquarters in urban areas having more than 10,000 inhabitants. A surprising feature of the Uruguayan political scene is the absence of any strong demand for greater autonomy for these local boards, a move that would be tantamount to the creation of a genuine system of local government. This lack of demand has been attributed variously to the lack of any cultural tradition of local self-government, the highly centralized political system, the weak development of community groups, and the absence of financial resources for such bodies (Bervejillo:16). Although a national law even permits the direct election of the local boards, Río Branco, a Brazilian border town, is the only place to adopt this practice.

Nevertheless, the election of the left-wing Frente Amplio coalition to the Department of Montevideo in March 1990 led to a major initiative in citizen participation (Pérez, 1992:93). Administrative deconcentration of municipal services, including solid waste management and public lighting, was pursued through the establishment of eighteen neighborhood offices, known as *centros comunales zonales* (CCZs), each with a zonal coordinator appointed by the mayor (Sierra et al.:77). Following a widespread process of consultation known as Montevideo en Foro, in July 1993 the departmental council approved a radical step to establish eighteen directly elected neighborhood councils (consejos vecinales). The membership of these councils would vary between twenty-five and forty people, and the councils would have consultative status with the CCZs. The success of the consejos vecinales was considered to be a major reason for the reelection of the left-wing municipal administration in November 1994.

PROSPECTS FOR LOCAL GOVERNMENT

The absence of a strong tradition of decentralization in Uruguay may be traced to the historical predominance of the unitary model of political organization over the opposing federalist thesis advocated by José Gervasio Artigas, the founder of Uruguay. To a large part, the enduring strength of the unitary model reflects the geopolitical reality of the extreme vulnerability of this small country, wedged between two major regional powers. As a result, throughout Uruguay's history, the debate between centralization and decentralization has not been divorced from the issue of national sovereignty (Pérez, 1988:76). Hence, even during periods of formal autonomy, the activities of local government have been closely circumscribed by central government.

Uruguayan departments operate under a legal framework for local government that was passed in 1935 and is now the most outdated in Latin America. As a result, the structure and performance of local government remains wedded to the past. Virtually all issues relating to local socioeconomic development are handled by central government. Local government confines itself to a limited number of increasingly anachronistic functions.

Yet the changing socioeconomic structure of the country has given a new urgency to the demands for decentralization. For example, modern agri-industrial investment is for the first time leading to the establishment of growth poles outside Montevideo; regional economic integration with neighboring countries through the Mercosur common market that came into force in 1995 has encouraged frontier departments to develop joint activities with their Brazilian or Argentine counterparts; and the fact that departmental government has ended its role as a form of social safety net (via gross overstaffing) has given rise to its emerging role as an agent for local development.

27

VENEZUELA

Venezuela is a federal nation divided into twenty-two states, the Federal District (Distrito Federal) of Caracas, and a collection of offshore islands collectively known as the Federal Dependencies. Below the state level, the country is covered by 282 municipalities. The administration of the capital city of Caracas is the most fragmented in the whole of Latin America. There is no metropolitan government; the Metropolitan Area of Caracas exists only as a descriptive entity and is usually defined as including the Federal District (which includes the two Municipalities of Libertador and Vargas) and seven municipalities within the adjoining State of Miranda.

There are enormous disparities among municipalities in terms of population size. In 1992 fourteen municipalities each had more than 250,000 inhabitants, seventy-six had populations of between 50,000 and 250,000, and 192 municipalities (equivalent to 68 percent of the total) each had fewer than 50,000 inhabitants.

HISTORICAL DEVELOPMENT

Venezuela has a deep-rooted tradition of municipal autonomy that is intimately associated with the process of nation building during the early years of independence. During the late nineteenth century and early twentieth century, however, the centralization of political, economic, and administrative powers in the hands of central government progressed to the point where the federal system of government became a fiction (Brewer-Carias, 1991:132–135). For much of this period, successive federal governments cynically exalted the importance of municipal autonomy simply in order to justify their assault on the rights of the states (Peñalva:388).

The 1961 Constitution completed this process of centralization by reducing state and local governments to residual functions and by legitimizing the appointment of state governors by the president of the republic. State functions became extremely limited. States had no freedom to raise their own revenue, and they relied almost exclusively on transfers from central government to finance their limited expenditure. For all practical purposes, Venezuela became a unitary rather than a federal nation.

Following the overthrow of the Pérez Jiménez dictatorship in 1958, the primary purpose of state and municipal government was to reward supporters of the two political parties that emerged, COPEI and Acción Democrática, with short-term employment and other benefits. The oil boom of the 1970s that enlarged the federal budget, as well as the funding of local government investment programs by central government transfers, greatly enhanced this "gift-giving" role of national politicians.

Although the 1961 Constitution had in theory recognized municipal autonomy, seventeen years elapsed before a municipal code was finally promulgated in 1978. In the meantime, the overcentralized and clientelist system of government resulted in the politicization of the public administration at all levels, a lack of continuity in government programs, and rampant inefficiency in the public sector (Ellner:91). The associated corruption and misuse of oil revenues led to widespread popular alienation from the political process, as evidenced by the low turnout at municipal elections, which fell from 73 percent in 1979, to 59 percent in 1984, and to 45 percent in 1989.

An extraordinary legislative anomaly continued for decades after the promulgation of the 1961 Constitution, under which councils existed only at the higher governmental level of the district, with members elected under a closed and blocked party list system. Meanwhile, at the lower, municipal level there was no provision for political representation, despite the vociferous demands from a powerful movement of citizen organizations.

The 1978 municipal code reinforced this role of municipalities as mere administrative subdivisions of district councils. In the absence of local elections, municipalities were administered by three-member committees (juntas municipales) who were appointed by the district council and who served a one-year term with the possibility of reappointment. The main purpose of these committees was to serve as a channel of communication between rural communities and the district council headquarters located in major towns. There was no comparable structure in urban areas. By the mid-1980s the system of local government was characterized by an extreme lack of political accountability and the absence of mechanisms for citizen participation (Brewer-Carias, 1988:306–310).

In 1984 a presidential committee for the reform of the state (COPRE) was established in order to counter the growing threat that citizen alienation posed to the political system. In December 1989 this initiative finally bore fruit in the form of two pieces of enabling legislation that provided the basis for a program of decentralization. The primary focus of this reform, however, was the devolution of responsibilities from central to state government, rather than to local government. The 1989 decentralization law, known as the LODT, provided for the gradual transfer of service delivery functions from federal to state governments through a series of bilateral agreements. A new 1989 municipal code, Ley Orgánica de Régimen Municipal No. 4,109, abolished the district tier of government and established local councils henceforth at the municipal level only. It also allowed local government to cooperate with federal and state government in the provision of water, sewerage, solid waste disposal, and primary health care, and it introduced the notion of accountability in budget preparation, auditing, and investment programming.

ORGANIZATIONAL STRUCTURE

Venezuelan local government comprises a unipersonal executive head, or mayor (alcalde), and a legislature (consejo municipal). The number of councillors (consejales) varies between a minimum of five in municipalities with populations of fewer than 15,000 and a maximum of seventeen in those with populations of more than one million. The introduction of a clear separation of executive and legislative responsibilities in local government dates only from the state reform program of the late 1980s, which was designed to reduce the "democratic deficit" at the municipal level. For several decades prior to 1978, the council leader (presidente municipal), elected from among the councillors, also served as the executive head of the municipality. In addition to problems arising from this fusion of legislative and executive roles, the arrangement led to considerable instability in decisionmaking because the council leader was elected annually, with the same person rarely serving for the full five-year mandate of the council.

The 1978 municipal code introduced the post of municipal administrator for municipalities with populations of more than 50,000, modeled on the idea of a city manager in the United States. The administrator was appointed by the council to serve during its own five-year term, and he or she was subject to dismissal by a majority vote of councillors. Selection criteria for the post included a university education or relevant experience in public administration. Despite this reform, in practice executive power remained in the hands of the council leader, who retained the authority to dismiss municipal staff and to appoint staff from shortlists proposed by the administrator. This collegiate executive system often led to conflict between council leaders and administrators, and this had a negative impact on municipal management (Peñalva:399). This system was replaced under the 1989 municipal code, which led to the disappearance of the posts of council leader and municipal administrator. And in the Federal District of Caracas, the presidentially appointed governor was replaced by a directly elected mayor.

In recent years, Venezuela has experienced the most radical reform of the local government electoral system in the whole of Latin America. Until the mid-1980s the system was extremely unaccountable. Councillors were elected according to a single closed and blocked party list system, and the names of candidates did not even appear on the ballot paper. As part of the state reform program, this approach was replaced in the 1989 municipal elections by separate elections for the mayor and by a Swiss-style panachage (open and nonblocked list) system for councillors. Even though the relevant legislation was approved only three months before the election, and although publicity about the new system was scanty, over 30 percent of voters exercised their right to preference voting instead of simply voting by list. Twenty-five percent of councillors were elected on the preference vote, of whom 60 percent represented intraparty defeats (i.e., the displacement of one candidate who would have been elected on a pure list system by another who placed lower in the list but attracted more preference votes) (Molina:14). In 1992, in a second reform, the "list" electoral system for councillors was replaced by a mixed system, similar to the German model and unique in Latin America, under which two-thirds of councillors were elected on a ward basis, with the remaining one-third elected according to party lists.

In addition, the period of office for both mayors and councillors was reduced from five to three years, with the possibility of reelection in both cases. This reform had the effect of delinking local government elections from national government elections. Previously, local government elections were held six months after the elections for presidential and congressional office. This had ensured a built-in advantage for the party that won the national elections because that party was still benefiting from the "honeymoon" effect with the electorate at the time of local government elections.

FUNCTIONAL RESPONSIBILITIES

Under the 1961 Constitution, central government imposed an obligatory "minimum service" provision on local government. This covered basic services such as water supply and sewerage; urban planning; housing; pavements; traffic; urban transportation; public lighting; road construction; cemeteries; environmental protection; solid waste management; slaughterhouses; markets; fire service; cultural, recreational, and sports facilities; and parks and gardens. But it also stated that these functions were not necessarily the exclusive domain of local government. This legislative sleight of hand, later also incorporated in the 1978 municipal code, legitimized the concentration of power in the hands of central government through the Ministry of Urban Development (MINDUR), which acted as the major financing and coordinating institution for service provision by central government agencies at the local level. As a result, many of the functions attributed to local government in the Constitution were shared with or directly carried out by central government agencies, and very few services were provided exclusively by local government (Peñalva:405–406). For decades this denial of municipal responsibility was accepted by municipal authorities because the party list system and the absence of separate mayoral elections minimized political accountability to the electorate.

A reform of the municipal code in 1989 continued to fudge the question of municipal responsibilities, even though it was promulgated in the context of heightened concern for decentralization. A list of eighteen functions, including gas, electricity, water supply, and urban public transportation, were defined as municipal competencies. Five other areas were identified in which municipalities were required to cooperate in accordance with central government guidelines: public hygiene, primary health care, social services, local economic development, and road construction and maintenance. Furthermore, each municipality was required to guarantee a minimum range of service provision, which varied according to the size of its urban population.

PERSONNEL SYSTEM

In 1988 there were 26,400 municipal employees, accounting for 2 percent of total public sector employment in the country. As in the rest of the Venezuelan public sector, a career structure hardly exists in local government. Instead, national political parties have imposed clientelist practices in the selection, promotion, and dismissal of staff at all levels. Until recently these practices were encouraged by the divided nature of executive authority, which was split among the administrator, the council leader, and those councillors who were heads of committees. Repeated attempts to professionalize public administration failed in the face of entrenched opposition from political parties (De la Cruz:49).

A paradoxical consequence of the formal autonomy of local government, as enshrined in the 1961 Constitution, was that local government employees were not covered by the provisions of the national public administration personnel system that formed part of the 1971 civil service law. Instead, each municipality was responsible for establishing ordinances to regulate its own administrative system. Although Article 135 of the 1978 municipal code obliged all municipalities to establish procedures for the selection and promotion of staff on merit and for payment according to work done, in practice very few municipalities have implemented such measures. Nevertheless, as in the rest of the public administration, job stability in local government was heavily enforced as a result of pressure from powerful trade unions that forged strong links to clientelist political parties. This combination of job stability and weak human resource management has led to a degree of overstaffing and inefficiency in local government that is unparalleled in Latin America.

FINANCIAL STRUCTURE

In 1989 local government accounted for 6.5 percent of total public sector expenditure, compared with the 16.0 percent accounted for by state governments and the 77.5 percent spent by central government. In the same year, by contrast, local government accounted for only 3.0 percent of total public sector revenue, with the difference accounted for by financial transfers from central to local government (Nickson:6). Central government is highly dependent on oil revenue, which accounted for 75 percent of its total revenues in 1990. Meanwhile, income tax accounted for only 8.4 percent of central government revenue because of widespread evasion. Given the insignificance of both income tax and indirect taxation (because of the absence of a value-added tax), subnational tiers of government are highly vulnerable to variations in national oil revenue, which remains by far the major source of transfers from central government.

The single most important source of income for most municipalities is the transfer from central government, mediated through state governments. According to the 1961 Constitution, 15 percent of the estimated current income of central government, known as the *situado constitucional,* had to be transferred to state governments and allocated among them in the following manner: 30 percent in equal parts and 70 percent in proportion to the population of each state. For over a decade, the proportion of this transfer that was then redistributed to municipalities was left to the discretion of each state; it varied between 0.76 percent and 20.0 percent in 1970 (Savio:84). In 1975 legislation was passed to ensure that 50 percent of the situado received by state governments, henceforth known as the *situado co-ordinado,* was earmarked for investment and effectively subject to control by central government in the way it was spent. The remainder, known as the *situado no co-ordinado,* could be spent freely. In turn, 10 percent of the latter, which was known as the *situado municipal,* had to be transferred to municipalities by the respective state government on the following basis established by the 1978 municipal law: 50 percent in equal parts and 50 percent in proportion to the population of each municipality. Half of the amount received in this form by local government had to be spent in a manner approved by the state government, and the remainder could be spent freely. Between 1978 and

1987, local government received 48 percent of its income in the form of this central government transfer mediated through state governments.

As part of the state reform program, under the 1989 LODT, central government transfers through the situado procedure were substantially increased in order to strengthen the fiscal resources and autonomy of states and, indirectly, of local government. The situado constitucional was increased from 15 percent to 16 percent in 1990, with provision for an annual increase thereafter of 1 percent up to a maximum of 20 percent by 1994. The distinction between situado co-ordinado and situado no co-ordinado was abolished and replaced by the requirement that at least 50 percent of the total transfer received by each state should be used for capital expenditure. The situado municipal was increased from 10 percent to 11 percent of the current income of central government in 1990, with provision for an annual increase thereafter of 1 percent up to a maximum of 20 percent by 1999.

The formula for distributing revenues to state and local government (situado constitucional and situado municipal) is broadly progressive with regard to interjurisdictional equity, insofar as the states and municipalities with smaller populations (which benefit from a 50 percent equal allocation factor) tend to be those with a relatively high proportion of poor residents. Compared with those of other Latin American countries, the Venezuelan formula has the advantage of simplicity, predictability, and transparency.

The other major source of local government finance is own revenue generation. This typically ranges between 35 percent of total income for smaller municipalities and 65 percent for larger municipalities. Local revenue is typically generated by taxes (88 percent) and user charges (12 percent). Venezuelan municipalities have considerable discretion to vary the level or rate of taxation levied in their area of jurisdiction, an unusual feature in Latin America. Nevertheless, the long-standing tradition of applying absolute rather than percentage rates has had an extremely detrimental effect upon local revenue yields as a result of rising inflation during the 1980s.

The three major sources of municipal taxation are (1) the business tax, which is levied at a variable rate of 0.2–1.0 percent of total sales; (2) the property tax, which is levied on both urban residential and nonresidential users; and (3) a vehicle road tax, which is levied at a flat rate based on vehicle weight rather than engine size. As a result of the failure to update the flat rate over thirty years, the effective tax rate on the sale price of a new passenger car fell from 1.67 percent in 1962 to 0.0067 percent by 1992. At such low rates, yields are often insufficient even to cover collection costs. Other taxes include a tax on entrance tickets to cinemas and sporting events, a betting tax on horse racing and lotteries, and a tax on posters, billboards, lighting, and other advertising. Although a betterment levy exists, it is little used in Venezuela. Municipal borrowing in order to finance investment is extremely limited.

Although the 1989 municipal code gave additional revenue-raising

powers to local government in the form of a rural land tax, a tax on commercial advertisements, and a tax on gambling, there remains considerable
untapped potential for municipalities to raise the revenue yield from the
major local taxes. Municipalities could achieve this revenue increase in four
major ways: (1) by converting the assessment for the business tax from a
turnover basis to a profits or value-added basis; (2) by abolishing the existing exemptions for public sector properties; (3) by improving property tax
administration via updating the cadastre, increasing registration, and
empowering municipalities to enforce compliance; and (4) by radically raising the rate of the vehicle road tax by converting it from a flat rate to a percentage basis.

INTERMUNICIPAL COOPERATION

Although a national municipal association, the Asociación Venezolana de
Cooperación Intermunicipal (AVECI), was established in 1967, it remains
extremely weak and ineffective.

SUPPORT SERVICES

Since 1962 local government training has been carried out by the Fundación
para el Desarrollo de la Comunidad y Fomento Municipal (FUNDACO-
MUN), a state body whose president and executive director are named by
the president of the republic. During the 1960s, FUNDACOMUN was
regarded as a model institution of its kind in Latin America. It received
U.S.$30 million from USAID and technical assistance from the Institute of
Public Administration in New York, and it operated a wide range of services
for municipalities. These services included legal assistance; fiscal administration training, especially cadastral surveying; urban planning; general
management training; the promotion of local economic development; and
the provision of matching soft loan finance for public service investments,
especially solid waste management, bus terminals, and slaughterhouses.
FUNDACOMUN also boasted a strong commitment to promoting community participation in local government.

But the achievements of FUNDACOMUN fell far short of initial expectations. The organization suffered from poor leadership as a result of political interference. One incoming director fired all professionals who had been
employed under the previous administration. Another sought to convert
FUNDACOMUN into the government's principal agent for upgrading
squatter settlements. Yet another director was the young and inexperienced
daughter of the president of Venezuela; she had only recently graduated
from university. By 1988, according to one of its early advisers, FUNDA-

COMUN was a pale imitation of its former self, an organization barely alive and involved chiefly with minor incursions into community development (Boyce:4–7).

CITIZEN PARTICIPATION

Venezuelan municipalities retain a deep-rooted tradition of clientelism, and until very recently, citizen participation in local government was extremely weak by comparison with the rest of Latin America. Beginning in the 1960s, independent neighborhood organizations (*asociaciones de vecinos*) sprung up in urban areas in response to growing middle-class alienation from the corrupt two-party political system. In 1971 they formed a national federation, the Federación de Asociaciones y Comunidades Urbanas (FACUR). Although neighborhood organizations were given official recognition by the 1978 municipal code, municipal authorities generally refused to grant them consultative status. By 1988 FACUR had grown into a powerful movement for municipal reform, with over 8,000 member organizations.

The situation changed following the 1989 municipal code, which for the first time introduced measures to encourage citizen participation in local government. Parish councils (juntas parroquiales) were introduced at the submunicipal level, with five representatives in urban areas and three in rural areas. Initially they were elected according to the voting share of parties in council elections. A subsequent amendment to the municipal code introduced direct elections based on a party list system for the first time in December 1992. Municipal councils were also obliged to hold open sessions every three months in order to consider matters that pressure groups had requested to be aired in public. Councils had to invite community organizations, such as trade unions, social clubs, and sports clubs, to participate in these meetings.

In December 1990 the municipal code was amended to strengthen the consultative role of citizen associations in municipal affairs. At the same time, in order to promote citizen participation, the minimum number of members required to found an association was reduced to fifty in urban areas and twenty in rural areas. The reform empowered citizen groups to present ordinances for consideration by the council. Similarly, a petition signed by 10 percent of those on the electoral register required the council either to reconsider ordinances or else to submit them to a referendum. For example, in June 1992 two municipalities (Pampater in Nueva Esparta, and Cajigal in Anzoátegui) held referendums to decide whether to revoke the mandate of their mayors; and in the Municipality of Ezequiel Zamora in Monagas a referendum was held to decide on the relocation of a community displaced by environmental pollution.

PROSPECTS FOR LOCAL GOVERNMENT

In the midst of a profound political crisis, in the mid-1980s modernizers inside the Venezuelan political elite sought to radically reform a decadent political system. A decentralization program has played a major part in the reform process and has given high priority to the transfer of functions such as education, health, and public housing from federal to state government. But progress has been slow; in 1993 the first agreements were signed between the federal government and six states for the transfer of responsibility for public health services.

By contrast, the transfer of functions to local government has been accorded low priority. Imprecision in the enabling legislation has led to problems in the implementation of the program. Although a clear timetable was agreed upon for the increase in the situado budgetary assignment, there was no similar timetable for the transfer of expenditure responsibilities, which have lagged far behind. This mismatch between the enhanced allocation of revenue shares without corresponding expenditure obligations runs the risk of creating the kind of macroeconomic instability experienced in Brazil.

State governments will be the major beneficiaries of central government interjurisdictional transfers under the new situado mechanism. By 1994 states already received an estimated 20 percent of central government recurrent income. By contrast, local government will receive an annual nonconditional grant equivalent to only 4 percent of central government ordinary revenue by 1999. This is not very high by Latin American standards, and it does not bode well for the attainment of improved equity, although states and municipalities that assume new expenditure responsibilities have been promised extra budgetary allocations by central government, to be based on current expenditure levels.

Perhaps more than anywhere else in Latin America, clientelism poses a serious challenge to the decentralization process (Ellner:103). Under the 1989 LODT, COPRE can impose neither a unified career structure nor a unified pay-and-reward system upon state governments. Instead, it has sought to influence new legislation on personnel matters currently under consideration in several states. In the meantime, the transfer of major functions and competencies from central government could be seriously threatened by the lack of human resource management at the state and municipal levels.

Appendix 1

The Declaration
of Quito

The mayors, deputy mayors, council members, leaders of municipal development agencies, and experts in local government from Latin America and the Caribbean, gathering in Quito between 22 and 25 November 1988 on the occasion of the biennial meeting of the Latin American Chapter of the International Union of Local Authorities (IULA) and the international seminar "The Role of the Municipality as Agent for Development and Decentralization in Latin America," hereby declare:

1. Latin America and the Caribbean face a situation of economic crisis and social decline characterized by a foreign debt of around U.S.$400 billion, by an increase in the level of poverty that already afflicts more than 40 percent of Latin Americans, and by national circumstances that include both low economic growth and problems of acute economic, social, and political inequality.

The root cause of these problems may be traced back to the profound differences in the existing level of development between the great economic powers of America, Europe, and Asia, and our Latin American countries. As a result of unequal trading relations, technological differences, and an excessive financial burden, a significant part of our resources goes abroad, contributing to the accentuation of the economic crisis and social backwardness. Given these realities, the municipalities of Latin America and the Caribbean must assist our peoples in the forging of a greater Latin American unity that will facilitate the economic and political integration that is so necessary to strengthen our national economies.

2. The centralizing and exclusionary nature of the style of development that prevails in most of the countries of the region is a clear expression of the situation of backwardness referred to above. The tendency toward the spatial concentration of the population in a few urban centers, the structural concentration of production in the formal or modern sector of the economy, and the functional concentration of wealth in high-income social groups are all easily observable phenomena. These tendencies are reproduced within

the structure of government itself, in which central government usually retains over 90 percent of fiscal revenue, in contrast with the chronic financial weakness of regional and local governments.

3. Although it was undoubtedly necessary during certain periods in our countries' history to strengthen central government in order to ensure the creation and consolidation of the nation-state, the tendency toward the concentration of political power and resources in the central nucleus of the public administration has outlived its usefulness. Just at a time when the potential of Latin American public administration is urgently needed in order to overcome the crisis, the deficiencies of that administration are plain to see: its inability to raise the growth rate, its incapacity to redistribute social expenditure in favor of the poorest, its bureaucratic sloth, and, what is more, its grave cases of corruption.

Modernization of the state and replacement of the current centralizing structures are indispensable in order to overcome the crisis. In opposition to the proposals to simply dismantle the public sector there exist the alternatives of decentralization and of strengthening local government.

4. The municipality is local government par excellence. Its mission is to represent and mobilize citizens, productive enterprise, social organizations, and other institutions within its area of jurisdiction in pursuit of actions for collective development and welfare. Although its particular functions vary from country to country, and even within countries, according to tradition and the law, its role as a catalyst for local economic development and as a corrector of social inequalities at the local level is, in essence, the same everywhere.

In order to function properly, the municipality must possess a high degree of political autonomy; must count on its own resources, the stability of which is recognized by law; must be legitimated by the democratic election of its principal authorities; and in particular must be supported by the active participation of the community in all aspects of its operation.

Furthermore, it must mobilize the human and material resources of its communities through effective mechanisms of social participation and through professional and technical support from state and private institutions in each locality.

5. However, in a similar fashion to other levels of the state apparatus, municipalities suffer from deficiencies that must be corrected:

- The functions of authority must be sufficiently dignified and technically qualified. The mayor or council leader must combine the qualities of community leader with those of a good public administrator. In this sense, political parties and the political system must carry out a proper selection of candidates for electoral office, providing them with adequate technical assistance and training.

- Municipal staff should be recruited through open competition according to their capacities and professional and technical qualifications. They should receive systematic training and motivation, and should receive a salary commensurate with their responsibilities and tasks. The maximum degree of job stability should be sought for the good public servant, particularly for those occupying high technical levels and functional responsibilities.

- The finances of local government should be assured both through its own fiscal effort, which can provide it with a considerable level of income from its own locality, as well as through transfers from the national public finances, particularly in the case of municipalities in economically deprived and isolated areas. Municipalities should also obtain financial resources through voluntary contributions from the community and from the private sector.

- Municipal activities should be ordered in time and space by the elaboration of plans and programs that are adapted to local reality, that encourage a responsible use of natural resources in order to preserve the environment, and that are compatible with the municipality's own availability of human and financial resources. These plans should be drawn up with the maximum participation of the community. Local development planning is not an end in itself, but rather an instrument to improve the efficiency and efficacy of municipal activities.

- Municipalities should seek, wherever possible, to provide services that are self-financing. To achieve this, it is necessary to establish realistic tariff systems, which are complemented, if necessary, with redistributive mechanisms so as not to unduly affect low-income groups. The administration of public services should enjoy a sufficient degree of internal autonomy, for example, through decentralized municipal companies, in order to guarantee the technical competence of its management.

6. In the promotion of economic development, national and local government have different although complementary functions. There should be an equitable redistribution of tasks and resources between the two that can assure that the central level may concentrate on strategic decisionmaking linked to issues of national sovereignty, to macroeconomic management, and to the establishment of overall social policies, while shedding those innumerable smaller decisions that have to do with the implementation or local application of the former.

At the local level, on the other hand, the municipality can fulfill the role of comprehensive government by assuming all those tasks and decisions related to the effective promotion of development.

7. Central governments can assist municipal strengthening through the execution of programs of technical assistance, credit, and training, insofar as these are carried out in a spirit of strict respect for municipal autonomy. However, these programs should be subsidiary in character; in other words, they should not do what municipalities or their associations can do by themselves.

8. The formation and proper functioning of regional and national municipal associations are extremely useful in ensuring a fluid and positive dialogue between central and local government. In addition, these groups can undertake important tasks such as intermunicipal cooperation at national or international level, training, technical assistance, and other actions in favor of municipal development.

9. International development agencies—both bilateral and multilateral—can play an important role in strengthening municipalities and local power to the extent that they assign resources to programs of local development and municipal strengthening. However, the municipality should try to ensure that this assistance is mainly in grant form. Foreign loans should be obtained on the best possible conditions, that is, at low rates of interest and with adequate repayment periods. In this way, municipalities will be able to avoid having to earmark limited resources to debt servicing, thereby reducing the amount available for local development.

Furthermore, the commitments acquired with these agencies should not depend upon the prior approval of central government. In this sense, the channeling of aid for development exclusively through central government reinforces centralization and does not necessarily ensure the optimal use of resources.

10. Localities that depend upon central government are not fully developed localities. Decentralization is therefore an imperative for development. It presupposes, first, the transfer of resources, as well as decisionmaking capacity regarding their use, from central government to the regions, localities, and communities; it implies, second, that these bodies become progressively more capable of generating their own resources.

11. Although the strengthening of municipalities and local power is by no means the only possible form of decentralization, it is one of the most important means of promoting growth in the social base, the improvement of civic and political culture of communities, and a spatially more equitable improvement in the living conditions of the whole population, particularly the poorest social groups.

In this sense, cultural development and a strengthening of civic consciousness among local communities so as to forge their own destiny should precede, or at least accompany, purely material or physical growth.

Quito, 25 November 1988

Appendix 2

The Declaration of Tegucigalpa

The mayors and the representatives from municipal associations and development institutes supporting municipal development in Guatemala, Honduras, El Salvador, Nicaragua, Costa Rica, and Panama, gathering in the city of Tegucigalpa, M.D.C., for the regional seminar "The Role of the Municipality: The Essential Elements of Municipal Activity," 19–21 November 1991,

Considering

That municipalities are the natural scene for citizen life and constitute the basic cell of public administration and, for this reason, the government level at which the basic needs for life and collective well-being can be satisfied;

That the countries from the Central American isthmus confront the challenge of overcoming political, institutional, economic, and social crisis through the restructuring of the state, which should assure economic growth and peace based on social justice and the full recognition of the rights of all citizens;

That the people of the Central American isthmus have expressed their will to confront these development challenges through democratic systems that guarantee full citizen representation and new opportunities for coordination;

That the development of democracy fundamentally depends on it being fully exercised at the local government level;

That it is critical to strengthen the integration process, which should be focused on jointly confronting some of the basic problems that our development demands;

We Declare

1. The expressed will of mayors throughout the region and of the local communities that we represent to demand greater and better participation of local governments in the decisions and development of our communities;

2. The urgent need to entirely restructure the state in all of our countries such that the satisfaction of community needs takes place in an efficient, equitable, and democratic manner;

3. Our expressed and manifest support for political, fiscal, and institutional decentralization;

4. That within the decentralization process, it is necessary to devolve to municipalities the functions that guarantee full attention to the fundamental needs of our communities, along with the transfer of technical and financial resources necessary to adequately attend to such needs. This transfer should guarantee a greater and fairer distribution of resources among the communities in our nations. We reclaim these functions as a fundamental attribute of local government;

5. Our will to assume the exercise of these restored functions, which should be transferred gradually and selectively, as commonly agreed upon by the national government and municipalities of each country and as a function of the needs, capacities, and relative level of development of each municipality;

6. Our full commitment to confront the challenge of directly satisfying the vital needs of our communities under the conditions defined above. In this context, we commit the efforts of local government in supporting a more democratic and efficient administration for the collection and utilization of resources;

7. Our conviction that municipalities possess important comparative advantages that make it possible to better and more directly attend to local demands. These comparative advantages include: proximity to the user, which implies a lower cost in the implementation of public works projects and in the provision of services; greater receptivity to the demands and particular needs of local communities; the possibility for "co-development" and "co-responsibility" with these communities; and the possibility of subjecting development to citizen control;

8. That municipal development requires greater legitimacy and political representation to guarantee the credibility and support of the citizenry for the municipal execution of mandates. Consequently, we demand that local leaders be selected through direct and universal elections that occur on dates different from that of national elections and that are based on the local debate of platforms proposed by candidates to support and carry out community interests. The formation of city councils should be based on the principle of proportional representation;

9. That, in order to achieve the above, we reiterate our will to strengthen national municipal associations under the principles of free asso-

ciations and political independence. To these associations we give the tasks of: developing and supporting municipal political will that the process of state restructuring and decentralization will demand; municipal representation in national discussions and decisions that affect municipal interests and responsibilities; and the management of support services that allow the technical and administrative strengthening of local governments such that they can fully and efficiently exercise their functions;

10. Our full support for the Federation of Municipalities from the Central American Isthmus (FEMICA) as the most appropriate entity for representing and supporting us for the basic purpose of politically and economically strengthening municipal governments and administrations. In particular, we stand behind the work of FEMICA in its search for strategies and mechanisms that will mobilize political support as well as obtain support from actual national decentralization efforts. We expressly entrust FEMICA with the role of being our representative and speaker in regional integration efforts and request that FEMICA present this declaration in the next summit of Central American presidents.

We entrust FEMICA and the national municipal associations with promoting and executing the conclusions of this seminar and the plans set forth in this Declaration of Tegucigalpa.

APPENDIX 3

DIRECTORY OF MAJOR MUNICIPAL SUPPORT INSTITUTIONS IN LATIN AMERICA

ARGENTINA

CENTRO—Estudios Sociales y Ambientales
Roque Sáenz Peña 1142 - 5 Piso
1035 Buenos Aires
Tel: (54) 1 382-7040
FAX: (54) 1 325-7712

Centro de Estudios Urbanos y Regionales (CEUR)
Av. Corrientes 2835
Cuerpo A., 7º Piso
1193 Buenos Aires
Tel: (54) 1 961-2355
FAX: (54) 1 961-1332

BOLIVIA

Instituto de Investigación y Desarrollo Municipal (INIDEM)
Av. 6 de Agosto 2376
Casilla Postal 12355
La Paz
Tel: (591) 2 366-921
FAX: (591) 2 373-586

BRAZIL

Instituto Brasileiro de Administração Municipal (IBAM)
Largo IBAM No. 1
Humaitá
22282 Rio de Janeiro, RJ
Tel: (55) 21 537-7595
FAX: (55) 21 537-1262

Confederação Nacional de Municípios (CNM)
Av. Paulista 1776 - 6 andar
São Paolo - SP 01310-200
Tel: (55) 11 284-0740
FAX: (55) 11 284-1667

CHILE

Asociación Chilena de Municipalidades (ACM)
Estado No. 360, Of. 702-B
Santiago
Tel: (56) 2 633-7077
FAX: (56) 2 633-7263

COLOMBIA

Escuela Superior de Administración Pública (ESAP)
Diagonal 40 No. 46-A-37
Apartado Aéreo 29745
Bogotá
Tel: (57) 1 222-4700
FAX: (57) 1 222-4356

Federación Colombiana de Municipios (FCM)
Carrera 8a. 11-73
Bogotá
Tel: (57) 1 342-1572
FAX: (57) 1 342-1668

COSTA RICA

Instituto de Fomento y Asesoría Municipal (IFAM)
Apartado 10187-1000
San José
Tel: (506) 233-3714
FAX: (506) 233-1817

Unión Nacional de Gobiernos Locales (UNGL)
Apartado Postal 7696
San José
Tel: (506) 238-072
FAX: (506) 827-805

DOMINICAN REPUBLIC

Liga Municipal Dominicana (LMD)
Av. Correa y Cidrón esq. Jiménez Moya
Centro de los Héroes
Apartado 1471
Santo Domingo
Tel: (809) 533-3181
FAX: (809) 533-5882

ECUADOR

Asociación de Municipalidades Ecuatorianas (AME)
Apartado 17-01-2654
Quito
Tel: (593) 2 242-166
FAX: (593) 2 442-865

Centro de Investigaciones Ciudad (CIUDAD)
Av. La Gasca 326 y Carvajal
Casilla Postal 17-08-8311
Quito
Tel: (593) 2 230-192
FAX: (593) 2 402-362

EL SALVADOR

Instituto Salvadoreño de Administración Municipal (ISAM)
Calle Loma Linda 154
Col. San Benito
Código Postal 01-173
San Salvador
Tel: (503) 2 231-313
FAX: (503) 2 981-526

Instituto Salvadoreño de Desarrollo Municipal (ISDEM)
49 Avenida Sur
725 San Salvador
Tel: (503) 2 981-973
FAX: (503) 2 236-287

GUATEMALA

Instituto de Fomento Municipal (INFOM)
8A. Calle 1-66, Zona 9
Ciudad de Guatemala
Tel: (502) 2 310-168
FAX: (502) 2 314-950

HONDURAS

Asociación de Municipios de Honduras (AMHON)
Apartado Postal 3596
Tegucigalpa, D.C.
Tel: (504) 387-168
FAX: (504) 376-827

Banco Municipal Autónomo (BANMA)
Apartado 289
Tegucigalpa, D.C.
Tel: (504) 376-946
FAX: (504) 376-946

MEXICO

Centro Nacional de Desarrollo Municipal (CNDM)
Secretaría de Gobernación
General Prim No. 21
Col. Centro
C.P. 06040
Cuauhtémoc
México D.F.
Tel: (52) 5 535-6653
FAX: (52) 5 535-4175

Centro de Estudios de Administración Estatal y Municipal
Instituto Nacional de Administración Pública (INAP)
km 14.5 Carretera México-Toluca
Col. Palo Alto
C.P. 05110
Cuajimalpa
México D.F.
Tel: (52) 5 570-4643
FAX: (52) 5 570-0532

Instituto para el Desarrollo Técnico de las Haciendas Públicas (INDETEC)
Av. Lázaro Cárdenas No. 3289
Colonia Chapalita
Apartado Postal 5-866
45040 Guadalajara, Jal.
Tel: (52) 36 213-621
FAX: (52) 36 222-945

NICARAGUA

Instituto Nicaragüense de Fomento Municipal (INIFOM)
Carretera a la Refinería
Apartado Postal 3097
Managua
Tel: (505) 2 666-429
FAX: (505) 2 664-905

PANAMA

Instituto Panameño de Desarrollo Municipal (IPADEM)
Vista Hermosa
Vía Fernández de Córdoba
Apartado Postal 87-2108
Panamá 7
Tel: (507) 614-190
FAX: (507) 614-437

PARAGUAY

Instituto de Desarrollo Municipal (IDM)
Ygatimí No. 705, esq. J. O'Leary
Apartado Postal 1161
Asunción
Tel: (595) 21 444-542
FAX: (595) 21 442-079

PERU

Asociación de Municipalidades del Peru (AMPE)
Malecón Armendáriz 193
Miraflores, Lima 18
Tel: (51) 14 655-560
FAX: (51) 14 652-948

Instituto de Investigación y Capacitación Municipal (INICAM)
Apartado Postal 27-0187
San Isidro, Lima 27
Tel: (51) 14 473-838
FAX: (51) 14 473-838

Instituto Para la Democracia Local (IPADEL)
Elías Aguirre 180
Miraflores, Lima 18
Tel: (51) 14 460-835
FAX: (51) 14 469-121

VENEZUELA

Fundación para el Desarrollo de la Comunidad y Fomento Municipal (FUN-DACOMUN)
Apartado Postal 50218
Caracas 1050
Tel: (58) 2 952-0223
FAX: (58) 2 952-0185

Asociación Venezolana de Cooperación Intermunicipal (AVECI)
Apartado 2029
Caracas
Tel: (58) 2 811-590
FAX: (58) 2 810-162

REGIONAL ORGANIZATIONS

Centro Latinoamericano de Administración para el Desarrollo (CLAD)
Apartado Postal 4181
Caracas 1010-A
Venezuela
Tel: (58) 2 923-297
FAX: (58) 2 918-427

Federación de Municipios del Istmo Centroamericano (FEMICA)
Avda. Cervantes, Edif. Principal
Frente Catedral Metropolitana, 3 piso
Tegucigalpa, D.C.
Honduras
Tel: (504) 220-018
FAX: (504) 220-242

Instituto Centroamericano de Administración Pública (ICAP)
Apartado Postal 10025
San José
Costa Rica
Tel: (506) 341-011
FAX: (506) 252-049

International Union of Local Authorities—Centro de Capacitación y Desarrollo de los Gobiernos Locales (IULA-CELCADEL)
Casilla 17-01-1109
Quito
Ecuador
Tel: (593) 2 469-365
FAX: (593) 2 435-205

GENERAL BIBLIOGRAPHY

Aguiluz, D. "Democratización del estado y descentralización," *Revista Centroamericano de Administración Pública* (San José), No.18 (Jan.–June 1990), pp.5–36.

Ahumada, J. "El gobierno y la administración local: Tradición y cambio en los 80's," *Revista Interamericana de Planificación* (México), Vol.19, No.75–76 (Sept.–Dec. 1985), pp.197–223.

Allen, H.J.B. *Cultivating the grassroots: Why local government matters.* Bombay: IULA and All-India Institute of Local Self-Government, 1990.

Annis, S., and Hakim, P. (eds.) *Direct to the poor: Grassroots development in Latin America.* Boulder, Colo.: Lynne Rienner Publishers, 1988.

Arboleda, M. (ed.) *Finanzas municipales: Estudios breves en 8 países latinoamericanos.* Quito: CELCADEL-IULA, 1990.

Arocena, J. "Descentralización e iniciativa: Una discusión necesaria," *Cuadernos del CLAEH* (Montevideo), No.51 (Dec. 1989), pp.43–56.

Bervejillo, F. "Gobierno local en América Latina: Casos de Argentina, Chile, Brasil y Uruguay," in Nohlen, D. (ed.) *Descentralización política y consolidación democrática: Europa—América Latina.* Caracas: Nueva Sociedad, 1991, pp.279–299.

Blanksten, G. I. "Bibliography on Latin American politics and government," *Inter-American Review of Bibliography,* IV (1954), No.3, pp.191–214.

Boisier, S. "Decentralization and regional development in Latin America," *CEPAL Review* (Santiago), No.31 (April 1987), pp.133–144.

Borja, J. *Descentralización del estado: Movimiento social y gestión local.* Santiago: FLASCO, 1987.

Borja, J., Calderón, F., Grossi, M., and Peñalva, S. (eds.) *Descentralización y democracia: Gobiernos locales en América Latina.* Santiago: CLACSO/SUR/CEUMT, 1989.

Boisier, S. *Centralización y descentralización territorial en el proceso decisorio del sector público.* Santiago: ILPES, 1985.

Burkholder, M. A., and Johnson, L. L. *Colonial Latin America.* New York: Oxford University Press, 1990.

Campbell, T., et al. *Decentralization to local government in LAC: National strategies and local responses in planning, spending and management.* Washington, D.C.: World Bank, Latin America and the Caribbean Technical Department, 1991.

Carrión, F. (ed.) *La investigación urbana en América Latina: Caminos recorridos y por recorrer—estudios nacionales.* Quito: Ciudad, 1989.

———. (ed.) *Municipio y democracia: Gobiernos locales en ciudades intermedias de América Latina.* Santiago: Ed. SUR, 1991.

Castells, M. "Administración municipal, democracia política y planeamiento urbano en América Latina," in Borja, J., et al. *Organización y descentralización municipal*. Buenos Aires: Edit. Universitaria de Buenos Aires, 1987, pp.163–173.

Chirinos, L. A. "La participación vecinal," in Pease, H. (ed.) *Construyendo un gobierno metropolitano*. Lima: IPADEL, 1991, pp.87–138.

Clichevsky, N. *Construcción y administración de la ciudad latinoamericano*. Buenos Aires: IIED, 1990, ch. 4.

Conyers, D. "Decentralization and development: A review of the literature," *Public Administration and Development*, Vol.4, No.2 (April–June 1983), pp.187–197.

Coraggio, J. L. "Poder local, poder popular," *Cuadernos del CLAEH* (Montevideo), No.45–46 (August 1988), pp.101–120.

Cornelius, W., and Kemper, R. (eds.) *Metropolitan Latin America: The challenge and the response—Latin American Urban Research, Vol.6*. Beverly Hills, Calif.: Sage, 1978.

Cunill, N. *Participación ciudadana*. Caracas: CLAD, 1991.

D'Alessandro, R., et al. *Administración y reforma tributaria municipal en América Latina*. Caracas: CLAD—Capítulo Latinoamericano de IULA, 1987.

Davey, K. *Sectoral adjustment: The case of municipal development*. Birmingham: Development Administration Group, University of Birmingham, 1992.

Davis, H. E. (ed.) *Government and politics in Latin America*. New York: Ronald Press, 1958, ch. 13.

De Mattos, C. A. "La descentralización: Una nueva panacea para impulsar el desarrollo local?" *Cuadernos del CLAEH* (Montevideo), No.51 (Dec. 1989), pp.57–75.

Dillinger, W. *Urban property taxation in developing countries*. Washington, D.C.: World Bank, 1988 (Policy Planning and Research Department, Working Paper No.41).

Domínguez, Francisco. *Estudios sobre las instituciones local hispanoamericanas*. Caracas: Academia Nacional de la Historia, 1981.

Edelman, D. (ed.) *Coloquio técnico sobre gestión de áreas metropolitanas: Informe final*. Caracas: CLAD, 1990.

Fox, J. "Latin America's emerging local politics," *Journal of Democracy*, Vol.5, No.2 (April 1994), pp.105–116.

Galilea, S. "La planificación local: Nuevas orientaciones metodológicas," *Cuadernos del CLAEH* (Montevideo), No.45–46 (August 1988), pp.123–141.

Gall, P. M. *Municipal development programs in Latin America: An inter-country evaluation*. New York: Praeger, 1976.

Gilbert, A. G. *The Latin American city*. London: Latin America Bureau, 1994.

Gilbert, A. G., et al. (eds.) *Urbanization in contemporary Latin America*. London: John Wiley, 1982.

Graham, C. "Mexico's solidarity program in comparative context: Demand-based poverty alleviation programs in Latin America, Africa and Eastern Europe," in Cornelius, W. A., et al. (eds.) *Transforming state-society relations in Mexico: The national solidarity strategy*. San Diego: University of California, Center for U.S.-Mexican Studies, 1994, pp.309–327.

Graham, L. S. "Latin America," in Rowat, D. C. (ed.) *International handbook on local government reorganization: Contemporary developments*. Westport, Conn.: Greenwood Press, 1980, pp.487–498.

Guarda, G. C. "A new direction in World Bank urban lending to Latin American countries," *Review of Urban and Regional Studies*, Vol.2 (1990), pp.115–124.

Hardoy, J. E., et al. (eds.) *Ciudades en conflicto: Poder local, participación popular y planificación en las ciudades intermedias de América Latina.* Quito: El Conejo-CIUDAD, 1986.

Haring, C. H. *The Spanish empire in America.* New York: Oxford University Press, 1947, ch. 9.

Harris, R. L. "Centralization and decentralization in Latin America," in Cheema, G. S., and Rondinelli, D. A. (eds.) *Decentralization and development: Policy implications in developing countries.* Berkeley, Calif.: Sage, 1983, pp.183–202.

Herzer, H., and Pírez, P. "Municipal government and popular participation in Latin America," *Environment and Urbanization,* Vol.3, No.1 (April 1991), pp.79–95.

Hijano, M. "El municipio iberoamericano en la historiografía española," *Revista de Indias,* Vol.50, No.188 (1990), pp.83–94.

Humes, S. *Local governance and national power: A worldwide comparison of tradition and change in local government.* Hemel Hempstead, England: Harvester Wheatsheaf, 1991.

Hurtado, J. "Probable contexto sociopolítico y económico del desarrollo local latinoamericano en los próximos veinte años," *Revista de la SIAP* (Guatemala), Vol.23, No.91–92 (Dec. 1990), pp.274–282.

Jacobi, P. "Descentralización municipal y participación ciudadana: Anotaciones para el debate," *Estudios Sociales Centroamericanos,* No.55 (Jan.–April 1991), pp.45–60.

Jickling, D. "The IULA centre in Quito: The first two years," *Planning and Administration,* Vol.12, No.2 (Autumn 1985), pp.60–66.

Kern, R. (ed.) *The caciques: Oligarchical politics and the system of caciquismo in the Luso-Hispanic world.* Albuquerque: University of New Mexico Press, 1973.

Kirkpatrick, F. A. "Municipal administration in the Spanish dominions in America," *Transactions of the Royal Historical Society* (London), 3rd series, Vol.9 (1915), pp.95–110.

Leal, F., and Dávila, A. *Clientelismo: El sistema político y su expresión regional.* Bogotá: Tercer Mundo, 1990.

Lordello de Mello, D. *Local government training needs in Latin America.* Paper presented to the Large Cities Forum promoted by Nairobi City Council and IULA. Nairobi, Kenya, 16–18 November 1982.

———. "Modernización de los gobiernos locales en América Latina," *Revista Interamericana de Planificación,* Vol.17, No.66 (June 1983), pp.185–202.

———. "Associação de Municípios: Experiência na América Latina," *Revista de Administração Municipal,* No.172 (July–Sept. 1984), pp.56–63.

Lowndes, V. "Decentralisation: The potentials and the pitfalls," *Local Government Policy Making,* Vol.18, No.4 (March 1992), pp.53–63.

Lynch, J. "Intendants and cabildos in the Viceroyalty of La Plata, 1782–1810," *Hispanic American Historical Review,* Vol.35 (August 1955), pp.337–362.

———. *Spanish colonial administration, 1782–1810.* London: University of London, Athlone Press, 1958, ch. 9.

———. "The institutional framework of colonial Spanish America," *Journal of Latin American Studies.* Vol.24 (1992), Supplement, pp.69–81.

McAlister, L. N. *Spain and Portugal in the New World, 1492–1700.* Minneapolis: University of Minnesota Press, 1984.

Macon, J., and Merino, J. *Financing urban and rural development through betterment levies: The Latin American experience.* New York: Praeger, 1977.

Marzahl, P. *Town in the Empire: Government, politics and society in seventeenth-century Popayán.* Austin, Texas: Institute of Latin American Studies, 1978.

Mawhood, P. "Decentralisation and the Third World in the 1980s," *Planning and Administration,* Vol.14, No.1 (Spring 1987), pp.10–22.

Montoya, M. (ed.) *Memoria del seminario latinoamericano de administración municipal del 16 al 20 de junio de 1980.* Lima: INAP, 1980.

Morse, R. M., and Hardoy, J. E. (eds.) *Rethinking the Latin American city.* Baltimore: Johns Hopkins University Press, 1992.

Mouchet, C. "Municipal government," in Davis, H. E. (ed.) *Government and politics in Latin America.* New York: Ronald Press, 1958, pp.368–392.

Nickson, R. A. "Democratisation and local government in Latin America," *Administrative Studies* (Helsinki), Vol.11, No.4 (1992), pp.219–231.

Nohlen, D. (ed.) *Descentralización política y consolidación democrática: Europa–América Latina.* Caracas: Nueva Sociedad, 1991.

Norton, A. *International handbook of local and regional government: A comparative analysis of advanced democracies.* Aldershot: Edward Elgar, 1994.

Orduña, E. *Bibliografía Iberoamericana de administración local.* Madrid: IEAL-AVECI, 1983.

Organization of American States (OAS). *The financial situation of the municipalities and the role of the central government in Latin America.* Washington, D.C.: Organization of American States, Public Administration Unit, 1968.

Parry, J. H. *The Spanish seaborne empire.* London: Hutchinson, 1966.

Pierson, W. W. "Some reflections on the cabildo as an institution," *Hispanic American Historical Review,* Vol.5, No.4 (Nov. 1922), pp.573–596.

Pike, F. B. "Public work and social welfare in colonial Spanish American towns," *The Americas,* Vol.13, No.4 (April 1957), pp.361–375.

———. "Algunos aspectos de la ejecucion de las leyes municipales en la America Española durante la época de las Austrias," *Revista de Indias,* Vol.18, No.72 (April/June 1958), pp.201–223.

———. "The municipality and the system of checks and balances in Spanish American colonial administration," *The Americas,* Vol.15, No.2 (Oct. 1958), pp.139–158.

———. "Aspects of cabildo economic relations in Spanish America under the Hapsburgs," *Inter-American Economic Affairs,* Vol. 13, No.4 (Spring 1960a), pp.67–86.

———. "The cabildo and colonial loyalty to Hapsburg rulers," *Journal of Inter-American Studies,* Vol.2, No.4 (Oct. 1960b), pp.405–420.

Population Concern. *1994 World Population Data Sheet.* London: Population Concern, 1994.

Portes, A. "Latin American urbanization during the years of the crisis," *Latin American Research Review,* Vol.24, No.3 (1989), pp.7–44.

Preston Moore, J. *The cabildo in Peru under the Hapsburgs.* Durham, N.C.: Duke University Press, 1954.

Raczynski, D., and Serrano, C. *Políticas sociales, mujeres y gobierno local.* Santiago: CIEPLAN, 1992.

Rehren, A. "El gobierno local en la ciencia política," *Política* (Santiago), No.29 (May 1992), pp.87–108.

Reilly, C. A. (ed.) *New paths to democratic development in Latin America: The rise of NGO-municipal collaboration.* Boulder, Colo.: Lynne Rienner Publishers, 1995.

RHUDO-SA and USAID. *La mujer y la cultura política local en Colombia y Venezuela.* Quito: IULA/CELCADEL, 1993.

————. *La mujer en la política y la administración local de Uruguay y Argentina.* Quito: IULA/CELCADEL, 1993.

Rofman, A. "El proceso de descentralización en América Latina: Causas, desarrollo, perspectivas," in Cunill, N. (ed.) *Descentralización político-administrativa: Bases para su fortalecimiento.* Caracas: CLAD, 1990, pp.9–45.

————. "Descentralización y gobierno local: Una polémica abierta," *Pensamiento Iberoamericano,* Vol.17 (Jan.–June 1990), pp.345–348.

Rosales, M. "Experiencias latinoamericanas de asociativismo municipal," in Martelli, G. (ed.) *Una asociación nacional de municipalidades en Chile.* Santiago: Fundación F. Ebert, 1992, pp.39–49.

Sanin, H. *Descentralización, o la devolución de poderes del gobierno central al gobierno local: Orientaciones para un proceso.* Tegucigalpa: USAID and RHUDO/CA, 1990.

Slater, D. (ed.) *New social movements and the state in Latin America.* Amsterdam: CEDLA, 1985.

Smith, B. *Decentralization: The territorial dimension of the state.* London: Allen & Unwin, 1985.

Stein, S. J., and Stein, B. H. *The colonial heritage of Latin America.* New York: Oxford University Press, 1970.

Tomic, B. "The reason for and feasibility of participation in development in Latin America," *Planning and Administration,* Vol.12, No.2 (Autumn 1985), pp.22–27.

Velíz, C. *The centralist tradition of Latin America.* Princeton N.J.: Princeton University Press, 1980.

Violich, F., and Daughters, R. *Urban planning for Latin America: The challenge of metropolitan growth.* Boston: Oelgeschlager, Gunn & Hain, 1987.

Wheaton, S. H. *A challenge for Central American democracy: A municipal agenda.* Washington, D.C.: PADCO, 1992.

Wiesner, E., and López, R. "Fiscal decentralization: The search for equity and efficiency," in Inter-American Development Bank. *Economic and Social Progress in Latin America: 1994, Report.* Washington, D.C.: Johns Hopkins University Press, 1994. pp.173–231.

World Bank. *World Development Report 1993.* New York: Oxford University Press, 1993.

BIBLIOGRAPHY BY COUNTRY

ARGENTINA

Díaz de Landa, M. "Descentralización nacional y regional en Argentina," in Nohlen, D. (ed.) *Descentralización política y consolidación democrática.* Caracas: Nueva Sociedad, 1991, pp.301–321.

FIEL. *Hacia una nueva organización del federalismo fiscal en la Argentina.* Buenos Aires: Fundación de Investigaciones Económicas Latinoamericanas, 1993.

Fundación Jorge E. Roulet. *Municipalismo y democracia: Encuentros municipales bonaerenses.* Buenos Aires: 1988.

Furlan, J. L,. and Moreno, A. R. *Municipal modernization: Imperatives and strategies* Córdoba: Ministerio de la Función Publica. Paper presented at the 15th World Congress of the International Political Science Association, Buenos Aires, 21–25 July 1991.

García, D., and Garay, A. "El rol de los gobiernos locales en la política Argentina," in Borja, J., et al. (eds.) *Descentralización y democracia: Gobiernos locales en América Latina.* Santiago: CLACSO/SUR/CEUMT, 1989, pp.13–67.

Hardoy, A., and Hardoy, J. E. "Building community organisation: The history of a squatter settlement and its own organisations in Buenos Aires," *Environment and Urbanisation,* Vol.3, No.2 (Oct. 1991), pp.104–120.

Herzer, H. *Local governments in Argentina.* Washington, D.C.: World Bank, 1992a (Infrastructure and Urban Development Department, Working Paper No.94).

———. *El caso de Córdoba, Argentina: Reflexiones metodológicas y conceptuales de investigación.* Santiago: CEPAL, 1992b.

———. *Gestión urbana en ciudades medianas seleccionadas de América Latina: El caso de la ciudad de Córdoba, Argentina.* Buenos Aires: CENTRO, 1992c.

Herzer, H., and Pírez, P. (eds.) *Gobierno de la ciudad y crisis en la Argentina.* Buenos Aires: IIED, 1988.

Pírez, P. "El municipio y la organización del estado en Argentina," *Medio Ambiente y Urbanización,* Year 7, No.28 (Sept. 1989), pp.5–13.

———. *Municipio, necesidades sociales y política local.* Buenos Aires: IIED, 1991a.

———. "Argentina: Descentralización y gobiernos locales," in Nohlen, D. (ed.) *Descentralización política y consolidación democrática.* Caracas: Nueva Sociedad, 1991b, pp.323–333.

———. "Gobierno local en el Area Metropolitana de Buenos Aires," *Medio Ambiente y Urbanización,* No.35 (June 1991c), pp.43–59.

Pírez, P., and Gamallo, G. *Gestión municipal de servicios: Residuos sólidos y vivienda social en Zárate.* Buenos Aires: CENTRO, Informe de Investigación 1/92, 1993.

Ternavasio, M. "Debates y alternativas acerca de un modelo de institución local en la Argentina decimonónica," in *La gestión municipal: Selección de lecturas básicas.* Buenos Aires: Fundación J. Roulet, 1990, pp.43–68.

Walter, R. J. *Politics and urban growth in Buenos Aires, 1910–1942.* Cambridge: Cambridge University Press, 1994.

BOLIVIA

Aramayo, F. (ed.) *Municipalidad y democracia.* La Paz: ILDIS, 1987.

Araujo, F. *El desarrollo municipal y la Ley 843.* La Paz: PROADE, 1994.

Araujo, F., and Gamarra, R. *Estudio comparado de los recursos financieros de la H. Alcaldía Municipal de El Alto.* La Paz: INIDEM, 1991.

Ardaya, R. *Ensayo sobre municipalidad y municipios.* La Paz: INIDEM, 1991.

Aron-Schaar, A. "Local government in Bolivia: Public administration and popular administration," in Heath, D. (ed.) *Contemporary cultures and societies of Latin America: A reader in the social anthropology of Middle and South America.* New York: Random House, 1974, pp.495–501.

Boye, O. "Descentralización en Bolivia," in Nohlen, D. (ed.) *Descentralización política y consolidación democrática.* Caracas: Ed. Nueva Sociedad, 1991, pp.217–223.

Da Rocha, L.A.M. *Reforma institucional de la Ley Orgánica de Municipalidades: Estudio preliminar.* La Paz: Proyecto de Fortalecimiento Municipal (World Bank), 1991.

Finot, I. *Democratización del estado y descentralización.* La Paz: ILDIS, 1990.

Graham, C. "The politics of protecting the poor during adjustment: Bolivia's emergency social fund," *World Development,* Vol.20, No.9 (1992), pp.1233–1251.

Jickling, D. "Municipal development in Bolivia," *Studies in Comparative Local Government,* Vol.8, No.1 (Summer 1974), pp.35–42.

Oporto, H. "Descentralización en Bolivia: Esperanzas y frustraciones," *Nueva Sociedad,* No.105 (Jan.–Feb. 1990), pp.46–54.

Ramírez, L. "Municipio y territorio," in Valencia, L. (ed.) *La legislación municipal en cuestión.* La Paz: INIDEM, 1993, pp.62–119.

Rivera, A. "Municipios y problemas urbanos en Bolivia," *Revista Mexicana de Sociología,* Vol.48, No.4 (Oct.–Dec. 1986), pp.109–121.

Rivera, S. "Liberal democracy and *ayllu* democracy: The case of northern Potosí, Bolivia," *Journal of Development Studies,* Vol.26, No.4 (July 1990), pp.97–121.

Rondinelli, D. A., and Evans, H. "Integrated regional development planning: Linking urban centres and rural areas in Bolivia," *World Development,* Vol.11, No.1 (1983), pp.31–53.

Tellería, W. "Los talleres populares de planificación urbana de Sucre," *Municipio y Participación* (INIDEM), No.1 (Spring 1993), pp.29–31.

Vacaflor, H. (ed.) *El régimen municipal: Aportes al debate.* La Paz: ILDIS, 1990.

Valencia, L. E. (ed.) *La legislación municipal en cuestión.* La Paz: INIDEM, 1993.

Van Lindert, P. "Collective consumption and the state in La Paz," *Boletín de Estudios Latinoamericanos.* Vol.41 (Dec. 1986), pp.71–93.

Vargas, H. "El municipio y la organización del Estado en Bolivia," *Medio ambiente y urbanización,* No.28 (Sept. 1989), pp.14–21.

Whitehead, L. "National power and local power: The case of Santa Cruz de la Sierra,

Bolivia," in Rabinovitz, F., and Trueblood, F. (eds.) *National-local linkages: The interrelationship of urban and national politics in Latin America—Latin American urban research, Vol.3.* Beverly Hills, Calif.: Sage, 1973, pp.23–46.

BRAZIL

Abrucio, F. L. *Descentralização/pacto federativo.* Brasilia: Escola Nacional de Administração Pública, 1993.

Alencar, E., et al. "Administração municipal e associações comunitarias," in *Anais do XV encontro anual da ANPAD.* Belo Horizonte: ANPAD, 1991.

Assies, W. "Urban social movements and local democracy in Brazil," *European Review of Latin American and Caribbean Studies,* No.55 (Dec. 1993), pp.39–58.

Batley, R. "Central-local relations and municipal autonomy in Brazil," *Local Government Studies,* Vol.10, No.3 (1984), pp.51–67.

―――. *Urban management in Brazil: Part 1—Common characteristics, Part 2— Recife, Part 3—Porto Alegre.* Birmingham: University of Birmingham, Development Administration Group, 1992.

Collins, C. *Military rule and the reform of local government in Latin America: The case of Brazil, 1964–1980.* Birmingham: University of Birmingham, Development Administration Group, 1985.

Davey, K. *Municipal government in Brazil: A case study.* Birmingham: University of Birminham, Development Administration Group, 1989.

―――. "The institutional framework for planning," in Devas, N., and Rakodi, C. (eds.) *Managing fast growing cities: New approaches to urban planning and management in the developing world.* Harlow, Essex: Longman, 1993, pp.153–175.

de Barros Loyola, C. *El sistema de mérito y la carrera administrativa en el servicio municipal brasileño.* Rio de Janeiro: IBAM, 1984.

de Souza, C. M. *Metropolização brasileira: Uma análise dos anos setenta.* Rio de Janeiro: Fundaçao Gertulio Vargas, 1985.

―――. "Gestão urbana na constituição de 1988," *Revista de Administração Municipal,* No.192 (July–Sept. 1989), pp.12–27.

Dias, J. M. "Desestabilização institucional no municipalismo brasileiro," *Revista de Administração Municipal,* No.163 (April–June 1982), pp.54–75.

Dillinger, W. *Urban property taxation: Lessons from Brazil.* Washington, D.C.: World Bank, Infrastructure and Urban Development Department Report INU 37, 1989.

Ferguson, B. W. "Protest to programs: Neighbourhood associations in a Brazilian municipality," *Grassroots Development,* Vol.16, No.1 (1992), pp.12–21.

Filho, J. R. "Participação comunitária e descentralização dos servicos de saúde," *Revista de Administração Pública,* Vol.26, No.3 (July–Sept. 1992), pp.119–129.

Gay, R. "Community organizations and clientelist politics in contemporary Brazil: A case study from suburban Rio de Janeiro," *International Journal of Urban and Regional Studies,* Vol.14 (1990), pp.648–666.

Grossi, M. "Situación y perspectivas de los gobiernos locales en Brasil," in Borja, J., et al. (eds.) *Descentralización y democracia: Gobiernos locales en América Latina.* Santiago: CLACSO/SUR/CEUMT, 1989, pp.73–139.

Hermann Netto, J. *Democracia feito em casa.* Brasilia: Cámara de Deputados, 1984.

Lewandowski, E. "Local and state government in the Nova República: Intergovernmental relations of the Brazilian political transition," in Graham, L., and Wilson, R. (eds.) *The political economy of Brazil: Public policies in an era of transition.* Austin: University of Texas, 1990, pp.26–38.

Lordello de Mello, D. *Local government in Brazil.* The Hague: IULA, 1958.

———. "Brazil," in Rowat, D. C. (ed.) *International handbook on local government reorganisation.* London: Aldwych, 1980, pp.473–486.

———. *Contribuição das atividades de treinamento do IBAM ao processo de desenvolvimento urbano.* Rio de Janeiro: IBAM, 1987.

———. "Brazil," in Humes, S. (ed.) *Local governance and national power.* Hemel Hempstead, England: Harvester Wheatsheaf, 1991, pp.155–167.

Lordello de Mello, D., and Reston, J. *El municipio en Brasil.* Rio de Janeiro: IBAM, 1990.

Machado Júnior, J. "Regionalisação ou municipalisação do Brasil," *Revista Brasileira de Estudos Políticos,* No.63–64 (July 1986–Jan. 1987), pp.171–183.

Mahar, D. J., and Dillinger, W. R. *Financing state and local government in Brazil.* Washington, D.C.: World Bank, 1983 (Staff Paper No.612).

Mainwaring, S. "Grassroots popular movements and the struggle for democracy: Nova Iguaçu," in Stepan, A. (ed.) *Democratizing Brazil: Problems of transition and consolidation.* New York: Oxford University Press, 1989, pp.168–204.

Martins, C. E., et al. *Municipalismo: Organização de Orestes Quércia.* São Paulo: CEPASP, 1986.

Medeiros, A. C. *Politics and intergovernmental relations in Brazil: 1964–1982.* New York: Garland, 1986.

Nunes, E., and Vigevani, T. "El municipio y la organización del Estado en Brazil," *Medio Ambiente y Urbanización,* No.28 (Sept. 1989), pp.22–26.

Nunes Leal, V. *Coronelismo: The municipality and representative government in Brazil.* Cambridge: Cambridge University Press, 1977.

Rabinovitch, J. "Curitiba: Towards sustainable urban development," *Environment and Urbanization,* Vol.4, No.2 (Oct. 1992), pp.62–73.

Shah, A. *The new fiscal federalism in Brazil.* Washington, D.C.: World Bank, 1991 (Discussion Paper No.124).

Sherwood, F. P. *Institutionalizing the grass roots in Brazil: A study in comparative local government.* San Francisco: Chandler, 1967.

Velloso da Silva, F. "A experiência catarinense em associaçoes municipais," *Revista de Administração Municipal,* No.164 (July–Sept. 1982), pp.48–65.

Villela, L. "Sistema tributario y relaciones financieras intergubernamentales: La experiencia brasileña," *Planeación y Desarrollo* (Bogotá), Vol.24, No.1 (Jan.–April 1993), pp.171–188.

CHILE

Araos, M. C., et al. *Gobernar la comuna: Manual de gestión municipal.* Santiago: CORDILLERA, 1992.

Baeza, R. *La Contraloría General de la República frente a las municipalidades.* Santiago: Corporación de Promoción Universitaria, 1992.

Castañeda, T. *Combating poverty: Innovative social reforms in Chile during the 1980s.* San Francisco: International Center for Economic Growth, 1992.

Castells, M., et al. *La ciudad de la democracia: Urbanismo, poder local y democracia.* Santiago: Vector, 1988.

Chaparro, P. *Organización y función del gobierno local en Chile, 1925–1973: Una apreciación crítica.* Santiago: Centro de Estudios Democráticos, 1985.

Contraloría General del Estado. *Informe gestión financiera del Estado 1991.* Santiago: Contraloría General del Estado, 1992.

Espinola, V. *Descentralización del sistema escolar en Chile.* Santiago: Centro de Investigación y Desarrollo de la Educación, 1991.

Espinoza, V., et al. "Poder local, pobladores y democracia," *Revista Mexicana de Sociología,* Vol.48, No.4 (Oct.–Dec. 1986), pp.123–140.

Etchepare, J. "Municipalidades: Instancia política o administrativo-local?" *Política* (Santiago), No.29 (1992), pp.13–60.

Garay, I., et al. *Gobernar la comuna: Manual de información y estadísticas básicas comunales y municipales.* Santiago: CORDILLERA, 1991.

ILPES. *Manual de capacitación municipal.* Santiago: ILPES/DIDESCO/UNDP, 1992.

Irarrázabal, I. (ed.) *Problemas y propuestas para el sistema de financiamiento municipal.* Santiago: Centro de Estudios Públicos, 1992.

Martelli, G. (ed.) *Una Asociación Nacional de Municipalidades.* Santiago: Fundación F. Ebert, 1992.

Oros, J. *Diagnóstico financiero—Municipalidad de San Esteban.* Quito: IULA/CEL-CADEL, 1992.

Portes, A. "Latin American urbanization during the years of the crisis," *Latin American Research Review,* Vol.24, No.3 (1989), pp.7–44.

Raczynski, D., and Cabezas, M. *Ingresos y gastos municipales: Chile (1977–87) y Gran Santiago (1985/86).* Santiago: CIEPLAN, 1988.

Raczynski, R., and Serrano, C. "Administración y gestión local: La experiencia de algunos municipios en Santiago," *Estudios CIEPLAN,* No.22 (Dec. 1987), pp.129–151.

———. *Planificación para el desarrollo local? La experiencia en algunos municipios de Santiago.* Santiago: CIEPLAN, Colección Estudios No.24, June 1988, pp.37–62.

Rosenfeld, A. "El municipio y la organización del estado en Chile," *Medio Ambiente y Urbanización,* No.28 (Sept. 1989), pp.39–45.

Rosenfeld, A., et al, "La situación de los gobiernos locales en Chile," in Borja, J., Calderón, F., Grossi, M., and Peñalva, S. (eds.) *Descentralización y democracia: Gobiernos locales en América Latina.* Santiago: CLACSO/SUR/CEUMT, 1989, pp.185–239.

Sassenfeld, H. (ed.) *Asociación Chilena de Municipalidades: Necesidad y viabilidad.* Santiago: Fundación F. Ebert, 1992.

SUBDERE. *Manual de gestión municipal.* Santiago: Ministerio del Interior, 1992.

Tomic, B., and González, R. *Municipio y estado: Dimensiones de una relación clave.* Santiago: PREALC/ILO, 1983.

Valenzuela, A. *Political brokers in Chile: Local government in a centralized polity.* Durham, N.C.: Duke University Press, 1977.

Valenzuela, E. "Educación y Salud: Diagnóstico y propuesta de alternativas de solución a los déficits municipales," in Maihold, G. (ed.) *La descentralización en Nicaragua: De la delegación de servicios a la transferencia de competencias?* Managua: Fundación F. Ebert and INIFOM, 1992, pp.117–135.

COLOMBIA

Bird, R. M. *Intergovernmental finance in Colombia: Final report of the mission on intergovernmental finance.* Cambridge, Mass.: Harvard Law School, International Tax Program, 1984.

Bird, R. M., et al. *Colombia: A review of recent fiscal decentralization measures.* Washington, D.C.: World Bank, 1986.

Castro, J. *La democracia local: Un nuevo régimen departamental y municipal.* Bogotá: La Oveja Negra, 1984.

Cifuentes, A. "Análisis sobre la carrera administrativa municipal," in Atehortua, C. A., et al. *Estado y nuevo régimen territorial.* Bogotá: FESCOL and FAUS, 1992, pp.117–159.

Collins, C. *Local government and its reform in Colombia: 1974–1986.* Unpublished Ph.D. thesis, Birmingham: University of Birmingham, Development Administration Group, 1987.

————. "Local government and urban protest in Colombia," *Public Administration and Development,* Vol.8, No. 4 (Oct.–Dec.1988), pp.421–436.

Díaz Arbelaez, J. "Gobierno local y finanzas municipales en Bogotá," *Bulletin de l'Institut Français d'Etudes Andines,* Vol.17, No.1 (1988), pp.123–142.

Díaz Uribe, E. *El clientelismo en Colombia: Un estudio exploratorio.* Bogotá: El Ancora, 1986.

Dugas, J., et al. *Los caminos de la descentralización: Diversidad y retos de la transformación municipal.* Bogotá: Universidad de los Andes, 1992.

Echeverri, B. E. *Ley 14 de 1983: El fortalecimiento de los fiscos municipales.* Bogotá: ESAP, 1985.

Eljach, S. "Las Juntas Administradoras Locales: En qué va este proceso?" *Revista Foro* (Bogotá), No.9 (May 1989), pp.91–104.

Forero, H., and Salazar, M. "Local government and decentralization in Colombia," *Environment and Urbanization,* Vol.3, No.2 (Oct. 1991), pp.121–126.

Gaitán, P., et al. *Comunidad, alcaldes y recursos fiscales.* Bogotá: FESCOL, 1991.

Gaitán, P., and Moreno, C. *Poder local: Realidad y utopía de la descentralización en Colombia.* Bogotá: Instituto de Estudios Políticos, 1992.

Gilbert, A. "Bogotá: Politics, planning and the crisis of lost opportunities," in Cornelius, W. A., and Kemper, R. V. (eds.) *Latin American Urban Research, Vol.6.* Beverly Hills, Calif.: Sage, 1978, pp.87–126.

Gonzáles, E. "El municipio y la organización del estado en Colombia," *Medio Ambiente y Urbanización,* Año 7, No. 28 (Sept. 1989), pp.27–38.

González, E. A. "El sistema de transferencias intergubernamentales," in Cárdenas, M. E. (ed.) *Descentralización y estado moderno.* Bogotá: FAUS and FESCOL, 1991, pp.23–61.

González, E. A., and Duque, F. "La elección de Juntas Administradoras Locales de Cali," *Revista Foro* (Bogotá), No.12 (June 1990), pp.77–88.

Jaramillo, I., and Castro, J. *La participación de los municipios en la cesión del IVA.* Bogotá: FESCOL, 1990.

León, H. "Una propuesta de categorización municipal," in Cárdenas, M. E. (ed.) *Descentralización y estado moderno.* Bogotá: FAUS and FESCOL, 1991, pp.81–141.

Linn, J. F. *The distributive effects of local government finances in Colombia: A review of the evidence.* Washington, D.C.: World Bank, 1976 (Staff Working Paper No.235).

Mendoza, E. *Perspectivas de la carrera administrativa en Colombia.* Bogotá: Departamento Administrativo del Servicio Civil, 1984.

Pulido, L. M. "Las Juntas Administradoras Locales: Propuestas de modificación a su reglamentación legal," in Gaitán, P., et al. *Comunidad, alcaldes y recursos fiscales.* Bogotá: FESCOL, 1991, pp.87–137.

Restrepo, D. "Transformaciones recientes en América Latina: La descentralización, mito y potencia. El caso colombiano," *Revista Paraguaya de Sociología,* No.79 (Sept.–Dec. 1990), pp.117–140.

———. *Descentralización y neo-liberalismo: Balance de un proceso.* Bogotá: CEIR, 1992.

Rodríguez, L. "El sistema municipal de Colombia," in Arboleda, M. (ed.) *Finanzas municipales: Estudios breves en 8 países latinoamericanos.* Quito: CEL-CADEL, 1990, pp.11–32.

Rojas, F., et al. *Propuestas sobre la descentralización en Colombia.* Bogotá: FCM/FAUS/FESCOL, 1990.

Santana, P. "La territorialidad de la democracia," *Revista Foro* (Bogotá), No.21 (Sept. 1993), pp.57–71.

———. "Gobiernos locales, descentralización y democracia en Colombia," in Reilly, C. A. (ed.) *Nuevas políticas urbanas: Las ONG y los gobiernos municipales en la democratización latinoamericana.* Arlington, Va.: Fundación Interamericana, 1994, pp.191–209.

Shugart, M. S. "Leaders, rank and file, and constituents: Electoral reform in Colombia and Venezuela," *Electoral Studies* Vol.11, No.1 (March 1992), pp.21–45.

Tamayo, E. *Administración municipal colombiana.* Bogotá: ESAP, 1987.

Uribe-Echevarría, F. "The decentralization debate in Colombia: Lessons from experience," *Planning and Administration,* Vol.12, No.2 (Autumn 1985), pp.10–21.

Vargas, C., et al. "Financiamiento del desarrollo regional: Situación actual y perspectivas," *Planeación y Desarrollo* (Bogotá), Vol.24, No.1 (Jan.–April 1993), pp.311–346.

Velásquez, F. E. "Local government in intermediate cities in Colombia: Municipal administration for whom?" *Environment and Urbanization,* Vol.3, No.1 (April 1991), pp.109–120.

Viviescas, F. "Identidad municipal y cultura urbana," *Revista Mexicana de Sociología,* Vol.48, No.4 (Oct.–Dec. 1986), pp.51–71.

COSTA RICA

Araya, C., and Albarracín, P. *Historia del régimen municipal en Costa Rica.* San José: IFAM, 1986.

Baker, C. E., et al. *Municipal government in Costa Rica: Its characteristics and functions.* San José: Associated Colleges of the Midwest Central American Field Project, School of Political Science, University of Costa Rica, 1972.

Castro, J. A. *Análisis histórico de la crisis municipal en Costa Rica.* San José: IFAM, 1977.

Chan, C., and Vargas, R. *Fortalecimiento municipal y transferencia de competencias de entidades nacionales a los gobiernos locales.* San José: IFAM, 1991.

IFAM. *El regimen municipal de Costa Rica.* San José: Instituto de Fomento y Asesoría Municipal, 1981.

Jagger, H. "IFAM, functions and services for local government in Costa Rica," *Planning and Administration,* Vol.12, No.2 (Autumn 1985), pp.52–59.

Lungo, M., and Pérez, M. "Area Metropolitana de San José: Coordinación de gobiernos locales o gobierno metropolitano," *Medio Ambiente y Urbanización,* No.35 (June 1991), pp.73–83.

Monge, L. A. *La carrera administrativa municipal en Costa Rica.* San José: IFAM, 1984.

Murillo, T. "El sistema municipal de Costa Rica," in Arboleda, M. (ed.) *Finanzas municipales: Estudios breves en 8 países latinoamericanos.* Quito: CEL-CADEL, 1990, pp.33–66.

Ortega, H. H. *San José, Costa Rica local government: Demands and decisions.* Unpublished Ph.D. thesis, University of Oklahoma, 1974 (University Microfilms, Ann Arbor, Michigan, Order No. 74–21,984).

Ortíz, E. *La municipalidad en Costa Rica.* Madrid: IEAL, 1987.

Quesada, L. A. *Municipalidad: Gobierno local con autonomía?* San José: n.p., 1991.

Soto, B. *Perfiles de la democracia costaricense: El sistema municipal de Costa Rica.* San José: IFAM, 1985.

DOMINICAN REPUBLIC

Aybar de Sanabria, F. *Apuntes sobre la organización y sistema tributario municipal.* Santo Domingo: Foro Urbano, 1989.

Chaves, L. J. *Apuntes sobre la evolución de régimen municipal y su papel en la estructura del estado.* Jarabacoa: Foro Urbano, 1987.

Jiménez, T., and Peguero, C. "Las administraciones locales y su participación en programas de desarrollo," in Instituto Nacional de Administración Pública, *Administración Pública y Desarrollo Regional.* Madrid: Ministerio para las Administraciones Públicas, 1991, pp.295–304.

Moore, M. *La carrera administrativa en el sector municipal dominicano y su relación con el adiestramiento.* Santo Domingo: Oficina Nacional de Administración y Personal, 1984.

Pérez, C. *Poder municipal, democracia y participación.* Santo Domingo: Foro Urbano, 1989.

ECUADOR

Allou, S., and Velarde, P. "Desarrollo urbano, organización popular y nacimiento de los poderes locales en Santo Domingo de los Colorados, Ecuador," in Carrión, D. (ed.) *Ciudades en conflicto: Poder local, participación popular y planificación en las ciudades intermedias de América Latina.* Quito: CIUDAD, 1986, pp.147–174.

Carrión, F. "La política del municipio en Quito," *Revista Mexicana de Sociología,* Vol.48, No.4 (Oct./Dec. 1986), pp.141–161.

Carrión, F., and Velarde, P. "El municipio y la organización del Estado en Ecuador," *Medio Ambiente y Urbanización,* Vol.7, No.28 (Sept. 1989), pp.46–54.

Fawcett, C. *FONAPAR: An institutional assessment.* Syracuse: Maxwell School,

Syracuse University, 1986 (Local Revenue Administration Project Occasional Paper No.107).

Fuhr, H. "Municipal institutional strengthening and donor coordination: The case of Ecuador," *Public Administration and Development,* Vol.14, No.2 (May 1994), pp.169–186.

Greytak, D., and Méndez, V. *The impact of intergovernmental grants on local governments in Ecuador: A study of FONAPAR.* Syracuse: Maxwell School, Syracuse University, 1986 (Local Revenue Administration Project Occasional Paper No.106).

Manglesdorf, K. "Administrative decentralisation and development: Some conflicting evidence from Ecuador," *International Review of Administrative Sciences,* Vol.54 (1988), pp.67–88.

Rosales, M. "El municipio ecuatoriano: Síntomas y razones de su fragilidad," in Borja, J., et al. (eds.) *Descentralización y democracia: Gobiernos locales en América Latina.* Santiago: CLACSO/SUR/CEUMT, 1989, pp.241–283.

———. "El sistema municipal ecuatoriano," in Arboleda, M. (ed.) *Finanzas municipales: Estudios breves en 8 países latinoamericanos.* Quito: CELCADEL, 1990, pp.89–116.

Rosales, M., et al. *El desafío local: El municipio como agente de desarrollo.* Quito: El Conejo, 1988.

Unda, M. "La relación entre sociedad política y sociedad civil en los municipios ecuatorianos," *Bulletin de l'Institut Français d'Etudes Andines,* Vol.17, No.1 (1988), pp.225–232.

EL SALVADOR

Giordano, J. M. *El municipio y la municipalidad.* San Salvador: ISAM, 1988.

INCAE. *Programa para el desarrollo local en El Salvador.* Alajuela, Costa Rica: 1991.

Molina, C. "La experiencia de la descentralización educativa en El Salvador," in Maihold, G. (ed.) *La descentralización en Nicaragua: De la delegación de servicios a la transferencia de competencias?* Managua: Fundación F. Ebert and INIFOM, 1992, pp.103–115.

Murphy, M., et al. *Improving municipal capabilities in El Salvador.* Annapolis Junction, Md.: International City/County Management Association, 1993.

Navas, C. "Centralización/descentralización del Estado en El Salvador en los años 80," in Martínez Assad, C., et al. (eds.) *Hacia un nuevo orden estatal en América Latina? Centralización/descentralización del Estado y actores territoriales,* Vol.5. Buenos Aires: CLACSO, 1989, pp.249–284.

Sollis, P. "Poverty alleviation in El Salvador: An appraisal of the Cristiani government's social programme," *Journal of International Development,* Vol.5, No.5 (1993), pp.437–458.

GUATEMALA

CEDAL. "El municipio en Guatemala," *Estudios Municipales* (Mexico), Vol.12 (Nov.–Dec. 1986), pp.39–72.

Echegaray, F. I. *El sistema municipal de Guatemala.* Guatemala City: INCAE, 1990.

———. *El papel de las transferencias fiscales del gobierno central al gobierno municipal y la descentralización: El caso de Guatemala.* Guatemala City: INCAE, 1991.

Instituto Nacional de Administración para el Desarrollo. *Informe del primer seminario nacional sobre administración para el desarrollo municipal.* Guatemala: ANM-INAD-CNPE, 1967.

Linares, L. "Estrategía para el fortalecimiento institucional del municipio," *Momento* (Guatemala City), Year 4, No.11 (1989).

McIntosh, T. "Local government in Guatemala and its relations with the central government," *Planning and Administration,* Vol.5, No.2 (Autumn 1978), pp.15–27.

———. "Municipal financing and development planning in Guatemala," *Planning and Administration,* Vol.7, No.1 (Spring 1980), pp.57–68.

Mencos, F. A. *Descentralización y gestión local: La experiencia guatemalteca.* Guatemala: INAP, 1991.

Sánchez, J. "El sistema municipal de Guatemala," in Arboleda, M. (ed.) *Finanzas municipales: Estudios breves en 8 países latinoamericanos.* Quito: CEL-CADEL, 1990, pp.117–143.

HONDURAS

AMHON. *El municipio como factor de desarrollo nacional.* Tegucigalpa: Fundación Alemana para el Desarrollo Internacional, 1987.

Fiallos, C. *Los municipios de Honduras.* Tegucigalpa: Ed. Universitaria, 1989.

Guzmán, A. "El sistema municipal de Honduras," in Arboleda, M. (ed.) *Finanzas municipales: Estudios breves en 8 países latinoamericanos.* Quito: CEL-CADEL, 1990, pp.145–177.

Moncada, E. *Comentarios preliminares a la nueva ley de municipalidades.* Tegucigalpa: Friedrich Ebert Stiftung, 1991.

Paz, E. *El municipio en Honduras: De la autonomía a la servidumbre.* Tegucigalpa: Ed. Universitaria, 1984.

———. *La evolución histórica del municipio en Honduras.* Tegucigalpa: n.p. 1987.

MEXICO

Batley, R. *Urban management in Mexico: Part 1—Common characteristics, Part 2—Hermosillo, Part 3—Campeche.* Birmingham: University of Birmingham, Development Administration Group, 1992.

Gershberg, A. I. *Decentralization and public finance in Mexico.* Washington, D.C.: The Urban Institute, 1990.

González-Block, N., et al. "Health services decentralization in Mexico: Formulation, implementation and results of policy," *Health Policy and Planning,* Vol.4 (1989), pp.301–315.

Hernández, M., and Mejía, J. *Experiencias de la planeación municipal y propuestas para su mejoramiento.* Mexico D.F.: CIDE, Doc. de Trabajo 1, 1992.

IHS. *Municipal development programme of Mexico: Institutional strengthening study, Vol.1.* Rotterdam: Institute for Housing and Urban Development Studies, 1993.

INDETEC. "Criterios de distribución de participaciones federales a municipios en las entidades federativas," *Revista Hacienda Municipal,* No.44 (Sept. 1993), pp.41–53.

INEGI. *Finanzas Públicas Estatales y Municipales, 1976–1986.* Mexico D.F.: Instituto Nacional de Estadística, Geografía e Informática, 1990.

López, A. *La lucha por los ayuntamientos: Una utopía viable.* Mexico D.F.: Siglo XXI/IIS, 1986.

Martínez, C. *Municipios en conflicto.* Mexico D.F.: UNAM, 1985.

Martínez, C., and Ziccardi, A. "El municipio entre la sociedad y el Estado," *Revista Mexicana de Sociología,* Vol.48, No.4 (Oct.–Dec. 1986), pp.7–49.

———. "Política y Gestión municipal en México," in Borja, J., et al. (eds.) *Descentralización y democracia: Gobiernos locales en América Latina.* Santiago: CLACSO/SUR/CEUMT, 1989, pp.285–336.

Martínez, G. *La administración estatal y municipal de México.* Mexico D.F.: INAP, 1993.

Massolo, A. "La descentralización de la gestión pública: La reforma municipal de 1983," in Garza, G. (ed.) *Una década de planeación urbano-regional en México.* Mexico D.F.: El Colegio de México, 1989.

———. "Descentralización y reforma municipal: Fracaso anunciado y sorpresas inesperadas?" *Revista Interamericana de Planificación,* Vol.26, No.101–102 (Jan.–June 1993), pp.196–230.

Medina, A., and Mejía, J. *Sistemas administrativos de control: Un estudio descriptivo en los municipios.* Mexico D.F.: CIDE, Doc. de Trabajo 9, 1992.

OCDE. *Mexico: Estudios económicos de la OCDE.* Paris: Organización de Cooperación y Desarrollo Económico, 1992.

Olmedo, R. *El desafío municipal.* Mexico D.F.: CNEM, 1982.

Rodríguez, V. E. "Mexico's decentralization in the 1980s: Promises, promises, promises . . ." in Morris, A., and Lowder, S. (eds.) *Decentralization in Latin America: An evaluation.* New York: Praeger, 1992, pp.127–143.

———. "The politics of decentralization in Mexico: From Municipio Libre to Solidaridad," *Bulletin of Latin American Research,* Vol.12, No.2 (May 1993), pp.133–145.

Vásquez, H. *El nuevo municipio mexicano.* Mexico D.F.: Secretaría de Educación Pública, Foro 2000, 1986.

Viviescas, F. "Identidad municipal y cultura urbana," *Revista Mexicana de Sociología,* Vol.48, No.4 (Oct.–Dec. 1986), pp.51–71.

Ward, P. M. *Mexico City: The production and reproduction of an urban environment.* London: Belhaven Press, 1990.

Witker, J. *La administración local en Mexico.* Madrid: IEAL, 1986.

World Bank. *Decentralization and urban management in Mexico: Urban sector study.* Washington, D.C.: IBRD, 1990.

NICARAGUA

Belli, C. *La situación municipal y el proceso de descentralización en Nicaragua.* Managua: INAP, 1993.

Downs, C. "Local and regional government," in Walker, T. (ed.) *Nicaragua: The first five years.* New York: Praeger, 1985, pp.45–63.

———. "Regionalization, administrative reform and democratization: Nicaragua

1979–1984," *Public Administration and Development,* Vol.7, No.4 (Oct.–Dec. 1987), pp.363–382.

Downs, C., and Kusnetzoff, F. "The changing role of local government in the Nicaraguan revolution," *International Journal of Urban and Regional Research,* Vol.6, No.4 (1982), pp.533–548.

Harris, R. "Municipal development in Nicaragua," *Economic and Industrial Democracy,* Vol.3, No.1 (1982), pp.83–90.

Gómez, W. "El sistema municipal de Nicaragua," in Arboleda, M. (ed.) *Finanzas municipales: Estudios breves en 8 países latinoamericanos.* Quito: CEL-CADEL, 1990, pp.179–200.

Ortega, M. La *Ley de Municipios: Estudio y propuesta de reforma.* Managua: Fundación F. Ebert and POPOL-NA, 1992.

Rodríguez, A. *Centralismo, municipio, regionalización y descentralización en Nicaragua (1979–1991).* Managua: Fundación F. Ebert, 1991.

———. *Sistema de financiamiento y modelo municipal en Nicaragua.* Managua: Fundación F. Ebert, 1993.

Villanueva, J. C. "Algunas reflexiones sobre areas de factible ejecución de la descentralización," in Maihold, G. (ed.) *La descentralización en Nicaragua: De la delegación de servicios a la transferencia de competencias?* Managua: Fundación F. Ebert and INIFOM, 1992, pp.59–69.

PANAMA

Alderfer, H. F. "Local Government in Panama," *Journal of Administration Overseas,* Vol.8, No.4 (Oct. 1969), pp.270–276.

González, M. "La descentralización y el financiamiento municipal," *Gobierno Municipal* (IPADEM), Jan.–March 1994, pp.30–38.

Gutiérrez, R. "Poder local y desarrollo rural en Panama," *Caravelle,* No.36 (1981), pp.41–61.

Pinilla, H. "The participation of local governments in the planning process of Panama," *Planning and Administration,* Vol.12, No.2 (Autumn 1985), pp.37–44.

———. *Leyes de los gobiernos locales en Panama.* Panama City: Author's 2nd edition, 1990.

PARAGUAY

Arditi, B. "Elecciones municipales y democratización en el Paraguay," in Arditi, B. *Adiós a Stroessner.* Asunción: RP/CDE, 1992, pp.121–139.

Barboza, R. *Municipalidades del Paraguay.* Asunción: Univ. Católica, Fac. de Ciencias Jurídicas y Diplomáticas, 1989.

Bareiro, O., and Duarte, M. "Paraguay: El no debate sobre la descentralización," in Nohlen, D. (ed.) *Descentralización política y consolidación democrática: Europa–América del Sur.* Caracas: Edit. Nueva Sociedad, 1991, pp.225–236.

Feierstein, M., et al. *Voting for greater pluralism: The May 26 1991 municipal elections in Paraguay.* Washington, D.C.: National Democratic Institute for International Affairs, 1992.

Furst, D. *Análisis del sistema financiero municipal.* Asunción and Hannover: IDM/GTZ, 1987.

Goldenberg, L. E. *Percepción y distribución del impuesto inmobiliario.* Paper presented by the president of IDM at the symposium Constitución Nacional y Administración Municipal, Asunción, 9–10 October 1992, organized by the Centro de Estudios Democráticos and Junta Municipal de Asunción.

Marín, E., Silvero, J., and Sosa, E. *La organización municipal en el Paraguay.* Asunción: C.D.E. and Fundación F. Ebert, 1992.

Nickson, R. A. *Consignas populares para las elecciones municipales de 1990.* Asunción: BASE-ECTA, 1989.

———. *Democratización y descentralización en Paraguay.* Asunción: BASE-IS, 1993.

Sosa, E. *Gobierno municipal y participación ciudadana: El caso paraguayo.* Asunción: C.D.E. and Fundación F. Ebert, 1990.

PERU

Allou, S. "Las finanzas municipales en Lima, 1981–1986," *Bulletin de l'Institut Français d'Etudes Andines,* Vol.17, No.1 (1988), pp.143–198.

Althaus, J. *Realidad de las municipalidades en el Peru.* Lima: Fundación F. Ebert, 1986.

Arnao, R., and Meza, M. *Economías municipales en la Provincia de Lima.* Lima: Fundación F. Ebert, 1990.

Austin, A. G. *The role of municipal government in the national development of Peru.* New York: New York University, Graduate School of Public Administration, 1969.

Austin, A. G., and Lewis, S. *Urban government for metropolitan Lima.* New York: Praeger, 1970.

Calderón, J. *Elecciones otra vez? Municipalidades, porqué y para que?* Lima: DESCO, 1980.

Castro-Pozo, H. *Ley No.23853 Orgánica de Municipalidades concordado y comentada.* Lima: IPADEL, 1991.

Chirinos, L. A. "Gobierno local y participación vecinal: El caso de Lima Metropolitana," *Socialismo y Participación* (Lima), Vol.36 (Dec. 1986), pp.1–27.

———. "La participación vecinal," in Pease, H. (ed.) *Construyendo un gobierno metropolitano.* Lima: IPADEL, 1991, pp.87–138.

Collier, D. *Squatters and oligarchs: Authoritarian rule and policy change in Peru.* Baltimore: Johns Hopkins University Press, 1976.

Dawson, E. "District planning with community participation in Peru: The work of the institute of local democracy—IPADEL," *Environment and Urbanization,* Vol.4, No.2 (Oct. 1992), pp.90–100.

———. "NGOs and public policy reform: Lessons from Peru," *Journal of International Development,* Vol.5, No.4 (1993), pp.401–414.

Díaz, J. *Municipio: Democracia y desarrollo.* Lima: CIDAP, 1990.

Figari, E., and Ricou, X. *Lima en crisis.* Lima: Universidad del Pacífico and L'Institut Français d'Etudes Andines, 1990.

Fuentes, M., and Garzón, H. *Estructura de los ingresos y gastos municipales de la Provincia de Jauja, Departamento de Junín, Peru.* Lima: USAID, 1983.

Garzón, H. *El impuesto predial en el Peru.* Lima: USAID, 1981.

Giesecke, A., and Hurtado, I. *Como funciona la administración pública peruana? La burocracia estatal y la regulación y gestión del desarrollo.* Lima: Fundación F. Ebert, 1987.

González, E., and Tokeshi, J. *Renglones de gestión municipal No.1: Elementos.* Lima: Fundación F. Ebert, 1988.

Granda, M. *Los recursos financieros de los gobiernos locales en el periódo 1985–1988.* Lima: INFOM, 1989.

Greytak, D. *Local government finances in Peru.* New York: Syracuse University, Maxwell School, 1982 (Local Revenue Administration Project Monograph No.8).

INFOM. *Síntesis del diagnóstico de gobiernos locales a nivel nacional.* Lima: INFOM-USAID, 1985.

Kim, S. H. "The political process of decentralization in Peru, 1985–1990," *Public Administration and Development,* Vol.12, No.3 (August 1992), pp.249–265.

Mejía, J. "Los estudios sobre la municipalidad peruana," *Gobierno Local* (INICAM), Sept.–Oct. 1988, pp.16–44.

Montoya, M. *La reforma a nivel local.* Lima: INAP, Cuadernos RAP, 1976.

Muñoz, R. *Manual de tributación municipal.* Lima: INICAM, 1988.

Murgia, J. *Gestión urbana en Trujillo, Peru: La perspectiva del municipio.* Santiago: CEPAL, 1992.

Olivera, L. "La gestión local en Lima Metropolitana," *Medio Ambiente y Urbanización.* No.35 (June 1991), pp.61–72.

Pease, H. *Democracia local: Reflexiones y experiencias.* Lima: DESCO, 1989.

———. (ed.) *Construyendo un gobierno municipal: Políticas municipales, 1984–1986.* Lima: IPADEL, 1991.

Pease, H., and Jibaja, P. "Los gobiernos locales en el Peru," in Borja, J., et al. (eds.) *Descentralización y democracia: Gobiernos locales en América Latina.* Santiago: CLACSO/SUR/CEUMT, 1989, pp.337–378.

Peattie, L. "Participation: A case study of how invaders organize, negotiate and interact with government in Lima, Peru," *Environment and Urbanization,* Vol.2, No.1 (April 1990), pp.19–30.

Polanco, C. "El sistema municipal en Peru," in Arboleda, M. (ed.) *Finanzas municipales: Estudios breves de 8 países latinoamericanos.* Quito: CELCADEL, 1990, pp.201–232.

Riofrío, G. "Lima en los 90: Un acercamiento a la nueva dinámica urbana," *Nueva Sociedad,* No.114 (1991), pp.143–149.

Schmidt, G. D. "Political variables and governmental decentralization in Peru, 1948–88," *Journal of Inter-American Studies and World Affairs,* Vol.31, No.1–2, (Spring/Summer 1989), pp.193–232.

Távara, J. I. "Participación popular en el gobierno local," in Sánchez, A., and Olivera, L. (eds.) *Lima: Una metrópoli/ 7 debates.* Lima: DESCO, 1983, pp.245–271.

Villafuerte, F. "Gestión municipal y participación popular: La experiencia en Cusco 1980–1987," *Bulletin de l'Institut Français d'Etudes Andines,* Vol.17, No.1 (1988), pp.213–223.

Wilson, P., and Garzón, J. M. "Prospects for political decentralization: Peru in the 1980s," *International Journal of Urban and Regional Research,* Vol.9, No.3 (Sept. 1985), pp.330–340.

Zaaijer, M., and Miranda, L. "Local economic development as an instrument for urban poverty alleviation," *Third World Planning Review,* Vol.15, No.2, 1993, pp.127–142.

Zavaleta, J. *Municipalidad y democracia: Guía para el lector.* Lima: Fundación F. Ebert, 1986.

URUGUAY

Arocena, J. "Las municipalidades uruguayas frente a los desafíos del desarrollo," *Cuadernos del CLAEH* (Montevideo), No.62 (Sept. 1992), pp.77–91.

Bervejillo, F. *La descentralización en Uruguay.* Montevideo: CLAEH, 1992.

Martins, D. H. *El municipio contemporáneo: Los gobiernos locales de occidente y del Uruguay.* Montevideo: Fundación de Cultura Universitaria, 1978.

Moreira, C., and Venezziano, A. *Relations between national and local government: The Uruguayan case, 1990–1991.* Montevideo: Universidad de la República. Paper presented at the 15th World Congress of the International Political Science Association, Buenos Aires, 21–25 July 1991.

Pérez, A. "Hacia la transformación del régimen local uruguayo," *Cuadernos del CLAEH.* No.45–46 (Aug. 1988), pp.73–86.

―――. "La descentralización en Montevideo: Un itinerario innovador," *Cuadernos del CLAEH,* No.62 (Sept. 1992), pp.93–107.

Sabelli de Louzao, M. *Régimen municipal uruguayo, 1830–1935.* Paper presented at the seminar El Municipio en una Sociedad Democrática y Participativa. Montevideo: CIESU-CLACSO, 11–13 September 1985.

Sierra, G., et al. *Participación ciudadana y relaciones de gobierno.* Montevideo: FESUR, 1993.

VENEZUELA

Boyce, C. "Confessions and experiences: The Venezuelan experience," in *The education of an international development consultant.* Boston: (forthcoming).

Brewer-Carias, A. R. "Municipio, democracia y participación: Aspectos de la crisis," in INAP, *Crónica del 11 Congreso extraordinario de la organización iberoamericana de cooperación intermunicipal: 1985.* Madrid: INAP, 1988, pp.301–317.

―――. "La descentralización política en Venezuela: 1990, el inicio de una reforma," in Nohlen, D. (ed.) *Descentralización política y consolidación democrática.* Caracas: Edit. Nueva Sociedad, 1991, pp.131–160.

Cannon, M. W., et al. *Urban government for Valencia, Venezuela.* New York: Praeger, 1973.

De la Cruz, R. (ed.) *Descentralización, gobernabilidad, democracia.* Caracas: Nueva Sociedad/COPRE/PNUD, 1992.

Ellner, S. "The Venezuelan political party system and its influence on economic decision-making at the local level," *Inter-American Economic Affairs,* Vol.36, No.3 (Winter 1982), pp.79–103.

Faddi, G. "Crisis urbana en el área metropolitana de Caracas," *Revista Mexicana de Sociología,* Year 48, No.4 (Dec. 1986), pp.87–108.

Kelly, J. (ed.) *Gerencia municipal.* Caracas: IESA, 1993.

Kornblith, M., and Maingón, T. *Estado y gasto público en Venezuela, 1936–1980.* Caracas: UCV, 1985.

Molina, J. *Beyond the party list: Electoral reform in Venezuela.* Maracaibo: Centro de Investigaciones y Estudios Políticos y Administrativos, Univ. de Zulia. Paper presented at the 15th World Congress of the International Political Science Association, Buenos Aires, 21–25 July 1991.

Navarro, J. C., and González, Y. *Organizaciones y participación comunitaria: Su contribución a la lucha contra la pobreza en Venezuela.* Caracas: IESA, 1993.

Nickson, R. A. *The potential contribution of local government to the improvement of delivery of social services in Venezuela.* Birmingham: University of Birmingham, Development Administration Group, 1993 (background paper for the Oxford University IADB mission to Venezuela).

Palumbo, G. (ed.). *El papel del alcalde en el gobierno municipal.* Caracas: IESA, 1990.

Peñalva, S. "Situación y perspectivas de los gobiernos locales en Venezuela," in Borja, J., et al. (eds.) *Descentralización y democracia: Gobiernos locales en América Latina.* Santiago: CLACSO/SUR/CEUMT, 1989, pp.379–433.

Savio, C. J. "Revenue-sharing in practice: National-state-local subventions in Venezuela," in Rabinovitz, F. F., and Trueblood, F. M. (eds.) *Latin America Urban Research: Vol.3.* Beverly Hills, Calif.: Sage, 1973, pp.79–93.

Shugart, M. S. "Leaders, rank and file, and constituents: Electoral reform in Colombia and Venezuela," *Electoral Studies,* Vol.11, No.1 (March 1992), pp.21–45.

Vallmitjana, M. (ed.) *Caracas: Nuevos escenarios para el poder local.* Caracas: Ed. Nueva Sociedad, 1993.

INDEX

ABOUT THE BOOK
AND AUTHOR

This pioneering study provides a detailed examination of the growing significance of local government in the Latin American development process.

Part 1 of the book offers an overview of local government in the region. Nickson traces the historical decline of local government since colonial times and explains the reasons for its resurgence starting in the 1980s. He then explores its structure, legal status, and electoral system, the range of services that municipalities provide, the growing financial resources at their disposal, and their internal organization. The new phenomena of citizen participation in local government and intermunicipal relations are also discussed.

Part 2 provides eighteen comprehensive country profiles—written in a common format—addressing the political, financial, and administrative aspects of local government.

The book includes a directory of municipal support institutions at the national and regional levels, as well as the first systematic bibliography on Latin American local government to be published.

R. Andrew Nickson is senior lecturer in development economics in the Development Administration Group, School of Public Policy, University of Birmingham (England). He currently manages the Programa Euro-Latinoamericano de Formación en la Administración Pública, a European Union–funded training program for administrative reform in the Rio Group countries of Latin America.